NATURAL RESOURCE REVENUES

This book is the third in a series based on the Economic Policy Conferences of the British Columbia Institute for Economic Policy Analysis.

Natural Resource Revenues Conference,
Victoria, 1975

NATURAL RESOURCE REVENUES:

A Test of Federalism

Edited by

Anthony Scott

Published for
THE BRITISH COLUMBIA INSTITUTE FOR ECONOMIC POLICY ANALYSIS

UNIVERSITY OF BRITISH COLUMBIA PRESS
VANCOUVER

NATURAL RESOURCE REVENUES

Canadian Cataloguing in Publication Data
Main entry under title:
Natural resource revenues
  (British Columbia Institute for Economic Policy Analysis series)
  "Essays originated in a set of papers presented to the Victoria Conference on
Natural Resource Revenues ... 1975."
  Includes index.
  ISBN 0-7748-0060-7
  ISBN 0-7748-0061-5 pa.

  1. Federal-provincial tax relations (Canada)* - Congresses. 2. Natural
resources - Taxation - Canada - Congresses. I. Scott, Anthony, 1923-   II.
Victoria Conference on Natural Resource Revenues, 1975. III. Series: British
Columbia Institute for Economic Policy Analysis. British Columbia Institute
for Economic Policy Analysis series.
HJ2451.N38   336.2'78'3338   C76-016077-5

International Standard Book Number
(Hardcover edition) 0-7748-0060-7
(Paperback edition) 0-7748-0061-5

Printed in Canada

Contents

The British Columbia Institute of
Economic Policy Analysis   WALTER D. YOUNG   vii

Foreword   MASON GAFFNEY   ix

Introduction   ANTHONY SCOTT   xi

Acknowledgments   xvi

Who Should Get Natural
Resource Revenues?   ANTHONY SCOTT   1

The Constitution: A Basis for
Bargaining   W.R. LEDERMAN   52

The Political Context of Resource
Development in Canada   DONALD V. SMILEY   61

Equalization Payments and
Energy Royalties   THOMAS J. COURCHENE   73

Note on Equalization and
Resource Rents   DOUGLAS H. CLARK   108

Natural Resource Revenue Sharing:
A Dissenting View   ANDREW R. THOMPSON   112

Resource Rent: How Much and for
Whom?   HARRY F. CAMPBELL
W.D. GAINER
ANTHONY SCOTT   118

Static Redistributive and Welfare
Effects of an Export Tax   T.L. POWRIE   137

Taxes, Royalties, and Equity
Participation as Alternative Methods
of Dividing Resource Revenues:
The Syncrude Example   JOHN HELLIWELL
GERRY MAY   153

A Comment on Natural Resource
Revenue Sharing: The Links
between Revenue Sharing and
Energy Policy   JUDITH MAXWELL   181

Rent vs. Revenue Maximization as an
  Objective of Environmental
  Management   HARRY F. CAMPBELL   185

Ontario Mining Profit Tax:
  An Evaluation   J. CLARK LEITH   206

Governments and Mineral Resource
  Earnings: Taxation with Over
  Simplification?   PAUL G. BRADLEY   214

Note on Federations and Risk Aversion   JOHN BUTLIN   232

A Note on the Economics of Oil-
  Financed Recovery Projects   G.C. WATKINS   235

The Concept of a Nation and
  Entitlements to Economic Rents   A. MILTON MOORE   240

The Volatility of Rents   ALBERT BRETON   246

A Comment on Decentralized
  Resource Control   IRENE M. SPRY   250

Biographical Notes   257

Index   259

The British Columbia Institute
for Economic Policy Analysis

The British Columbia Institute for Economic Policy Analysis was set up to foster independent research in public policy and to help bring the scholarly resources of the universities to bear on problems of government in specific areas: unemployment, public finance, industrial organization, and natural resource use. It acted as a halfway house between academe and action. The institute was established by the provincial government but was independent of it. It drew the income to support its functions from an endowment fund.

The institute as such did not endorse viewpoints. The only restrictions on work done under its auspices were that it bear constructively on public policy and be of high professional competence. Each individual assumed responsibility for his own findings. The institute encouraged individual researchers to develop their viewpoints into workable policy recommendations and to engage in creative dialogue with civil servants, business and labour leaders, citizen groups and public officials, and others. The institute sought to provide a forum where many doctrines might be tried.

The institute initiated and defined research topics and responded to requests for consulting. Where possible it allocated requests to researchers in the government or university system, using its contracts to serve as referral and coordinating agency.

To those ends the institute maintained a research staff, supported other scholars within the province's universities, sponsored seminars and symposia where findings could be advanced and criticized, published the results of its sponsored endeavours, and offered in-service training in economic analysis to public servants. As an adjunct of the university system in British Columbia it supported students and otherwise engaged them in its activities. For the public service in British Columbia the institute engaged civil servants in its activities and encouraged a climate to attract, train, and hold professionals in government.

Walter D. Young
Chairman, Board of Directors

Foreword

This is the third in a series of symposia sponsored by the British Columbia Institute for Economic Policy Analysis. The first is on British Columbia forest policy; the second on pricing of local services and effects on urban spatial structure. Later symposia in the series are on pollution control, the energy industry, and mineral leasing as an instrument of public policy.

The present volume centres on the concept of an economic rent, particularly rent yielded by mineral resources. The economist's concept of rent, i.e., surplus above costs, applies to all natural resources but in the recent Canadian context it has been applied mainly to minerals. This volume asks which crown should be the landlord, crown provincial or crown Canada?

The issue is timely because of the recent eruptions of federal-provincial conflict over resource revenues. One of the sages has said it is easier to face a common calamity than to share a surplus. Recent Canadian history bears this out, as rising values for primary products have caused many Canadian mineral deposits to yield noticeable surpluses. The federal government has gone after a share of the surpluses by means of tighter rules for income taxation, sometimes coupled with export price controls. Provincial governments have tapped the same surpluses by other devices open to them: royalties, mining taxes, property taxes, marketing boards, and others.

Certain kinds of natural resources have, by tacit convention, not been disputed. Thus British Columbia's right to raise rentals charged for use of its valuable falling water has not been challenged, nor its right to raise stumpage rates for provincially-owned timber, nor its right to control prices of wood chips sold in the province. Ottawa has let these go by, even though they involve rents generated by natural resources on crown land. Minerals and hydrocarbons, on the other hand, are a zone of conflict.

The issue boiled over on 6 May 1974, when finance minister John Turner brought down a budget in which provincial mineral royalties were, for the first time, made non-deductible in calculating taxable income. The ensuing uproar precipitated an election, threats of secession, and a variety of compromises, some of them shifting arrangements hard to grasp unambiguously. Ottawa appears to have made its point, but the dust has never quite settled and deep questions remain over what the point was and about the nature of Confederation before and after. O Canada, what art thou? There are also universal questions raised about the nature of any government and its relation to a national land base. There are hardly any more fundamental questions in history.

The editor, Anthony Scott, is a dean among Canadians and among economists. He was a pioneer in developing the discipline of resource economics; more recently he has focused on Canadian Confederation. The present volume unites these topics. It convenes a distinguished group of lawyers, economists, and political scientists to produce a uniquely balanced and outstanding treatment of a topic both timely and timeless.

Mason Gaffney

Introduction

ANTHONY SCOTT

In the tug of war between Ottawa and the western provinces over energy pricing and taxation, who ought to win? This question was much in the air in 1975 when the essays in this volume were written. Ottawa's powers of direct taxation, and its rights to regulate trade and commerce, were being vigorously asserted not only over firms in the oil and gas industry but also over mining and forest products companies. Nor was it obvious to all bystanders that the two governments had the only claims: there were many shareholders and consumers to argue that higher dividends, more employment, or lower final prices were more worthy of consideration than the choice of tax collector. In the press and in the legislatures, economic arguments were adduced, mixed in with generous slabs of constitutional law, party political platforms, history, environmental analysis, and personal invective.

In these essays we attempt to stay within the bounds of professional economists' competence by examining the "economic" arguments, leaving to others the investigation of claims based on legal, customary, historic, political, social, or environmental grounds. Most laymen would agree that these self-imposed limits would not bind the political economist significantly. They leave him free to investigate the economic impact of alternative assignments of resource taxation powers. Furthermore, they do not prevent him from pontificating about the "best," "optimum," or "neutral" tax and its assignment; that is, from assuming the role in which laymen usually see him.

However, economist participants were also requested not to turn their backs on the "distributive" question: *who* should benefit from increased government resource revenues? Many members of the public do understand this question and have preferred answers to it—John Butlin offers Scottish nationalists as an example. But it appears that how resource revenues do enter into income redistribution in Canada is so little understood (especially in the workings of the equalization formula for provincial grants) that economists are among the few groups of citizens who can be expected to take any informed view on the matter. In short, in this conference, fair distribution, just as much as efficient allocation, was declared to be among the goals of the practising economist. Not every speaker was willing to avail himself of this privilege, but many do, implicitly (e.g., Courchene) and explicitly (e.g., Moore).

Their contributions, and most others, deal with the federal-provincial division of the tax revenue base. But this is not the only division that is worth investigating. Some may feel that more important questions are about the total claims of all governments—why not let more surplus flow to consumers, or to producers (shareholders)?

The claims of consumers to lower prices are rarely mentioned in this volume (note, however, the piece by Powrie). Although government policy has shown that price-fixing of energy resources is feasible, so that an implicit rent or windfall can be passed on to final users, the economists' distrust of this means of redistribution of the national income is revealed here by almost every author's neglect of this subject. Instead, the usual presumption has been that oil, gas, and natural raw materials are sold at market-clearing prices in more or less competitive circumstances. The greater the scarcity of these materials, the higher their prices, and the more profit or surplus is available for taxation. The proceeds of taxation can be spent or redistributed to the public; which part of the public is determined by the choice of government that is to do the taxing. But it is the citizen, not the resource consumer, who is considered.

Nor does the shareholder get much sympathy herein. The authors argue, in many ways, that taxation should not kill the goose that lays the golden egg. That is, taxation should not be so onerous that firms will withdraw rather than produce. If this condition is met, the authors presume that shareholders are receiving something like a Marshallian normal profit, enough to justify their maintaining their investments and replacing their depleted resources in the face of profitable alternatives in other parts of the world. While few authors even mention any policy of making firms worse off—say, by expropriation—equally few suggest any inherent advantage in distributing any of the remaining surplus (after normal profit) to shareholders or capital.

Consumers, in other words, are assumed by most authors to pay what supply and demand dictate, and businesses to receive at least enough to keep each industry's output on about the same path as would be observed in the absence of taxation. These assumptions tended to fence most of the authors out of familiar territory. Normally, we would expect specialists in industrial organizations to analyze revenue raising's impact on corporate price-setting behaviour and concentration; while specialists in public finance dealt with the incidence of depletion allowances in profit taxation. In the present volume, however, such analyses were only of minor relevance, unless they suggested that the impact, or incidence, depended on which government raised the revenue. If the impact was independent of the jurisdiction that used the tax base, there was nothing to be said herein. For example—to take an idea that was *not* advanced seriously—if provinces are confined to gross royalties, while Ottawa is for some reason more inclined to use a net tax on output, it could be argued that because the former levy tends to be more distorting of efficient extractive programs, the privilege of collecting resource taxes should be assigned to Ottawa. Several authors do verge on propounding views of this general type, but few strong beliefs emerge.

The authors divided themselves into three groups. The first group was concerned with the taxation of the mining and energy industries and its connection with natural resource policy. My own introductory chapter attempts to indicate ways of linking the choice of tax collector with the likely effects of the alternative collector's chosen system of taxation. The linkage depends on whether the taxes are on resource "rent" and so are "neutral," or on whether they are on costs or prices and so likely to distort or affect private output and timing decisions. A thorough survey by Campbell and Gainer investigates, in a series of simplified agricultural and rent cases, in what sense rent can be neutral. A companion piece by Powrie examines export taxation.

A second group of revenue oriented papers started at an earlier stage: instead of assuming that certain methods of raising revenue tended to be neutral, they showed their recognition that the general literature says little or nothing that is authoritative on this subject. This recognition impelled them to make careful case studies of the effect of certain taxes and agnostic conclusions about their general tendency (that is, their tendency to distort the plans and production programmes that would exist without taxation.). Among these we would mention especially Bradley and Leith; the papers of Maxwell, Watkins, and Campbell also bear on this subject. Bradley's discovery of how intricate a neutral mining tax would have to be is of particular interest.

The paper by Helliwell and and May has a related theme. Concentrating on the sensitivity of Syncrude revenues to various possibilities (such as price and cost changes), it can be taken as suggesting that the shares to be received by the various investing governments do not affect the amount to be shared: the equity-share method of distribution is assumed to be, and may indeed be, neutral.

While maintaining an interest in the neutrality distortion problem, a third group of the writers in this volume reserved their force for the problem of entitlement to resource revenues. Lederman succinctly reviews the constitutional situation, advancing the notion that who may tax resources is not engraved in tablets of bronze: rather the written constitution gives the provinces and Ottawa basic bargaining positions on which each may stand while debating and exploring routes to the resolution of new conflicts. Smiley reviews the issues in an authoritative survey in which resource revenues are seen as only part of the landscape; Canada will not stand or fall on the rights-to-rents question.

The economists were fascinated with the effect of increased provincial revenues on the revenues of other provinces via the equalization formula. My own paper presents some sketchy estimates of the importance of this reflective effect. In a long and important paper Courchene updates his earlier investigation of the equalization formula. Clark's expert comments are of value here.

Two authors remind us that choice of a government as a resource manager might well carry stipulations. It should not be assumed that, just because a province is close to a resource problem, its management will be efficient. Irene Spry points to the distorted pricing of resources used by Ontario Hydro as an example of what should be avoided. And Albert Breton, from another point of view, indicates how considerations of the costs of adjustment and of co-ordination inherent in managing natural resources should bear upon this question.

We were fortunate that at least two speakers felt able to put it all together. Moore's thoughts on the proper distribution of income were loosely linked to the neutrality discussions of the resource experts, strongly influenced by the estimates of Courchene and others of the importance of rents to nationwide equity in taxation and transfer payments. Thompson too was not neutral. But he was less concerned about the technicalities of non-distorting tax incidence than with the importance of resource management by the provinces and management's intimate association with taxation.

Thus the authors do rise to the occasion. While the industry expert's approach warns us against offhanded judgements about the impact of resource taxation, not all writers were inhibited from looking for, and propounding, a moral.

My own impression, as editor, is that among these authors a split verdict points to their support for a particular compromise policy. Resource revenues are connected with resource management: a variety of additional considerations then brings a consensus to the view that the levying of taxes and the charging of fees and royalties is best assigned to the provinces. But then provincialism wanes. Should redistribution of rents and windfalls be confined to the boundaries of the resource rich provinces? Several authors could find arguments in the affirmative, but few wished to press them heavily. Here nationwide redistribution, by "divisioning" (Gainer and Powrie), "equalization," or other means, was in the ascendant. The provinces should be regarded as stewards and bailiffs, not landlords; as rent collectors and managers, not rentiers and owners.

Acknowledgments

This collection of essays originated in a set of papers presented to the Victoria Conference on Natural Resource Revenues, held at the Empress Hotel, Victoria, B.C., 5-7 June 1975. To hold an economists' conference on this subject was the idea of Mason Gaffney, in his role as director of the British Columbia Institute for Analysis of Economic Policy. The Institute remained involved not only in the essential financing of each step, but also in the organization and staging of the conference and in assisting in the revision of manuscripts and the publication of this volume. In addition to Dr. Gaffney, all concerned are much in the debt of Miss Jean Mohart, Executive Secretary, both for planning and for prompt and expert aid at every stage; and to Mr. Len Rouechė, who took time off from his own research to provide a summary of the discussion. My own preparatory work was greatly aided by Peter Gardner at U.B.C., who also co-operated in conference co-ordination and trouble-shooting.

Not all who eventually contributed to the volume did so in full at the conference, and I am especially grateful to those authors who enlarged on their comments to make our published treatment more complete. I also wish to record the participation of the following economists (and experts in other fields), whose interventions both enlivened the conference and also led to improvements of many of the main papers: Professor R. Cheffins, University of Victoria; Professor Parzival Copes, Simon Fraser University; Mr. Richard Campbell, staff, Royal Commission on Forest Policy; Professor John Bossons, University of Toronto; Mr. G. Young, staff, Institute for Analysis of Economic Policy; Mr. A.J. Hepworth, staff, B.C. Energy Commission; Mr. Stephen Hollett, staff, Institute for Analysis of Economic Policy; Mr. George Post, Economic Council of Canada; Professor Meyer Bucovetsky, University of Toronto; Dr. John Young, Canada Department of Finance; Professor Peter Pearse, University of British Columbia.

In addition to helpful and constructive comments, Mr. R.W. Keyes of Cominco Ltd. contributed his own summary of the total discussion, a great help to the editor.

My task as editor has subsequently been greatly eased by the typing of Sheila Briggs and other secretaries at U.B.C. and the skilful editorial aid of Sanford Osler.

The contribution of the Institute and its members to this conference cannot be overrated, and I would like to conclude by thanking not only Dr. Gaffney but also Dr. Walter Young, Miss Mary Rawson, Mr. Alistair Crerar, and other members of the Board of Directors, who attended all sessions and who have kept a friendly eye on the preparation of this volume.

A.D.S.
August 1976

Who Should Get Natural Resource Revenues?

ANTHONY SCOTT *

I. INTRODUCTION

Who should get natural resource revenues in Canada? After the consumer and export prices have been set, the revenues are distributed. Much must go to the supplier of fuels, lubricants, and other materials. Most of the rest is spent on the purchase of the services of labour and capital. These amounts must not only be large enough to cover past contracts, but also adequate to satisfy the expectations of workers and capitalists that investing their time or funds will be, risk and uncertainty aside, rewarded in the future. After all these contractual and incentive needs are satisfied, we may find a surplus, signalling that the total revenue has been larger than strictly necessary. This is *rent*, the sum of the surplus of every type of earning over what could be earned in the best alternative.

In what follows, I simply assume that natural resource revenues emanate not from the taxation of these necessary earnings, but from the taxation of the rent. This assumption is made for convenience. But it could be defended by arguing that in fact the services of labour and capital used in Canadian resource industries are highly mobile and versatile—in fact, elastic in supply. It would follow that governments cannot in the long run successfully tax any part of resource sales revenues except the rent; attempts to do so would result in the contracting of industry to those shows and sites where the tax could be shifted from necessary factor earnings to rent.

Of course, it must be conceded that imperfections in the factor markets do result in some of the rent being spread around, being added here and there to wages and contractual capital payments. Furthermore, lack of intense competition in the product markets may result in consumers sometimes getting raw materials at bargain prices: here the rent may be thought of as being paid, as compared to arm's-length pricing, to the consumers. Nevertheless I shall assume that most of the rent accrues in the first instance as a residual profit or surplus to the firm, there to form a base for special natural resources taxes and fees, as well as the subject of special exemptions and allowances in personal income tax, corporation tax, and property tax administration. In brief, I am not trying to trace the rent that escapes the tax collectors' net.

Thus the subject I shall explore, put more precisely, is: who should tax the natural resource rents in Canada? The main contributions to an answer are, in Section II, a survey of certain abstract criteria that may automatically suggest themselves to professional economists; and, in Section III, certain estimates of the extent to which the question has been quantitatively an important one.

The question itself is not, I believe, capable of unified analysis by economists' methods. Its allocational and microeconomic aspects range from the definition of "rent" when resources are extractive rather than renewable, to the problems of incentive and uncertainty when exploration and discovery are also essential aspects of supply cost. And its distributional aspects are just as diffuse, combining three separate questions: who should receive pure rents (unearned surplus); how can income inequalities be reduced; and how large is the population over which redistribution should take place? Economists, accustomed to applauding the taxation of windfalls, normally dodge the latter two questions. But they will find that they are more or less inextricably intertwined here, and must be considered simultaneously.

Thus the integrity of the whole problem arises not from any tidy methodological unity, but from the fact that Canada, in the 1970's, is presented with both the allocational and the distributional aspects of the same problem: how should the revenues from natural resources be shared among governments?

II. SURVEY OF CRITERIA FOR THE ASSIGNMENT OF NATURAL RESOURCE REVENUES

The purpose of this section is to survey the various arguments, or criteria, which have been advanced to justify the assignment of natural resource revenues to one or another of the two levels of government. By "assignment" I mean the awarding of the revenues of natural resource activities not only as a base for taxation, as in the awarding of the power to levy a certain tax, but also as a source of income from the sale or lease of lands, both before their exploitation and afterwards (i.e., both in the form of a price charged for the right to exploit and a royalty for having done so). Canadian statistics, following the Canadian constitution, rightly attempt to keep these two forms of revenue distinct; but in this section I will recognize that they are essentially using the same base and thus should be scrutinized to decide the extent to which the conflict between them is necessary and costly.

This survey takes the present institutions of government in Canada, including the constitution, as having only limited relevance to the assignment question. This is not to deny that any tax reassignment, based on a balancing of the criteria listed, may have such a high cost of negotiation and implementation as to be of negligible merit. For each of us is deeply imbedded in a structure of taxes and powers and can change our position in that structure only at the high cost of having to reconsider many matters that have already been decided under the existing structure of taxes and responsibilities. In addition, as economists we must recognize that the mechanisms of adjustment and capitalization have already wiped out and diffused many of the windfall gains and losses that accompanied the tax, spending, and resource alienation policies of earlier generations. Furthermore, we must acknowledge that many of the bad allocational results of earlier tax assignments are now of little more than historical interest: some resources have already vanished; some populations have already waxed and waned; many capital goods, public goods, and transportation facilities have already made their apparently imperishable imprint on the economic and political map of our country.

These considerations serve to remind us that we can unwind the historical skein only to a modest length, and that at heavy (and largely unknown) cost. Thus the present exercise, attempting to ignore much of today's laws, property rights, tax rates, and legislative powers is made in full knowledge that extensive reform, if it were suggested, would be extremely difficult and probably unjust. Its advantage is simply that in freeing us from the bondage of trying to remember what is sacred, it allows us to understand better the full implications of the criteria to which we now turn.

Institutional Criteria

I begin by considering institutional or "non-economic" criteria, such as law, custom, and property rights. I suggest, briefly, that these rules are not sufficiently strong to offer clear guidance in the revenue assignment problem. Then I turn to a search for allocational (efficiency) criteria.

a. The Constitutional Law. I can be brief on this legal topic because of the subsequent contribution from Professor Lederman. There he makes two points. In spite of present litigation and controversy, there is no doubt about the rights of the provinces to exercise their ownership powers in the collection of royalty-like payments; and there is no doubt about the power of the federal government to impose direct taxes. Professor

Lederman goes on to argue that while these two sets of rights may very well conflict, the role of the constitution is not so much to prevent such conflict as to give each side a base from which it can negotiate.

In this survey I have nothing to add to that general conception of the present position. Instead, I scrutinize other distributional and allocational arguments to see which side they tend to favour.

b. Crown ownership. Economists tend to be impressed by property rights. Thus they tend to feel that the resource revenue question is already largely settled by the fact that, in many places, the provincial Crown not only has certain taxation rights and legislative powers bestowed by the B.N.A. Act, but, more important, has also what are essentially private property rights.

Professor Lederman's chapter suggests that such rights may be overly impressive to economists; they are conceivably subject to much moderation by the exercise of federal powers.

The purpose of this more economically oriented section is to suggest that when provincial ownership co-exists with federal taxation powers on provincial tenants, Crown ownership as a species of landlord status does not imply to economists any particular division of the excess over necessary factor payments.

The federal taxes on the resource base are generally direct: for the most part modifications and extensions of the corporate income tax. Provincial taxes are also direct, including not only the corporate (and personal) income tax but also variants of the real estate property tax. In addition to these taxes, provincial revenues have been greatly augmented by public domain revenues from the use or alienation of Crown lands: royalties, licence and and lease rentals, charges and fees, and bonus payments. In principle these are identical to payments agreed between a private landowner and a tenant or buyer. (They include certain payments in kind, such as the building of a railroad; and services originally or later rendered to the landlord.)[1]

Many such payments, being once-for-all consideration for freehold occupation of the resource, were made a century or more ago and no longer are Crown revenues. Others were for freehold resource use or occupation, but carried a commitment to pay some payment such as a royalty to the original landlord. Resources exploited by the private sector more recently still tend to be Crown property, and often must be handed back to (or reclaimed by) the Crown. It has been argued that it would be unjust (or would distort the efficiency of the different choices made by different provinces as to the mode of alienation of their resources) if some provinces were now to lose future royalties on virgin lands, while others have nothing to lose in the future. This point is not unimportant, as data to be presented later will show. If we examine the time series of provincial comprehensive resource revenues, we see that, even since 1900, a large part of these were earned before 1914 by some provinces, but were delayed till after 1945, or later, by some others. Furthermore, some provinces tend to take their resource revenues in such immobile forms as roadbuilding and other developmental outlays, while others prefer past, or future, cash.

If we assume that each province had a rational motive for its own timing and mode of resource alienation, a decision to turn only royalty revenue over to the federal government would be unjust. It would impose little burden on those provinces that had opted for early alienation and perhaps scattering of the proceeds; and a large burden on those which still looked forward to a future stream of such proceeds.

The mere fact of Crown ownership is usually regarded as a *prima facie* demonstration that all the rents should be returned to the Crown. "If the lands are provincial, the royalties are a contractual payment owing to the province." The difficulty is that such statements do not tell us how much of a rent should be captured by a landlord.

If we try the analogy with capturing of rent by private landlords, we find an essential difference. First, the provincial Crown has not acted like a competitive landlord. Most provinces have not, since Confederation, levied onerous royalties; some have levied none at all on some Crown tenures. There have been various reasons for this, [2] but none of them has suggested an owner who, faced with a derived demand for a resource in fixed supply, set out to extract the most that competitive bidding could bring in. Thus, if the Crown's motives were different from private competitive landlords', we cannot expect to learn much from a comparison with market institutions.

This flaw in the analogy between private and Crown rents is confirmed by a second observation. In taxation of such other industries as agriculture, the private landlord's share of the gross revenues is not so large as to leave nothing for the federal income tax collector. The farmer makes a payment to both.

The reason for this is obvious. In a simple theory textbook model, without government or taxation, the rent collector can capture 100 per cent of the surplus. And in a simple public finance model, the tax collector can take 100 per cent. But when both are out to capture the same surplus, there is no simple textbook rule about the division of this pie. The rent collectors may be attempting to capture all the residue *after* taxes; or the tax collector may be attempting to capture all the residue *after* rent payments; or both. Furthermore, neither may seek 100 per cent of their residue, but only a modest percentage. I believe that this is what we have witnessed in the past. If so, Canadian economic history offers no useful analogy to today's resource rent problem. More important from the point of view of the present survey, the mere fact of Crown ownership, surprisingly, offers no clear guidance to the distributional question.

c. The relevant redistributional group. The third and final redistributional criterion to be mentioned here is that of the optimum breadth of the income redistribution jurisdiction. The idea is as follows. An assignment of a revenue base to a particular jurisdiction (or level of government) is also an indication of the extent of the population among whom the revenues (and the profits, surpluses, and rents on which they are based) are to be redistributed. Thus a local school tax may redistribute a mine's revenues among only a few thousand citizens, whereas a national income tax on the same base would diffuse this rent among millions.

This contrast is rarely so vivid in practice. Local property tax revenues tend to be equalized and standardized; and national taxes tend to "return" some revenues to the locality or province where the base is. Furthermore, most resources are liable for both kinds of imposts, so that the question should be about the preferred combination of the two taxes. Nevertheless, the criterion suggested is clear: resource rents should be the base for the revenues of jurisdictions whose population most nearly approximates the group to whom rents ought to be redistributed.

What group is this? This is not a familiar question to Canadians. By far the majority of contributions to the literature of federal-provincial finance have been based on one or more of our six previous criteria, or with "national standards": the goal that all provinces should have at least the fiscal capacity to finance a minimum level of public services. These include various provincial social services and transfers. National unconditional grants, including equalization grants, are advocated as a means to this goal. Some of these same services and transfers are further assisted by national conditional grants. Indeed the whole pattern of national conditional and unconditional grants to the provinces is, it might be argued, tantamount to a scheme to offer uniform income transfers everywhere. In support of this interpretation of the goal of grant policy, we find that welfare payments and other social services are in many years nearly as high in the "poor" as in the "rich" provinces.

Nevertheless, there are limits to the extent of this actual equalization, and some of them stem from the confusion created by natural resource revenues in the present federal equalization formula. It could require that the federal government increase its taxes on all bases in all provinces in order to bring the adjusted fiscal capacity of the resource-poor provinces closer to the swollen average revenues of the resource-rich provinces. Swollen resource revenues do not get redistributed directly so that it is quite possible that if the base for federal taxes does not include many resource rents, they would not even get redistributed indirectly. Thus Ottawa has seen the enrichment of the Alberta treasury as a source of "cost" to Ottawa (and to federal taxpayers generally) in the undertaking to make equalization payments to provinces that Alberta has outstripped.

The more basic question, whether resource revenues *ought* to be redistributed within a local, or a nationwide area, and so *ought* to be assigned to a particular level of government, has never come up for explicit discussion in Canada. "Nationwide redistribution," being confined to intergovernmental equalization issues, has been implicitly defined merely as the equalization of fiscal capacity for all provincial services, rather than as the more ambitious nationwide sharing of natural resource economic rents, when and as they are realized. This perception is related to the Canadian attitude to "rights"—it is not clear that most Canadians believe they have any "right" to "horizontal equity."[3] While it is in general correct to say that in Canada federal tax rates are the same for taxpayers everywhere, there is actually no "uniformity" provision in the Canadian constitution. Tax abatements and "opting out" procedures indeed have led to an accepted inter-regional difference between the burden of federal taxes in the different regions (though some of this variability could be said to be matched by equal variations in services). Further, the acceptability of the idea that "property and civil rights" should remain at the centre of provincial powers would seem, to a non-lawyer, to imply acceptance of somewhat different sets of economic "rights" from coast to coast. I would suggest that this is a different attitude from that in the U.S., where a somewhat closer connection between national citizenship and uniform economic rights appears to be demanded. But more work would be necessary to establish the Canadian point of view (especially if I am correct that most Canadians have not, so far, thought about geographical redistribution beyond the possibility of equalizing provincial fiscal capacities).[4]

But that something is really at stake can be demonstrated. In Section III of this chapter we show how extensive natural resource revenues have been in each province, and what difference would be made to the revenues of each province if resource revenues were pooled and spread over the whole country. Three different variants of the present equalization formula are used. There it is shown that the "have" and "have not" provinces would substantially change places. Today's have provinces make less use of other taxes than do the have nots. An equitable nationwide sharing of resource revenues would, therefore, lead to a convergence of individual tax pressure on citizens in the two groups of provinces.

Allocational Criteria

I turn now to criteria which are not explicitly distributional in their orientation. Instead I seek "economic" as opposed to ethical reasons for preferring one level of natural resource tax collector rather than another.
a. Resource revenues as benefit taxes. The first of these is taken from the literature of public finance, and commences with traditional reasons for assigning certain taxes to "local" jurisdictions. While this idea does not take us very far, it does suggest a benefit tax or imputation motive for dividing the rent *between* the taxing levels of government.

In the literature of public finance, it is argued that because the benefits of government action are spatially restricted, it is desirable to confine a government's taxing power to the geographical area within which it supplies goods and services. The map of taxpayers, voters, and beneficiaries should be identical.

Some of this argument is far from compelling, being based on the assumption that jurisdictions cannot make bargains with their neighbours when net benefits spill across borders. If this assumption is not correct, then the efficiency of containing all government services, beneficiaries, and taxpayers within one frontier does not follow. It may, for example, turn out to be less costly to bargain with neighbours than to attempt to "internalize" all revenues and services.

Nevertheless, there is much to be said for a weaker maxim, traceable to Alfred Marshall and Ursula Hicks and utilized by Charles Tiebout.[5] It is based on the idea that the possibility of interjurisdictional migration enables people to reveal their preferences among the tax and benefit offerings of different, "competing" jurisdictions. Not only can people with different preferences choose their jurisdiction, but jurisdictions can attract the number of people they need to spread costs acceptably.

For this process to work, however, it is necessary that taxes be "localized." That is, people must be prevented from enjoying the region's services while escaping the region's taxes. It is a frequent conclusion to this line of reasoning that a land or property tax meets the desired localization specification. This is because it is, in large part, a levy on the rent of land.

This conclusion is not a familiar part of the theory of factor prices and distribution. There the rent of land is usually regarded as a pure windfall: a payment in excess of that necessary to provide any of the variable inputs used on the land. As such it can be distributed in any way, to any combination of persons (and tax collectors), without affecting the allocation of resources. What then is its connection with government services?

The missing link is supplied by the argument that society raises the demand for the services of land, and, land's supply being fixed, its value or rent. Thus the rent of land is not an exogenous windfall from society's point of view, but is a consequence of social actions and decisions.

Henry George's rather loose application of this argument was that "the rent of the land belongs to the people." In his case, it was not the government, but society as a whole, that created land value and so was entitled to it. Government's role was simply to capture the annual surplus from the landowners. If the amount of rent is unaffected by any government's actions, it follows that any particular government's claim to these rents could be based only on its capacity to collect taxes or on extraneous distributional arguments.

However, if the amount of rent is dependent on government services, then it may be argued that the rent is not a pure windfall, distributable anywhere, but is a source for a payment which is *necessary* to maintain itself. If it is not paid (if it is avoided or escaped), the mobility of tax-payers will cause the jurisdiction's revenues to be inadequate to supply the necessary services. Furthermore, within the larger area within which factors are generally mobile, the claim of any particular level of government to capture rents must be limited to that part of rent that its services have created.

To summarize, in this view the payment received by industry for the product of land or a natural resource is matched by a set of claims by suppliers of raw materials and purchased services, labour, capital, and by each of the hierarchy of government jurisdictions that has provided services either to complement other inputs or to expand final demand. Each of these payments is "necessary," in the long run. (On top of them all, of course, there may be a final unearned, unnecessary surplus that can be captured by anyone, or any government.)

On this approach, the assignment of natural resource revenues in Canada would require an expansion of the imputation process that underlies distributional theory beyond the basic factors of production to the various levels of government. A marginal procedure might be imagined, for example, notionally varying slightly the amounts of provincial, local, and national services, and observing each time the change in resource values and rents. There is implicit in much Canadian writing on this subject a prediction that this procedure would reveal provincial services to be most important. Provincial provision of such services as roads and highways would, it is believed, turn out to be much more important, dollar for dollar, for resource rents than expenditure on federal functions. In brief, provincial actions are thought to be necessary for the existence of taxable rent, but federal actions are not.

In any case, the theory itself is neutral as between levels of government. It has a cutting edge only when expenditure functions have already been assigned. While it may indeed lend extra support to provincial claims, its general effect is to suggest that both levels of government must get some part of the rent.

Notice that this long train of reasoning suggests a quick test. In the case of private services, non-payment of wages or interest leads to the withdrawal of inputs and the reduction of the value of output. In the same sense the "benefit" theory suggests that tax payments to a particular government are necessary. Thus, if the rents are not paid as resource revenues or are captured by another level of government, the result should be the withdrawal of government services. (Not out of pique, but because the necessary payments are not being received.) If this test is passed, certain resource revenues belong to the service-providing government as surely as wages belong to the worker.

b. Exhaustibility. The second efficiency criterion for the assignment of resource revenues has to do with the exhaustibility of resources. It was once argued by the Rowell-Sirois Commission, and it has not since been disputed, that exhaustibility justified assigning mineral taxation to the provincial governments. The Commission's argument was not dependent on some provinces' extensive ownership of Crown resources. Dealing with the contemporary provincial mining tax, the Commission argued that its proposal for its retention by the provinces

> recognizes the justice of the provincial claim to direct participation in the profits arising from the exploitation of their wasting assets...
> and will supply revenues both to amortize provincial expenditures on development and to prepare for the expenditures necessary when the resources are depleted. On the other hand, it should be recognized that, although the resources belong to the provinces, their profitable development depends to a large extent on Dominion tariff, trade and monetary policies, and on Dominion expenditures on transportation and development, and that the Dominion is also entitled to a direct share of these resource revenues in order to amortize its own expenditures on developing them.
>
> The mining tax rebate is recommended because the profits of these companies are made from the depletion of natural resources within the province. No similar proposal is made in the case of other natural resources such as forests...[6]

Nothing could be clearer. Recognizing that most resources belong to the provinces (and in other paragraphs recognizing too, that provinces obtain revenues under public domain powers), the Commission set out depletion as a separate criterion. They used it to justify their assurances that even those provinces that own none of their resources should receive enough to "amortize" development and managerial expenditures. The reader will recognize that this criterion is very similar to that outlined as the "benefit" principle above (see section "resource revenues as benefit taxes").

What is not so clear is the application of this criterion to the specification of how much of the net return from, say, mining, a province should receive. The problem arises because of mobility. Expenditure which has a wasting value is not only that which assisted directly in the "development" of the resources, but also that which was demanded to provide services for the provincial population which may or may not drift elsewhere after the resources are depleted. The picture suggested by the Commission's words, of an amortizable debt incurred in providing roads, etc., to assist resource development, which must be paid off quickly while the resource profit is still taxable, is rarely seen in practice. Instead we observe only the remnants of populations that have been attracted by a resource later having to cover public expenditures without the help of resource profits.

It does not seem to have mattered to the Commission that provinces may not actually use such revenues for quick amortization of durable public works or preparation for leaner years. Indeed, the Commission's whole approach demanded that the provinces should be free to decide how to use tax bases assigned to them.

But it should have mattered, for the decision is by no means of purely local importance. For future private decisions to migrate are much influenced by earlier public amortization decisions. This can be seen by comparing the effects of one extreme policy using local mining taxation to reduce the burden of other private taxation, with the opposite extreme, using it for early retirement of the local public debt. Compared with tax burdens in new agricultural regions where there is no exhaustion of resources, the former policy would enable residents to amortize their private expenditures early and to accumulate capital, but would prolong the tax burden for public works debt, perhaps beyond the life of the mines. The latter policy, in contrast, would allow the government budget to rise and fall with mineral production and employment in the mines. Individual tax rates would continue more or less on a par with those in agricultural regions.

Thus the former policy aggravates local population fluctuations. When workers are moving in, the especially light individual tax burden attracts many people whose successors or descendants will be driven away by the heavy tax burdens of a region now without a mining tax base. This policy may have much to recommend it, encouraging rather than slowing down the inevitable population movements of any mining frontier (as I argued in my 1965 Queen's paper).[7] However, in the present context, it should be pointed out that relative to the latter policy, it tends to place an extra tax burden for welfare and public works on the provinces to which the migrants move.[8] It is even possible that a policy superior to the two alternatives just compared would be to assign some of the mining tax revenues either to the potential emigrants, to carry with them, or to the government of the region to which they are migrating. Because either policy would be very costly to administer, it might be easier to assign part of the mining tax revenue to the national government.

This brief discussion should be sufficient to suggest the necessity to distinguish analytically two separable aspects of the wasting resource problem. One stems from resource depletion; the other from any subsequent depopulation.

As a resource is depleted, the local population becomes less able to sustain the burden of public works and the associated debts incurred when annual resource earnings were at their height. One problem arises out of market failure: the cleft between the planning of resource development and depletion and between public works investment and depreciation. One can imagine ways of overcoming this problem. If for example the rate of resource extraction and the amortization of public works was the business of the same decision-maker (public or private, as in a company town), then the optimum rates might well be reached; it might be predicted that these rates would be consonant with marginal values rising over time at the rate of discount. This planning problem would be the only problem if the public works were less durable than the exhaustible resources. However, if they were more durable, the Rowell-Sirois remedy would also be required. The shorter the life of the resources, the larger the percentage of the local resource rents neeeded by the local government. Proof is indicated by extreme cases. Imagine an immensely valuable deposit that could be profitably mined out only in one year. Special local roads and a townsite would therefore need to be amortized (after salvage values) over one year. If the local government had no access to a special large tax, it could provide no roads and the resource could not be exploited. Next imagine that it might be physically possible to spin out extraction over several years, paying for local roads with a smaller annual tax. But this would be more costly. Thus (in the absence of other social costs) a presumption is established that local power to levy a large tax on extraction would be more efficient than a limitation of that power to a small, or zero, tax. This seems to be a restatement of the Rowell-Sirois point.

The second aspect of exhaustibility is depopulation. Our conclusion about this phenomenon is less clear because depopulation of a jurisdiction, followed by migration to another jurisdiction, brings about a little understood "double burden."

One of these burdens is chiefly financial: the concentration of the burden of debt amortization and asset maintenance onto the shoulders of a diminished group of taxpayers. There may also be some real extra costs of adapting large-scale assets for a smaller population. The other burden is chiefly a real one: the cost of extra public services and goods to provide for the new migrants from the depopulated region. It may be borne partly by the new arrivals themselves, but the tax administration system may cause it to be spread over the entire body of taxpayers. Both burdens are real enough to those who bear them, and sufficient to justify special tax provisions if exhaustion does cause depopulation.

There are at least two sure-fire methods of preventing the double burden. One would be to finance durable social assets at the same time as resources are alienated; they might, for example, be a first charge on developers, leaving the developer free to choose any rate of extraction and the population any flow of emigration. Another would be to bestow the debt personally on the various members of the population: this would give them an incentive to ensure that the rate of resource extraction and their own planned emigration were harmonized. (Probably they would consent to live under such a system only if mineral shares, or royalties, were issued to them at the same time as they incurred part of the public debt.) While such schemes are fanciful, they do suggest ways in which emigrants, on arrival in their new communities, could afford to pay a special immigration levy to their new government, thus reducing the burden from double to single.

How should these various possibilities be taken into account, in assigning actual resource revenues? To be completely general, the criterion ought to be worded somewhat as follows: a local jurisdiction's share of total resource revenue should vary directly with the "exhaustibility" of its resources (e.g., the inverse of their expected life), and the durability of the public works (e.g., their expected service life) associated with the exploitation of the resources; and should vary inversely with the proportion of the original population expected to remain, after resource exhaustion, within the jurisdiction. The complexity of this condition suggests that the simple fact of expected exhaustion is not a sufficient criterion. It works, for example, to suggest that it might be a very good idea to assign a mining tax to Ontario but not so imperative to assign it to Saskatchewan, because the likelihood of population emigration subsequent to resource depletion seems to me least for Ontario. Both need the tax if they cannot harmonize resource extraction rates and public works depreciation. In principle, however, the greater the subsequent depopulation, the weaker any province's case for retaining mining revenues and the stronger the argument for assigning some revenues to adjoining or senior governments to help "prepare for the expenditures necessary when resources are depleted."

c. Time preference. If the province and the central government discount the future differently, who should have the revenue? The previous criterion has already suggested one way in which time preference matters. One jurisdiction may attempt to conserve resources and replace wasting assets so as to maintain social capital intact; another may in effect consume this capital by spending much of its revenues on current goods and services, or on reducing private taxes.

This difference should not be misinterpreted. A government that reduces individual taxes, increases transfers, or adds to pensions may be considered to have assisted its citizens to make their own private provisions out of increased disposable income for the future. It would differ from the conserving government only in its preference for private rather than public capital. [9] A difference between governments that is more important here is in their patience: their attitudes to increased public or private capital formation versus increased current public or private spending.

Should resource revenues go to impatient, or patient, governments? Often, there is no real difference. Most governments have access to the same capital markets, so that their borrowing or lending will tend always to bring their *marginal* rates of time preference (the revealed percentage rate at which they add to or draw down their financial assets) toward equality. Their *average* attitude to the future hardly comes into it. Thus differences in risk, scale of borrowing, or access to the central capital market will normally account only in the short run for revealed differences in governments' marginal time preference rates.

If for some reason differences in impatience do persist, they would surely suggest to an all-knowing constituent assembly fresh grounds for assigning resource revenues. Should not the propensity to reinvest be given weight? My problem is that I cannot proceed from here. Unless it is known that a government's capital market constraint is contrived, or unless it is known that different governments' reinvestment policies differ because of ignorance or stupidity, calling for paternalistic intervention, how should a constituent assembly choose between present-oriented and future-oriented levels of government?

d. Risk Aversion. When governments depend on natural resource revenues that vary with output grade or price they are sharing the risks of such variation with the taxpayers and managers. This is true for almost every revenue, even those that are payable before exploitation begins. It is true that a pre-exploitation bonus bid based on an offer by a firm that has made an evaluation of the risks ahead enables a government to accept a certain amount at one firm's price or premium for risk-bearing. But use of this system does not mean that governments can avoid resource risks. To the contrary. To see this, consider a government deciding whether to accept a stream of *ex ante* offers or a stream of *ex post* royalties for all the successive resource plays within its province. At the time before this choice between these alternative payment systems is made, both systems are subject to risk; neither has a certain present value. Selecting the system of *ex ante* offers for individual sites and plays leaves the government with a future revenue stream that is unknown and subject to future variability with output, grade, and price. While variations with this system may be less frequent and more discrete, they may be more violent than with the *ex post* system. I would expect both alternative streams to have about the same present value.

To me it seems that it is impossible in a competitive economy for a small government to avoid the cost of bearing risk. For firms in a competitive extractive industry, borrowing and lending on a worldwide capital market will tend to offer bids that, over time, over many plays, and over all firms, are risk-standardized. The industry as a whole will hedge its bets, for it will not be able to obtain capital for investments with unknown variability of outcomes. Thus over time and over all offers the residual cost of variability must be borne by the landlord—the government. The amount of this cost, however, will depend on whether the government decides to accept the industry's risk-bearing price or whether it decides to carry the variability itself.

Risk aversion might therefore be identified as follows. Consider the governments of two similar regions. A very risk-averse administration would attempt, without much investigation into future prospects, to find one giant firm or consortium that would make a single initial payment for the privilege of free exploitation of all the resources it could discover, with very little sensitivity to the implicit "premium" charged by industry. A very risk-prone administration, at the other extreme, would decide on the same slight information to carry out exploration itself, or to share all profits and losses proportionately with contractors. Any risk "premium" subtracted by industry from its bids would be too high.

However, such differences between governments' willingness to bear

risk need not reflect mental differences between their citizens or
ministers. They may well be determined by their capacity to deal with
highly variable resource revenues. In the first place, levels of
governments may differ in their access to the capital market. The level
with most imperfect access may be forced to pay more dearly for loans
to cushion it in periods of unexpectedly low resource revenues; it would
tend to convert this high cost into a preference for stable systems of
resource taxation. Secondly, the governments may differ in the cost of
adjustment of their public and private economies to variable revenues.
In a host of ways, including its ability to interrupt certain public
expenditure programmes and its power to suddenly raise the weight of
private taxation on other industries, one level of government may be
better equipped than another to cope with a variable stream of resource
revenues. This brings us to the powerful Samuelson and Arrow-Lind
analyses. Envisaging a single level of government with no access to a
wider capital market, their models suggest that higher levels of
government are better able to "pool" different sources of variable
revenue. [10]

Other explanations may also be offered. Recent explorations by P.A.
Neher of political decisions by a changing majority of an electorate
changing through time may suggest that the younger a jurisdiction's
population, the more inclined it would be to a safety-first approach. [11]
(Here the boundary between time preference and risk aversion becomes
hazy.) And, of course, there is nothing absurd in the idea that people do
differ temperamentally in their zest in, or aversion to, variable revenues
or taxes.

Is the risk-aversion criterion likely to help with the problem of
assigning resource revenues? Not if all levels of government are hooked
into a central capital market. All would be expected to behave similarly in
the presence of risk.

If they were not equally able to borrow, which level of government
ought to be favoured? The public sector as a whole would tend to pay
more to the private sector as a whole for safety from revenue variability,
the lower the level of government chosen to receive these revenues. Some
readers of this paper have argued that, in those circumstances, it would
be inefficient to assign resource revenues to lower level governments that,
unable to withstand risk, tended always to go for the most secure,
invariable tax and tenure systems of resource alienation. While one must
sympathize with this conclusion, one must warn that a resulting
assignment to higher levels would not be based purely on allocational
grounds unless the lower level of government, having resource revenues
taken from it, were compensated by grants from the higher, more risk-

prone, level. This assignment would then achieve something like hooking the lower level into the world capital market. Otherwise, it would not be possible to argue that Canadian welfare was damaged if the most risk-averse levels of government continued to receive the most risky of revenues.

Much more research needs to be done before this tentative conclusion can be regarded as comprehensive.

This section of the paper has contained both institutional or distributional and allocational or non-distributional criteria for assigning resource revenues in a federation. In the next few lines I attempt to summarize the latter.

It is surprising that for what seems a purely distributional question— who should get the resource revenues?—several efficiency criteria can be suggested. But so it has turned out. To review them, they appeared as follows: a. resource revenues are essentially benefit taxes and should be paid to the governments that provide the benefits; b. resource revenues arise from exhaustible assets and should accrue to the level of government that incurs the burdens arising from exhaustion and depopulation; c. resource revenues raise questions of time preference and should be collected by the level of government most able to make efficient allocations over time; d. resource revenues raise questions of the burden of risk of revenue variability and should be collected by the level of government least prone to pay highly for a risk-free stream of revenues.

My discussion of these four arguments has shown that there are circumstances in which they might be compelling. None of them is trivial. When a level of government is highly specialized in serving few people or providing few services, the criteria must be given weight.

But, in Canada, where the provinces are each large, varied, and hooked into the same capital market as serves the federal government, criteria c. and d. tend to fade away. Then we are left only with a. and b. These may well survive, as they have in the past. Provinces should collect revenues for the special services that they provide, especially when such expenditures must be amortized over a short period of time. But the same criteria arguments point to a division of the revenues. The federal government also provides special services to the resource industries. It may also serve as the proxy collector of revenues needed for the special expenditures necessitated by the immigration from regions where resources have been exhausted.

III. HOW MUCH REVENUE IS THERE TO REDISTRIBUTE?

It would be highly satisfying to be able, in this section, to present an estimate of the amount of natural resource *rent* available to be taxed, by one jurisdiction or the other. But this ideal is unattainable. Not only data, but also rigorous definition of "taxable rent" are non-existent. Instead we first present estimates of actual *revenues* from natural resources collected by or paid to the provinces since 1900. In the following subsections we will compare these figures with the outcome if the federal government had collected the revenue and redistributed it on the basis of the current federal "equalization" formula.

1. Comprehensive Natural Resource Revenue

Considering how often resource revenues have been discussed in Canada, it is surprising that no agreed figure has been calculated. In what follows, I have taken it on myself to define a "comprehensive natural resource" total, as follows.

We use as our base the concept "provincial natural resource revenue" as it has emerged from work by tax study committees. Its definition is complex but it includes provincial Crown mineral and forestry stumpage, dues, leases, licences, royalties, fees from provincial public domain lands, and resources; *plus* logging and mining profits taxes; *plus* identifiable property tax-like revenues on forest, timber, mineral, etc. assessed values or acreages, some of them labelled school taxes; *plus* certain revenues from fishing and trapping. (Similar revenues accrue to the northern territories, and to the federal government directly, but are ignored here.)

This total, connected with the calculation of equalization grants, is now published annually by Statistics Canada. Our job has been (1) to push it back toward 1900; and (2) to add to it revenues collected as (provincial) corporation taxes on natural resource extraction; while (3) making sure that we exclude agricultural land, activity, or profit. With these adjustments, we have an approximation to a measure of provincial revenue from the holding and/or exploitation of (mostly extractive) natural resources in the provinces. Some individual and farm income and rent is thereby omitted when ideally it should be included. Furthermore, much revenue is omitted that is collected as provincial sales taxes, business taxes, and so forth, which has, no doubt, a substantial effect on the rent that would otherwise exist as a base for more direct proprietorial revenues. These calculations are presented and described in detail in the attached Appendix.

The derivation of our total for a recent year (1971) is illustrated in Table 1.

Are such totals large or small? We can gain some perspective by temporarily ignoring our new "comprehensive" series and using published series for a comparison of *public domain* revenues with total provincial government revenues. Naturally, they are most important in the resource-

TABLE 1

	British Columbia	Ten provinces
"Natural resource revenue," as published by Statistics Canada	151	641
Of which public domain revenues mining and logging taxes	134	
Other	17	
Provincial corporation tax on natural resource extraction	3	25
"Comprehensive natural resource revenue," "total"	154	666

rich provinces: they were equal to 12 per cent of B.C.'s, 30 per cent of Alberta's, but only 6 per cent of all provinces' combined gross provincial revenues from *all* sources. The latter, Canada-wise percentage may be compared with some earlier dates: for all provinces, roughly similar public domain revenues, rents etc. would have been about almost 20 per cent in 1913, 17 per cent in 1921, 15 per cent in 1926, 10 per cent in 1930, 9 per cent in 1937, 9 per cent in 1939, 11 per cent in 1949, and 12 per cent in 1950. Just what one should make of this graceful trend, and of its subsequent precipitate drop in 1970 to 6 per cent is not clear.

In looking at the raw data I got the impression that in the 1920's and 1930's public domain revenues were more stable—less volatile—both than they are today and than other revenue sources. Many of them were specific, being essentially per acre fees and charges, so this is not surprising. Today, however, being based heavily on royalties, profits taxes, and bonus payments, they are more sensitive to prices and outputs and are thus more closely correlated with the base of other taxes. It is also clear that their relative importance to most provinces has greatly declined. One reason for the decline is that tax rates on bases such as retail sales, personal income, and corporations have increased as the provinces have gained new grants, transfers, and shared tax sources and as immigration and economic development generally have tended to reduce the "hewer of wood and drawer of water" role of taxable industries.

Whatever the explanation, the trend and changing provincial distribution are both suggested by these rough estimates. In 1913, and in the interwar period, the average province depended heavily, but to a diminishing degree, on resource revenues. Nearly every province (except the prairies) shared. [12] This downward trend has continued. However, the dependence of the resource-rich provinces on such revenues has actually increased.

Details of this trend, and the distribution, of public domain revenues can

FIGURE 1

PROVINCIAL NATURAL RESOURCE REVENUES:
FOUR ALTERNATIVE EQUALIZATION FORMULAE

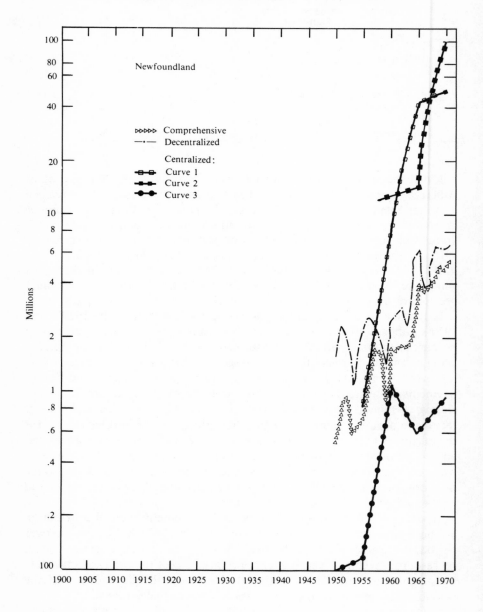

FIGURE 1A

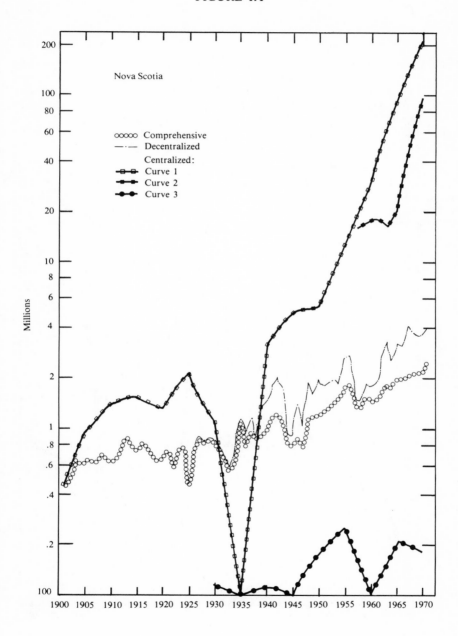

22

FIGURE 1B

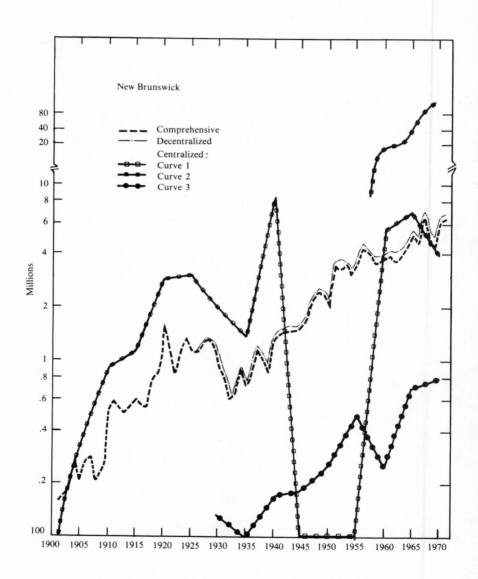

FIGURE 1C

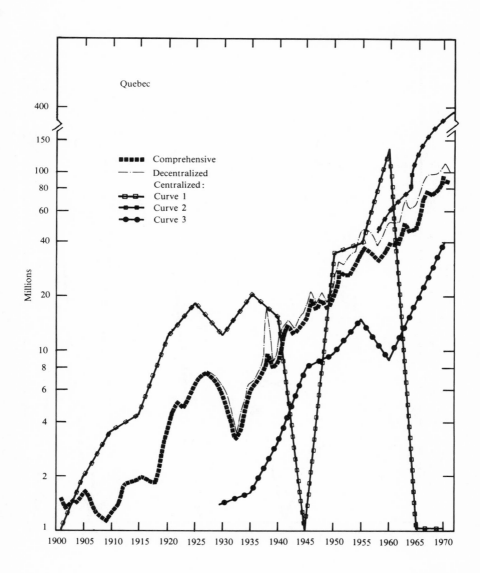

24

FIGURE 1D

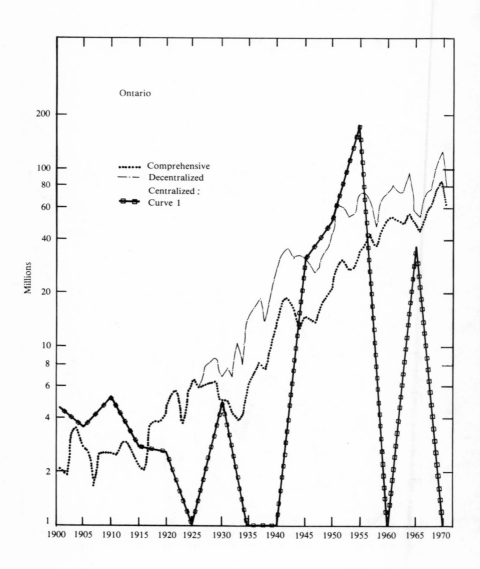

Ontario

Comprehensive
Decentralized
Centralized :
Curve 1

Millions

200

100
80

60

40

20

10
8

6

4

2

1

1900 1905 1910 1915 1920 1925 1930 1935 1940 1945 1950 1955 1960 1965 1970

FIGURE 1E

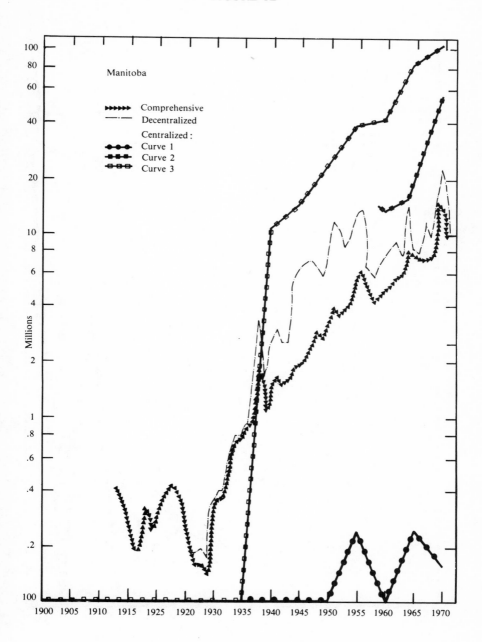

FIGURE 1F

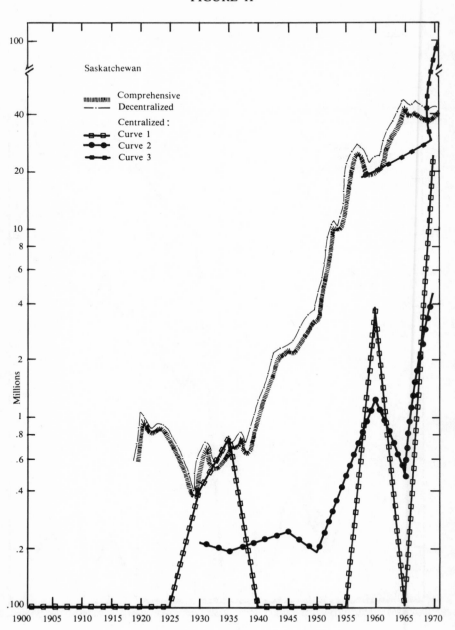

FIGURE 1G

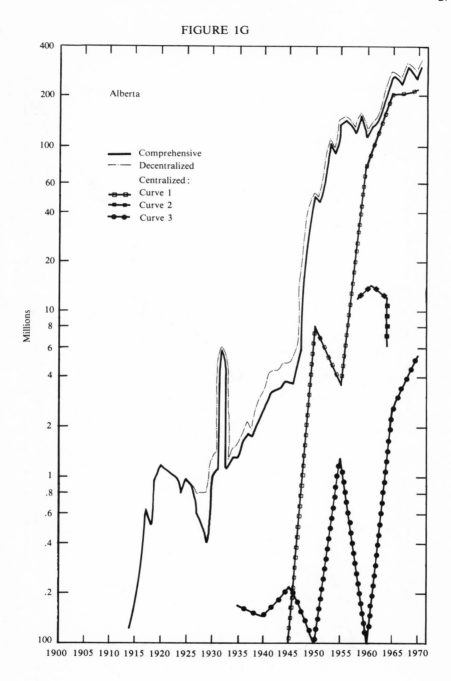

FIGURE 1H

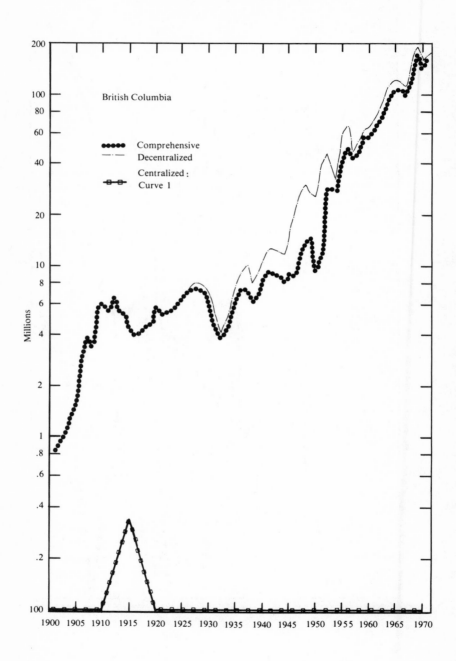

British Columbia

Comprehensive
Decentralized
Centralized :
Curve 1

Millions

TABLE 2

COMPREHENSIVE RESOURCE REVENUE
AS PERCENTAGE OF GROSS PROVINCIAL REVENUE

1913	25	(33) *
1926	18	(22) *
1930	12	
1939	12	
1950	12	
1970	5	

* Note: In these years, the resource revenues of the prairie provinces were very small, being received instead by Ottawa. If we add all Ottawa's territorial resource revenue to the provinces', the first two figures above would be in 1913 and 1926 as shown in parentheses.

be shown more generally by recourse to our comprehensive figures. These are set out by province, since 1900, in Appendix Table 1 and also are charted with a solid line in Figure 1 (note that on this semi-log chart, the vertical scale changes slightly between provinces). As a percentage of gross provincial revenue, for all provinces, they would come out as shown in Table 2.

For one particular province, British Columbia, they would fall from about 50 per cent in 1913 to 10 per cent in 1970. Thus the familiar public domain figure tends to fall about 10 per cent below our comprehensive revenue estimate.

An alternative and revealing way of comparing the time series of natural resource revenue is shown in Figure 2. Here we show the data in *per capita* terms, by province. While the numbers are greatly in need of simplifying and smoothing, three interesting patterns stand out.

First, ever since 1900 British Columbia has been one of the "have" provinces (the resources boom of the 1900's, terminating in 1913, is clearly visible).

Second, Alberta and Saskatchewan, with British Columbia, moved far ahead of other provinces in the 1950's, and Nova Scotia fell well behind. Presumably this reflects *inter alia* the oil and gas booms.

Third, from 1900 to 1950 the per capita revenues of the provinces grew at surprisingly similar rates. British Columbia aside, it is possible to see a convergence around the Ontario-Quebec path. This may well constitute yet another illustration of the staple approach to Canadian development. [13] Resource revenue per capita may be regarded as a proxy for the carrying power of a region. When revenue rises, so does population; when it falls, population moves out. Thus the curves (apart from the oil and gas regions, where more sophisticated hypotheses are visibly necessary) illustrate how people are attracted or repelled by changing resource rents.

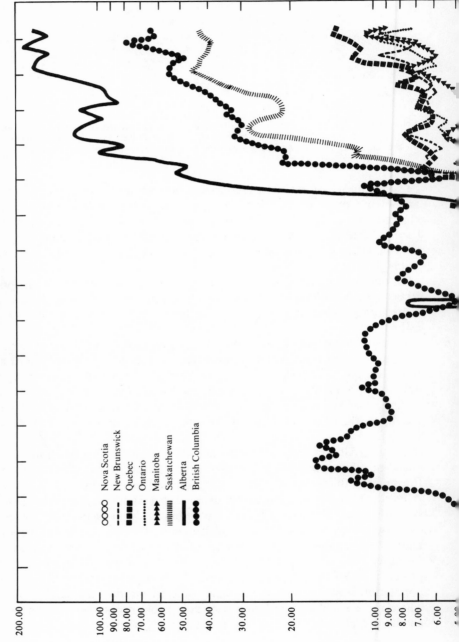

FIGURE 2

PER CAPITA NATURAL RESOURCE REVENUE,
BY PROVINCE, 1901-1971

Nova Scotia
New Brunswick
Quebec
Ontario
Manitoba
Saskatchewan
Alberta
British Columbia

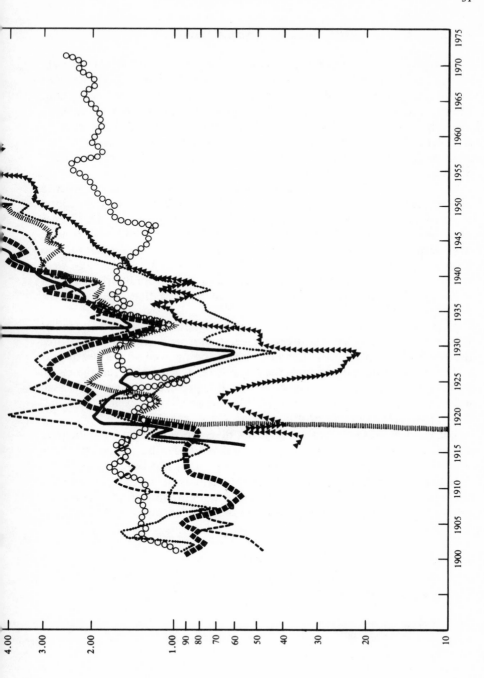

2. The "Decentralized" Resource Revenue Series

Where to draw the line between natural resource revenues and corporate profits must be decided on essentially arbitrary judgements. If the attempt is to capture rent, then care must be taken to exclude rewards to capital, labour, and especially enterprise. The opposite danger, of rent slipping through into other tax bases, is just as important. In this subsection we discuss estimates consistent with an assumption that the corporation income tax (both provincial and federal), to the extent that it is based on the profit of extractive activity only, is a tax on rent. [14]

To do this we contrast our comprehensive revenue series with a decentralized series. In it we add to the comprehensive series the federal share of combined federal and provincial corporate revenues. This series could be thought of as the outcome of a conference in which it was decided that, so far as natural resources are concerned, all "direct" taxation and proprietorial revenues would accrue to the provinces in which they were levied. Any remaining federal share would come only from indirect taxes or from the direct taxation of industries and persons that deal with the extractive industries. [15]

This series is also charted, as an almost parallel line on each panel of Figure 1, in dots and dashes. It can be seen that it tends mainly to reinforce the revenues of provinces that are already doing well in terms of our comprehensive measure of resource revenue (as is shown by the figures in Table 3), but doing relatively more for the provinces where the taxed industries have not been too lavishly blessed with exemptions and deductions from taxable profits.

The chief interest in Figure 1 is in the divergence of the comprehensive and decentralized curves. The greater the divergence, the greater the share of (what we assume to be) the same tax base that has been going to the federal government's corporate tax. The closer the lines lie together, the less consequential is federal taxation. A casual examination of the figure, for example, suggests that Ottawa has never been a keen taxer of Alberta's oil

TABLE 3

(MILLIONS OF DOLLARS, 1971)

	British Columbia	*Ten Provinces*
Comprehensive natural resource revenues	$154	$666
Federal tax on extractive corporate incomes	12	73
Total decentralized provincial natural resource revenue	$166	$739

and gas rents: the provincial government has, one way or another, captured by far the larger part. The implication is that a further decentralization than now exists of the collection of natural resource taxes would not, during the last sixty years, have added much to provincial revenues.

3. The "Centralized" Resource Revenue Series

The new data presented so far have shown graphically how unevenly natural resource revenues are spread, absolutely and per capita, across the country. Indeed I have suggested that the data understate the inequality because of the attractiveness to migration of the rents on which these revenues are based.

The purpose of this subsection is to provide a "centralized" comparison with the comprehensive series. I do so by calculating how much each province would receive if comprehensive resource revenues were *all* remitted to Ottawa, then distributed among the provinces in rough accordance with a rough "equalization" formula. Because this calculation must be carried back to 1900, I have invented my own equalization formula. Each province receives natural resource revenue in proportion to the deficiency of its per capita provincial revenues (excluding all natural resource and equalization payments but including statutory subsidies) and the average over all provinces. This means that provinces above this average receive no natural resource revenue whatsoever. (When the series is equal to zero, I have plotted it along the horizontal axis of the semi-log chart. Only the comprehensive series is published here. Other calculations are available on request.) The resulting data are plotted for every fifth year (as dots) as Curve 1 in Figure 1. Taking Nova Scotia as an example, we see her receipts owing to her per capita deficiency. As an approximation to the present equalization formula, this series suffers from being based only on revenues, not on either fiscal capacity or need.

Curve 2 is taken from the changing pattern of equalization payments among recipient provinces since 1957. The formula actually used has, since the 1960's, differed from the underlying Curve 1 not only in attempting to measure deficiencies in fiscal capacity as revealed by returns from one, two, up to eventually nineteen different revenue sources, but also in the effect of actual natural resource revenues. In Curve 1, a resource-rich province might have low revenues from other sources and thus show up as a have-not, or claimant province. In Curve 2 this could hardly happen even in the earliest years; in the later years shown, bountiful natural resource revenues would tend to place a province in the non-claimant category for equalization payments.[16] Thus for both Nova Scotia and Alberta, Curve 2 lies below Curve 1.

Curve 3 reflects an attempt to take account of regional differences in need. It shows the results of equalization of natural resource revenue according to deficiencies in each province's per capita personal income below the nationwide average per capita income. These levels are quite different from those in Curves 1 and 2. Both the former are affected by the provincial government's natural resource revenues, while the latter is more or less independent of all tax bases or revenues and depends heavily only on average personal income. The three curves are by no means parallel. [17] But, to return to my Nova Scotia example, it is striking that this province would gain from pooling of all provinces' comprehensive natural resource revenues only if some close variant of the present equalization formula were used. The same is true of Manitoba. B.C., Ontario, and Alberta would be best advised to avoid pooling under any of the three distribution formulas.

Note that Curves 2 and 3 do not appear for Ontario and British Columbia. They are have provinces in every sense. Alberta, on the other hand, appears as a have-not province when other provincial revenues are used as the criterion.

The general impression received from these calculations is as follows. Even the "wealthy" provinces of Canada have depended heavily on their natural resource revenues to make up their provincial budgets. In the absence of these revenues, they frequently would have fallen well below the national average provincial revenue per capita. In the early years of this century, their equalized share of the nation's resource revenues would have been adequate to raise them close to the national average. But in later years, the smaller relative importance of natural resource revenues would have left even Ontario and Quebec below the national average. Their equalization grants would not have been enough to have raised their total receipts to the national average.

This application of an equalization formula thus tends to show that those who are concerned about national horizontal equity cannot look with favour on the regional concentration of resource revenues, even before the energy crisis of the middle 1970's. If the federal government had received all these funds it may well be that many regional differences not only in government services but also in personal incomes (after taxes and transfers) would have disappeared.

But, I must stress, this is far from being a final conclusion. To start with, my equalization formulae are not those that actually would be used, making only rough use (in Curve 2 only) of the key concept of "fiscal capacity." Further, my conclusion ignores population mobility, attracted either by fiscal or by labour market incentives. It ignores the fact that regional differences may be closely correlated, positively with the amounts to be redistributed, and negatively with the amounts transferred. Thus nothing is proved by the calculation about what would be best for Canada.

The most that I can claim is to have shown how the respective provinces would fare if, keeping present tax rates, they lost their comprehensive resource revenues but gained equalization grants.

What is need next is to examine *other* ways of redistributing the rents through price controls, subsidies, and of course, market channels.

4. A Saudi-Arabian Estimate of Natural Resource Revenues

In the previous subsection we mentioned that certain provinces chose to sell the natural resources belonging to them, outright or for a small royalty, at an early date. These provinces now have very small public domain revenues and fairly small comprehensive or decentralized totals. Was this imprudence? It will occur to any economist that such provinces might possibly have been wise to have disposed of their natural wealth early, so long as it can be assumed that the proceeds since then have earned a return in their liquid or transformed use at least as great as the increase in their value that would have accrued had their exploitation been delayed until the present.

The ramifications of such a comparison are a challenge to statistical ingenuity: what would the early Ontario oil fields, the eastern Canadian spar trees, the Queen Charlotte spruce, be worth today? How could we find out?

Instead of responding to this challenge we have briefly attempted another, simpler, calculation. If the provinces had followed the advice now being taken by the leaders of Saudi Arabia and other O.P.E.C. countries, and invested their revenues from the public domain only in interest-bearing assets, what would be their interest income today? We have worked this out for eight provinces, but only since 1900. All comprehensive revenues have been assumed to be accumulated, not at interest. The provinces are assumed to consume the interest in lieu of the foregone resource revenue contributions to their consolidated general funds. In British Columbia, by 1971, the capital fund so accumulated would have risen to $1.9 billion. Interest earnings on such a sum, at 8 per cent, would yield $153.8 million in 1971. How does this compare with what did happen? By coincidence, the actual comprehensive earning of B.C. in 1971 were also about $154 million. Thus by now it would be possible, after twenty or thirty years of building up a nestegg, both to own a sizable stock of wealth and to get interest from it.

Table 4 shows that this B.C. result would have been fairly general: at most interest rates, all provinces would have been somewhat better off in 1970-71 if their ancestors had invested natural resource revenue in a fund paying today's generation only interest on this fund. This generalization depends of course on assumed rates of return, price, inflation, and on

TABLE 4

COMPARISON OF HYPOTHETICAL INTEREST INCOME
AND ACTUAL COMPREHENSIVE REVENUE

	Amount in fund, 1974 ($ millions)	Annual Fund Income		Actual Comprehensive Revenue
		at 6%	at 10%	
Nova Scotia	75	4.5	7.5	2.4
New Brunswick	138	8.3	13.8	6.3
Quebec	1,348	80.8	134.8	87.3
Ontario	1,338	80.3	133.8	82.6
Manitoba	166	10.0	16.6	9.5
Saskatchewan	614	36.9	61.4	41.6
Alberta	3,706	222.3	370.6	296.7
B.C.	1,922	115.3	192.2	154.4

whether the province's extractive activity peaked, as it were, in the past, or is peaking today.

These calculations are difficult to interpret and cannot therefore be conclusive. The results are compatible with either of the following views. Every jurisdiction can be assumed to have reinvested past resource revenues. Thus their present resource revenue is not consumable, but merely the current contribution to the provincial fund; the actual consumable wealth is the interest on this fund. Alternatively, today's decision makers can be assumed to have available today the *sum* of the last two columns: the interest on the fund plus today's actual resource revenues.

IV. CONCLUDING REMARKS

The numbers and graphs in the previous section show that it does "matter" who gets the natural resource revenue. The amounts are not small; estimates by T. Courchene also show that a good deal is involved. For some regions of the country, getting more or less of the nation's global resource rent makes all the difference between being a have and a have-not province. This may seem obvious, but I believe it has not been generally recognized how much was at stake even as early as 1971, before the energy crisis.

The "fund" calculations in the last section are a reminder that the amounts involved can be, and have been, allocated over time. This allocation is largely a matter of deliberate choice, both by government and by the exploiting firm. The connection of this general point to the present debate is this: some provinces have large revenues today precisely because they have foregone them earlier. Other provinces decided (or had the matter decided for them) to alienate their resources decades or centuries ago. Thus it would not follow that differences in current regional resource revenue, or even rent, reflect inequalities in original resource endowment. Nor, as the calculation showed, need they even reflect differences in present gains from those original endowments.

In general, I believe that the answer to the "who should get..." question can be answered on distributional or equitable principles alone. The first main section's survey of criteria did not suggest any efficiency argument of persuasive strength, for favouring provincial or national government. Different revenue assignment setups have different efficiency costs of resource management attached to them, but these costs may not be unacceptable, and do not point uniformly to extreme revenue centralization or decentralization. We are left without conclusive efficiency criteria. Nothing in the nature of natural resources themselves, nor in the rents they produce, signals an answer to this assignment question.

Notes

* I am very grateful for the participation of Peter Gardner and for his pioneering exploration of the magnitudes of resource revenues since 1900, reported herein.

1. Resource ownership is further complicated by the common law theory that all land ultimately belongs to the Crown, even when it has passed fully into private hands. Furthermore, the sovereignty of Parliament allows government to disregard property rights. Which level of government can act, and when, are matters discussed by Professor Lederman.

2. See Anthony Scott, "Resourcefulness and Responsibility," *Canadian Journal of Economics and Political Science* XXIV, 2 (May 1958): 203-15.

3. Equal economic treatment of equals.

4. The Carter Commission, for example, did not have much to say about the idea of geographical equalization of incomes, confining itself instead to the desirability of even-handed federal taxation.

5. Mrs. U.K. Hicks, in her *Public Finance* (Oxford, 1948), has pushed this line of argument. Part of it goes back to Marshall's distinction between "beneficial" and "onerous" local government expenditures. Much of it is, of course, inherent in all analyses of the property tax, stretching from Henry George to Netzer and Tiebout.

6. *Report of the Royal Commission on Dominion-Provincial Relations* (Ottawa, 1940),

Volume II: Recommendation, p. 114. A footnote, citing briefs from several provinces, is omitted here.

7. See my "Policy for Declining Regions: A Theoretical Approach" in W. Wood and R. Thoman, eds., *Areas of Economic Stress in Canada* (Queen's University, 1965), pp. 73-93.

8. Public finance economists will recognize a problem most recently discussed by J. Buchanan and C.J. Goetz, "Efficiency Limits of Fiscal Mobility...," *Journal of Public Economics* I,1(April 1972): 25-45, and in different guise by F. Flatters, V. Henderson, and P. Mieszkowski, "Public Goods, Efficiency and Regional Fiscal Equalization," *Journal of Public Economics* III, 2 (May 1974): 99. Buchanan would point out that no problem would arise if the new province could levy a fee on new immigrants. Neither paper takes into account the durability of the public works that are a special element in the depleting resource problem.

9. For discussions of alternative ways of conserving capital, see my *Natural Resources: The Economics of Conservation* (Toronto: McClelland and Stewart, 1972).

10. For a summary, up to 1969, see J. Hirshleifer and D.L. Shapiro, "Treatment of Risk and Uncertainty," in R.H. Haveman and J. Margolis, eds., *Public Expenditures and Policy Analysis* (Chicago: Markham Publishing, 1970), pp. 291-313. See also Hayne Leland, R. Norgaard, and S. Pearson, "An Economic Analysis of Alternative Outer Continental Shelf Petroleum Leasing Policies" (1974), report prepared for the Office of Energy Research and Development Policy, National Science Foundation (September 1974). Also to be published in M. Crommelin, ed., *Mineral Leasing as an Instrument of Public Policy* (Vancouver: U.B.C. Press, 1976).

11. Philip Neher, "Democratic Exploitation of a Replenishable Environment," *Journal of Public Economics* 5, 3 (April 1976): 361-71.

12. Mineral, forestry, and pulp and paper developments were spread over most provinces.

13. At least, of the Scott version. See "Policy for Declining Regions," cited above.

14. Detailed justification of this assumption is unnecessary. We make the calculation because we find it difficult to accept any clear dividing lines between the bases of, say, bonus or stumpage payments, mining and logging taxes, and corporate income taxes on extractive activities. Of course, the allowances, deductions, and exemptions differ vastly.

15. The picture produced by this calculation depends entirely on the accuracy with which the Department of National Revenue has succeeded in attributing profits (a) to regions and (b) to extractive, as opposed to processing, activities.

16. Full details of the present formula are published in the *Canada Gazette*, part II (24 January 1973), pp. 128ff. For discussion of this and earlier formulae since the 1950's see D.H. Clark, *Fiscal Need and Revenue Equalization Grants* (Toronto: Canadian Tax Foundation, 1969); A.M. Moore, J.H. Perry, and D.I. Beach, *The Financing of Canadian Federation* (Toronto: Canadian Tax Foundation, 1966); Canadian Tax Foundation, *National Finances, 1974-75* (Toronto, 1975), chapter 11; and the papers by Courchene *et al.*, "Federal-Provincial Tax Equalization: An Evaluation," *Canadian Journal of Economics* VI, 4 (November 1973): 483-502, and the contribution published as the Courchene paper.

17. J.H. Lynn suggested that our Curves 2 and 3 would not be similar for a given province. See his *Comparing Provincial Revenues Yields* (Toronto: Canadian Tax Foundation, 1968), pp. 47ff. His treatment also suggests to me that for most provinces Curves 1 and 2 would distribute nationwide natural resource revenue similarly.

Appendix

THE CALCULATIONS BEHIND THE COMPREHENSIVE NATURAL
RESOURCE REVENUE SERIES

The following paragraphs give in considerable detail the sources used in Peter
Gardner's research to obtain the comprehensive natural resource revenue series back
to 1900. It will be seen that the greater part of the series, going back to about 1917, is
on fairly firm ground because of the predominance of public domain revenues.
These had been made comparable by D.B.S. in the 1920's.

We have had to take many liberties with the corporation income tax. Our aim was
to obtain estimates of federal and provincial collections, by province, from
extractive industries. This was bedevilled in various periods by changing provincial
tax statutes, wartime security, non-publication, and non-classification by province
or by industry taxed. To meet these problems, various interpolations were used.
Heavy reliance for provincial collections was placed on federal taxation in the same
province over some years. The resulting series seems plausible, but the reader must
not forget that many special assumptions have been made.

Forestry statistics and tax data are notoriously weak in Canada, and this is true
also of the forestry components of the corporate tax. The problem shows up most in
trying to rid the published series of farm or agricultural profit tax components. The
notes below show the means used for doing this, which are rough enough; what must
be recalled is that forest and logging data may be, to an unknown degree, present in
the agricultural series.

The comprehensive natural resource revenue series consists of "natural resource
revenues" as defined by Statistics Canada (D.B.S.) (1) plus provincial share of
corporate income tax from natural resource industries. This is the record of total
actual revenues received by provinces from their natural resources. For reasons
discussed below the series can be assumed to represent revenues derived from value-
added only, by the process of extraction of the natural resource up to but not
including the primary processing stage.

The Dominion Bureau of Statistics was formed in 1918. In the area of provincial
finances and income taxes we have relied on their figures when available. They were
able to push the figures back to 1916 but anything earlier we have obtained from
other sources (except for dates for 1913). Apart from occasional interpolations, our
series since 1945 can be said to be almost completely consistent with D.B.S.'s
treatment. Our series from 1921 to 1944 contain more of our own estimates owing to
gaps in the figures, but we believe the errors are likely to involve less than 5 per cent
deviation from actual. Data from 1901 to 1920, of course, presented the greatest
challenge owing to the lack of consistent provincial reporting before 1916 and
continuous problems with making the figures comparable between provinces and
fiscal years. (In splicing the series together an effort was made to make sure that no

more than 12 months of data appeared in any one year. Thus the years do not refer to fiscal years but to the years in which most of the months of that fiscal year appeared.)

Fortunately, in the early period, most provinces copied each other's legislation. As a result, figures reported in the *Canada Year Books* and elsewhere as Public Accounts figures are very often comparable, the only difference being in the name used. (For example, timber land taxes are very similar to timber berth taxes.) It is possible that errors of estimation could cause deviations of as much as 15 per cent from the actual figures, in the period 1901 to 1920. However, the figures for 1913 are completely comparable with the figures for 1921 due to the efforts of D.B.S. (2) for the Rowell-Sirois Commission and can be considered consistent with post-1920 figures. For example, the D.B.S. Public Domain revenue for 1913 for Nova Scotia was 853, while the figure we compiled from the other sources was also 853; for New Brunswick the figures are 502 and 503; for Quebec they were 1,866 and 1,656; for Ontario they were 2,887 and 2,043; for Manitoba, Saskatchewan, and Alberta there were no other figures; and for B.C. the actual was 72 below the calculated 4,470. For almost every province it will be noticed that the calculated figure is lower than D.B.S.'s. Thus it is likely that figures from 1910 to 1920 are underestimates of the "actual" amounts, although, as discussed below, our figures have been adjusted upward to obtain our final series.

Table 1 is composed basically of three series which have been recorded historically for "natural resource revenues" in Canada. The first is Public Domain revenue; the second is revenue from indirect provincial taxes on the resource in question; and the third series is revenue from corporation income tax levied on those firms in natural resource industries. Decisions about classification of tax bases between natural resource and primary processing were made by provincial tax collectors beginning with Ontario in 1907. From 1917 these classifications came under the scrutiny of the federal department of finance and may therefore be regarded as agreed.

From 1910 to 1949 our first series, Public Domain revenue, included revenue from (A) mines and mining - (1) coal royalties, rentals, and permits (2) oil and natural gas rentals (3) metals royalties, fees, and dues (4) sand, gravel, and quarrying rentals; (B) forest, timber, and woods royalties, stumpage, rentals, and permits; (C) grazing rentals and fees; (D) streams and hydraulic service rentals; (E) land rental, fees, and sales (including capital receipts from sales of land for forestry or mining reasons); (F) fur licences, taxes, and sales; (G) fishery licences; (H) park fees and other miscellaneous. The major source was the Public Domain series developed by D.B.S. (2) for the Rowell-Sirois Commission. This series was available for the years 1913, 1921, 1925 to 1939. For the years 1937, 1938, 1939, 1941, and 1943 D.B.S. (3) prepared a Public Domain Series for the Dominion-Provincial Conference on Reconstruction which is comparable to D.B.S. (2).

From 1901 to 1949, the second series, direct provincial taxes on the resource, consisted of wild land taxes, timber land taxes, coal land taxes, timber berth taxes, and mining (profit) taxes. (There were no logging [profit] taxes prior to 1949.) Wild land taxes were imposed mainly on alienated land which had been completely logged or, more rarely, mined, and was lying idle. The tax was imposed, at quite high rates, to encourage private owners to allow it to return to the Crown. Mining taxes were levied as a form of royalty but on income before major deductions rather than on production. Although these taxes are on natural resources they are found in sections such as corporation taxes and land and property taxes rather than under Public Domain (often because reported by different provincial departments).

For the years 1901 to 1915 the source for series 1 and 2 is Perry (4) pp. 642-65; for 1913 we also had Public Domain and mining taxes revenues from D.B.S. (2). The difference was applied, as a set of multipliers, to Perry's Public Domain figures from 1901 to 1912, 1914, and 1915. These adjusted Perry Public Domain figures were added to the unadjusted series two direct taxes figures to arrive at our Natural Resource Revenue (series 1 plus 2) for 1901 to 1915.

From 1916 to 1924 Public Domain figures were compiled from D.B.S. (5) and D.B.S. (6). Capital receipts (which appeared only for B.C.) were obtained from Perry (4) as were the series 2 figures. Once again there were problems with matching year ends. However, the Public Domain figures available for 1921 from D.B.S. (2) matched quite closely those compiled from the other sources. Once again there were deviations in the Public Domain figures and a set of 1921 multipliers designed to adjust was applied to the series for 1916-20 and 1922-24. The adjusted Public Domain series was then added to the unadjusted series 2 figures to give Natural Resource Revenue from 1916 to 1924.

From 1925 to 1939 the series 1 Public Domain figures given by D.B.S. (2) were used. The series 2 figures were compiled from the National Finance Committee (7), from D.B.S. (5) from D.B.S. (6), and from Perry (4). The mining tax figures were taken from D.B.S. (2). The only province which presented serious difficulties was B.C., but comparisons of the D.B.S. (2) figures with the disaggregated figures suggested that although D.B.S. was not including full capital receipts they must have been including at least 50 per cent of them. (This is one area where it was decided to stick with the D.B.S. (2) figures with the uneasy feeling that they may not be correct. One possibility is that capital receipts included sales of land for agricultural use which D.B.S. (2) deducted. After 1932 the inclusion of capital receipts appears to be almost 100 per cent so the B.C. problem disappears.) The series 1 and series 2 figures were summed to give Natural Resource Revenue from 1925 to 1939.

From 1940 to 1949 Public Domain figures were compiled from D.B.S. (5), which for 1941 and 1943 was checked against D.B.S. (3). The source for series two was D.B.S. (6), D.B.S. (5), and Perry (4). The Natural Resource Revenue from 1940 to 1949 was obtained by adding series 1 and 2 together.

Individual problems which occurred on an isolated basis in the compilation of Natural Resource Revenue from 1901 to 1949 were the following. First, no figures were available from any source for Manitoba, Saskatchewan, and Alberta for the period 1901-12, 1914, and 1915. Estimates were available in 1913 from D.B.S. (2) and in 1916 from D.B.S. (6). To bridge the 1914, 1915 gap the difference between 1913 and 1916 for each province was filled by linear interpolation. But the figures prior to 1913 were not available. Second, licences and permits issued for natural resource activities were not disaggregated from all licences and permits until 1932. In the figures from D.B.S. (2) they have been included, but in the other years where Public Domain figures have been compiled, natural resource licences and permits were left out. Fortunately, the amounts are probably so small as to be negligible. From 1932 to 1949 licences and permits were disaggregated and could be included. Third, Ontario waterpower and storage charges are inseparable from Ontario Hydro income until 1926. As the major part of Ontario Hydro income is not derived from water and storage charges it was simply left out. After 1926 a distinction was made and therefore water charges could be included. Fourth, as noted above, there was a problem created by B.C.'s practice of classifying land sales separately. It is not clear from Perry's (4) figures the extent to which agricultural land sales have been excluded. A reading of the records prior to 1913 would indicate that these capital

APPENDIX A   TABLE 1
COMPREHENSIVE NATURAL RESOURCE REVENUE BY PROVINCE 1901-71

Year	Newfoundland	Nova Scotia	New Brunswick	Quebec	Ontario	Manitoba	Saskatchewan	Alberta	British Columbia	Federal Government of Canada
		444	157	1,494	2,073				832	1,605
		495	168	1,280	1,862				958	1,307
		629	191	1,500	3,230				1,077	1,775
		594	273	1,410	3,620				1,376	1,539
1905		624	208	1,670	2,800				1,617	1,383
		623	266	1,530	2,560				2,852	1,766
		612	278	1,230	1,650				3,743	1,501
		672	208	1,180	2,550				3,307	1,975
		615	233	1,100	2,580				5,815	2,236
1910		607	512	1,250	2,570				6,266	2,971
		642	582	1,360	2,485				5,314	3,210
		791	578	1,792	2,840	100	100	100	6,539	3,872
		853	503	1,866	2,887	427	49	57	5,401	3,508
		761	554	1,878	2,496	349	40	127	5,333	3,147
1915		727	592	1,979	2,191	271	30	197	4,283	2,953
		816	547	1,956	2,036	193	21	267	3,921	2,396
		744	541	1,862	3,614	189	24	645	4,133	4,272
		660	794	1,861	3,310	330	20	531	4,491	5,161
		634	852	2,691	3,280	229	597	992	4,558	4,340
1920		695	1,557	3,478	4,636	293	1,062	1,154	5,540	8,263
		739	1,164	4,609	5,303	345	707	1,112	5,205	5,924
		583	840	5,182	5,663	392	874	1,083	5,469	5,449
		756	1,097	4,817	3,663	436	924	1,004	5,504	5,282
		774	1,317	5,426	5,625	372	902	812	6,041	5,142
1925		449	1,121	6,581	6,668	275	825	970	6,722	6,011
		744	1,103	7,258	5,851	189	740	914	7,177	6,835
		800	1,206	7,580	6,047	155	627	627	7,443	7,220
		805	1,301	7,281	6,253	160	532	507	7,362	8,470
		852	1,206	6,639	6,330	140	353	413	7,168	9,130
1930		821	937	5,790	4,943	333	599	957	6,107	5,169
		733	780	4,587	4,974	362	746	1,109	4,647	4,436
		649	598	3,561	4,238	360	593	5,554	3,307	4,088
		541	647	3,220	3,831	592	562	1,115	4,172	8,974

Year										
		680	871	4,639	1,300	625	741	4,275	5,162	5,367
		1,001	720	6,130	1,295	719	748	6,140	6,373	11,542
1935		775	800	6,412	1,624	729	905	7,029	7,437	13,355
		949	1,145	7,541	1,798	807	914	7,919	7,396	13,426
		854	1,033	9,350	1,745	681	1,814	7,426	6,290	11,686
		895	855	7,922	2,199	343	1,021	9,589	6,662	15,779
		969	1,293	8,377	2,592	1,023	1,459	13,372	8,243	21,076
1940		1,173	1,402	12,461	3,045	1,350	1,627	17,323	9,405	38,706
		1,223	1,451	13,875	3,288	1,605	1,482	18,549	9,603	35,629
		1,104	1,473	12,272	3,381	2,121	1,576	16,398	8,989	30,546
		806	1,485	13,290	3,771	2,193	1,821	12,747	7,922	36,212
		784	1,553	14,900	3,707	2,370	1,837	14,452	9,066	40,051
1945		879	1,717	19,617	3,663	2,241	2,048	14,117	8,819	41,736
		745	2,220	16,737	5,111	2,591	2,359	13,677	11,380	46,902
		1,147	2,414	19,321	17,474	2,902	2,884	16,438	13,923	49,323
	100	1,165	2,378	16,918	38,815	3,343	2,586	19,087	14,753	46,012
	551	1,197	2,010	19,566	49,646	3,402	3,154	20,942	9,451	63,793
1950	838	1,285	3,428	27,795	45,690	4,935	3,813	27,095	11,593	101,809
	922	1,325	3,278	26,142	64,460	6,746	3,510	30,371	28,156	85,015
	589	1,429	3,539	26,696	103,969	10,310	3,760	26,918	28,356	69,758
	503	1,516	3,091	29,040	89,255	9,911	4,207	27,723	30,288	70,535
	698	1,760	3,469	35,574	135,861	13,780	5,642	33,918	42,196	107,473
1955	1,102	1,813	4,345	38,093	142,476	23,834	6,352	36,399	49,622	107,567
	1,698	1,360	4,129	36,073	134,035	26,639	4,864	42,002	43,423	69,280
	1,681	1,328	3,626	31,998	119,229	24,404	4,162	36,005	46,235	50,678
	865	1,539	3,690	34,607	151,169	20,154	4,550	45,217	56,832	70,624
	1,766	1,497	3,811	39,355	113,125	20,940	4,866	51,497	56,567	75,566
1960	1,665	1,455	3,960	39,368	127,470	21,554	4,999	52,997	63,946	90,205
	1,797	1,634	3,719	40,175	132,379	29,155	5,720	51,388	70,506	89,928
	1,787	1,810	3,944	52,291	180,395	33,516	5,736	48,831	82,602	105,132
	2,173	1,722	4,381	46,195	215,462	37,577	7,803	56,045	99,511	125,101
	3,915	1,970	5,095	48,807	260,036	44,912	7,526	48,845	105,827	85,915
1965	3,676	1,948	4,721	68,529	252,960	41,618	7,008	44,707	106,374	82,313
	3,805	2,057	6,299	71,637	235,714	42,940	7,011	55,248	97,413	116,692
	4,397	2,106	4,955	74,457	299,281	39,703	7,091	60,528	130,826	122,623
	5,010	2,163	4,526	78,835	274,173	38,925	8,562	78,016	172,702	133,533
	9,745	2,121	6,064	91,926	255,143	40,861	14,065	87,403	131,453	170,006
1970	5,479	2,482	6,329	87,363	296,735	41,586	9,467	62,610	154,410	109,662

receipts were in fact derived from sales of timber and coal lands only. As a result, figures prior to 1913 may overestimate natural resource revenue for B.C. However, as discussed below, series 3, corporate income taxes, for B.C. were not included before 1924. In fact B.C. had a corporate income tax before 1901. Therefore, the excessive inclusion, if there is any, of land sale receipts for B.C. might compensate for our inability to include the early corporate income tax on resource industry profits.

From 1950 to 1971 the Dominion Bureau of Statistics combined series 1 and 2 into a series called natural resource revenue. D.B.S. (8) p. 27 describes series 2 as "specific natural resource based industry taxes which are levied on corporate profits [which] are excluded from corporate income tax in favour of natural resource revenue." In D.B.S. (8) pp. 29-30 Natural Resource Revenue (the previous series 1 and 2 combined) is described as revenue derived from the exploration, development, and exploitation of natural resources, other than that received under income tax legislation and that derived through a government enterprise engaged in natural resource oriented operations. Five subclassifications identify specific resources from which the bulk of the revenue arises; a residual subcategory is provided for miscellaneous resource revenues not elsewhere classified. The specific inclusions are as follows:

a. Fish and game—revenue from hunting and fishing licences and permits; royalties on furs; fishing royalties.
b. Forests—revenue from taxes on logging operations, whether on profits, income, or other bases; leases and rentals of Crown lands; timber berth dues and rentals; stumpage dues and timber royalties; timber and fuel-wood licences and permits, timber sales; scaling fees; lease and contract fees, permits, and rentals; selective cutting fees, log-driving charges; ground rents, and management and forest protection charges.
c. Mines—(excluding quarrying, sand, gravel, and peat but including coal) revenue from taxes on mining income receipts or profits; taxes pursuant to mineral taxation acts; taxes on acreages, concessions, claim leases, and on particular minerals and royalties; exploration, development, and exploitation licences and permits; leases and rentals and other permits; royalties on mineral production; miners' certificates and licences; ground and building rents.
d. Oil and gas—revenue from sale of Crown leases and reservations, bonus bids, drilling reservation rentals, leases, and permits; oil and gas and producing tract taxes; natural gas taxes; oil and natural gas royalties, lease rentals, fees, and permits; helium permits and royalties, oil and gas mineral taxes, oil sands rentals, fees, and royalties.
e. Water power rentals—revenue from water power privileges; water storage reservoirs; water systems operations; water rental contributions; recording fees and royalties on electricity generated.
f. Other—revenue from sand and gravel, peat and quarry site leases, rentals and royalties; park and campground permits, feeds rentals, concessions, and sales; sales of leases and rentals of Crown lands; alkali rentals and royalties; and miscellaneous natural resource taxes, fees, and charges.

Thus Natural Resource Revenue from 1950 to 1971 was taken directly from D.B.S. (1).

As revenues from natural resources represent such a small fraction of total federal revenue it was difficult to find the disaggregated figures necessary to compile an accurate series. However, later comparisons with the figures given by D.B.S. (2)

Appendix 1 and D.B.S. (3) showed that the best method was the sum of revenue from Dominion Lands (including farm lands and homestead lands and fisheries for each year from D.B.S. (6). Thus Natural Resource Revenue from 1901 to 1912 and 1914 to 1920 and 1922 to 1924 is taken from D.B.S. (6). The same series for 1913, 1921, 1925-39 is taken from the Public Domain revenue recorded in D.B.S. (2). And in 1940, 1942, 1944-49 the series was compiled from D.B.S. (6), while in 1941 and 1943 it was taken from Public Domain revenue given by D.B.S. (3). As the federal government levies no direct taxes on natural resources, there is no series 2. Thus series 1 and the Natural Resource Revenue series are identical. From 1950 to 1971 D.B.S. (9) gave natural resource revenue for the federal government.

Series 3 does not accurately reflect true provincial revenue from corporate taxes. The reason is that prior to 1939 other forms of tax, such as capital tax, brought in far more revenue than income tax. However, it is impossible with the data sources available to discover what corporate taxes were derived against natural resource industries, except for the ones recorded in series 2. In fact, provincial income tax statistics broken down by industry are not available at all. In 1917 the federal government imposed an Income War Tax on corporations. Although some provinces had at one time or another attempted to levy corporation income tax, only B.C. had had one continuously.

After the federal legislation, B.C. introduced a bill changing its own legislation to conform more closely with that of the federal government. As each province imposed corporate income taxes over time its legislation was based on the federal one. As a result the net income tax base reported by the federal government for each province conformed quite closely to the provincial net income tax base. Because of this, and because there are no figures on provincial corporate income tax (except sporadically) it was decided to apply provincial corporate income tax votes to the federal corporate income tax revenues until 1943, and to the federal corporate income base after 1944.

The Dominion Bureau of Statistics (10) through its General Statistics Branch issued statistics called "Income Assessed for Income War Tax in Canada 1932-1941." It should be noted that this was for tax years 1930-39, i.e., two years prior to the imported year. In 1946 the Department of National Revenue started publishing Corporate Income Taxes. Once again fiscal 1946 meant statistics for tax year 1944. They published these statistics until 1966—i.e., until tax year 1964. At that date the Dominion Bureau of Statistics (11) once again started publishing them. Thus there is a complete record of net corporate income on which federal taxes are payable by the natural resource industries for taxation years 1930 to 1939, 1944 to 1954, 1957 to 1971.

For the period 1930 to 1939 actual federal taxes paid on natural resource corporate income are available for each province. The following describes the extrapolation of this federal series back to 1927 and forward to 1943. For the period 1927 to 1929 federal corporate income tax is available for each province for all industries. Accordingly the natural resource corporate income is calculated by applying the average percentage of total tax paid by natural resource industries in 1930, 1931, and 1932 to the all-industry tax figures for 1927, 1928, and 1929, by province. As the total natural resource corporate taxes paid in Canada for those years are available, the following comparison shows the discrepancy between the actual total and the total of the estimates made for each province on the above basis. In 1927 the total actual natural resource taxes was $2,656 thousand while our estimate is $2,590 thousand; in 1928 the actual was $3,617 thousand, the estimate is

$3,160 thousand; in 1929 the actual was $4,211 thousand, the estimate is $3,530.

For the year 1940 and 1941 the corporate income tax revenue on all industries was available by province. This time the 1939 percentages of total corporate tax accounted for by natural resource taxes was applied against the provincial totals for 1940 and 1941. Total natural resource corporate income tax for Canada is not available to compare as above to check the discrepancy.

For the years 1942 and 1943 the only federal natural resource revenue statistics available were for total corporate income taxes in Canada. An estimate based on the 1939 actual per cent of corporate income tax accounted for by natural resource corporate taxes was applied to the 1942 and 1943 figures. Then the estimated total was broken up by province according to the 1939 percentages. The reason for the heavy reliance on 1939 figures rather than on averages is that revenues from natural resource sources rose dramatically during the war. Unfortunately, this increase was only partially recorded in 1939 as the discrepancy is bad between the actual total natural resource revenue in 1944 and an estimate made for comparison based on the above method. The actual figure for 1944 was $34,212 thousand and the estimate was $23,526 thousand. Presumably the discrepancy would be smaller for 1942 and 1943.

Thus, including these guesses, we have a complete series of federal corporate income taxes paid by the natural resource industries, by province, from 1927 to 1943. In the case of B.C., total provincial corporate income tax was given back as far as 1924 by Perry (4) p. 258 and Perry (12) pp. 233-54, 365-66. Once again, using the average proportion of total corporate tax revenues accounted for by natural resource industries in 1930, 1931, and 1932 an estimate was made for 1924, 1925, and 1926. Thus for B.C. alone, including estimates, we have federal corporate income taxes paid by natural resource industries in B.C. from 1924 to 1943.

For 1917 to 1926 we used rougher estimates. For all provinces combined, federal corporate income taxes from 1927 to 1939 from natural resource industries were available from D.B.S. "Incomes Assessed for Income War Tax in Canada" 68-D-21 (10). The average proportion of natural resource industry taxes to total taxes was 8.5 per cent for 1927, 1928, 1929, 1930, and 1931. Applying this percentage to the total corporate income tax statistics which were available from 1917 to 1926, an "estimate" was made of the natural resource corporate income tax revenues received by the federal government.

For the years 1940, 1941, 1942, and 1943 the natural resource corporate income tax paid to the federal government was calculated in the same manner as for the provincial governments.

Thus, including rough estimates, a series of figures giving natural resource corporate income tax paid to the federal government was available from 1917 to 1926, for all provinces combined, and by province from 1927 to 1943. (For B.C., three extra years, 1924-26, were available.) In 1941 the provinces entered an agreement with the federal government which allowed the latter to rent the field from the provinces. Thus from 1941 to 1943 the federal government collections were the only collections made in each province. Income tax statistics for corporations included excess profits taxes levied during the war. There was no breakdown by province or by industry. Our estimates of the taxes paid by resource industries in this period are probably understatements, if the comparisons for 1944 also apply in 1941-43. This is also likely to be the case for our federal government revenue estimates, 1917-26, as natural resource industries declined steadily in influence in other totals such as public domain revenues, etc. Thus our multipliers based on 1927 to 1931 are likely to underestimate the actual proportions in those early years. Finally, in 1917-43 the industrial breakdown is labelled Natural Resource Industries. Although this breakdown is not exactly the same as that after 1944 it is probably very close. First of all because there was also a separate category in the early period for agrarian industries, one can assume there was no agricultural corporate income included in natural resource revenue. Second, for reasons discussed earlier, the federal government has always been keen to distinguish between value added due to extraction and that due to primary processing. Thirdly, a comparison between pre-1944 revenue categories and post-1944 does not show any sharp change.

Next, to estimate the actual flow of natural resource corporate income tax into each provincial treasury a ratio of the provincial corporate tax rate to the federal corporate tax rate was applied to the above estimate of federal income tax paid in that province. For example, in 1935, the federal corporate taxes paid by natural resource industries in Manitoba was $62 thousand. The federal corporate income tax rate was 15 per cent of net taxable income and the Manitoba corporate income tax rate was 5 per cent. Thus 5/15 of $62 thousand or $21 thousand was the estimate of corporate income tax paid by natural resource industries to Manitoba in the taxation year 1935.

As discussed earlier, B.C. had a corporate income tax before 1901 but figures were not available until 1924. In addition, the breakdown of that total corporate income into industry categories was not available until 1930. Estimates of this breakdown back to 1924 were made as explained above. Perhaps this is as far back as such estimates should be made. Given these limitations, corporate income tax paid by natural resource industries was first recorded for B.C. in 1924. In 1931 Manitoba was the next province to impose a corporate income tax at 2 per cent. The federal and provincial rates were obtained from Perry (4) pp. 258, 700 and Petrie (13) p. 34. In 1932 Quebec, Ontario, Saskatchewan, and Alberta, in 1938 New Brunswick, and in 1939 Nova Scotia imposed corporate income taxes. This rate-ratio method of calculation was used until 1944. The Perry and Petrie volumes were used for rates until 1940.

From 1941 to 1944 due to the rental agreement discussed earlier an estimate had to be made of the amount which accrued to the provinces through the rental agreements. The D.B.S. (6) *Canada Year Books* (in the Subsidies and Loans to Provinces section) for this period explain the basis of the rental agreement but there are no substitute tax rates in it. As a result it was decided to use a rate of 5 per cent for each province even though in 1940 some rates had been higher and others lower. The justification is that in 1947 when the tax agreement was negotiated the federal government was prepared to abate 5 per cent of net taxable corporate income to those provinces which levied their own corporate taxes. The basis was an assumption made by the federal government that this would have been the average benefit derived by the provinces from corporate income taxes.

Data from 1944 to 1954 was published by the Department of National Revenue (14) on net taxable corporate income and federal taxes paid. The first category included corporate income from agriculture, forestry, fishing, and trapping. The second category contained corporate income from mines, quarries, and oil wells. The problem was to get agriculture only out of the combined series. A fine breakdown was not available until 1965. This was compared with the breakdown between agrarian and natural resource corporate income in 1938. To extract the agricultural component from both net taxable income and federal taxes paid, a measure was made of the proportion of total agricultural, forestry, fishing and game, mines, quarries, and oil wells represented by forestry, fishing and game, mines, quarries, and oil wells for the years 1965, 1966, and 1967. This proportion was then weighted equally with that of natural resource to natural resource plus agrarian income in 1938 to get an interpolated proportion for the intervening years. For example, in B.C. the proportion was 94.6 per cent over 1965, 1966, and 1967. The other proportion, in 1938, for B.C., was 98.6 per cent so that the required average of the two was 96.6 per cent.

This final average percentage was then applied to the natural resource corporate net income and corporate federal taxes to arrive at the adjusted, non-agriculture series. (The final averages were 93.7 for Nova Scotia, 93.9 for New Brunswick, 98.7 for Quebec, 90.8 for Ontario, 87.9 for Manitoba, 85.3 for Saskatchewan, 89.6 for Alberta, 96.6 for B.C.) If the final adjusted series was larger than for mines, quarries, and oil wells it was retained; if it was smaller it was rejected and that for mines, quarries, and oil wells only used instead. This often occurred in provinces such as Ontario where the mines, quarries, and oil wells corporate income category was far larger than that for the agriculture, forestry, fishing, and game category.

From 1944 to 1954 an adjusted series for net income was derived as was an adjusted series for federal taxes. The provincial corporate tax rates were then applied directly to adjusted net income by province to derive the flow of corporate income taxes to each province.

From 1944 to 1946 the rate corporate income tax was 5 per cent for each province based on the abatement rates in the tax agreements. From 1947 to the present Quebec has levied its own corporate income tax. From 1947 to 1951 and from 1957 to the present Ontario levied its own corporate income tax. From 1947 to the present the remaining 8 provinces have switched from renting the tax field to imposing their own corporation taxes levied and collected by the federal government. The actual rates of corporation tax by province are not available until 1962 in D.B.S. (15). Under the 1947 agreement (refer to *Canada Year Books* for details) from 1947 to 1952 the abatement rate was 5 per cent. Quebec's rate was 5 per cent and Ontario's rate was 7 per cent. Under the 1952 agreement the abatement rate was changed to a tax credit of 7 per cent for those provinces re-entering the corporate tax field. Thus from 1953 to 1956 the tax rate used was 7 per cent for all provinces re-entering the corporate tax field. Thus from 1953 to 1956 the tax rate used was 7 per cent for all provinces. Under the 1957 agreement the tax credit was raised to 9 per cent. This was the corporate rate used for all provinces except Ontario, which levied a rate of 11 per cent in 1957. In 1958 Quebec raised its rate to 10 per cent, the others stayed at the 1957 rates. In 1959 and 1960 the rates were the same. In 1961 Quebec raised its rate to 12 per cent, Ontario stayed at 11 per cent, and the rest at 9 per cent. In 1962 the rates were first recorded by D.B.S. (15) and in subsequent years the rates were given by the same publication.

Thus from 1944 to 1954 using the methods outlined above a series was derived for both federal corporate income taxes paid and provincial corporate income taxes paid by natural resource industries in each province.

In 1955 and 1956 the Department of National Revenue (14) did not publish either corporate net income or federal corporate taxes by province and industry. Totals were available for Canada, however, and the 1954 percentages of total natural resource corporate net income were applied to arrive at provincial totals. It was decided not to line with 1957 results (the first year when the data were published again) as 1957 was a year of extremes due to the recession, whereas 1954 was more normal. Once again provincial corporate rates were applied to the estimates to arrive at the flow of natural resource corporate income tax to each province.

To arrive at the federal tax paid in each province in 1955 and 1956 the ten-province federal natural resource corporate income revenue was taken as a per cent of natural resource corporate net income, and this per cent was applied to our estimate of net income already made for each province. In 1955 this per cent was 44.6 and in 1956 it was 44.0.

From 1957 to 1964 provincial net income data by industry were again published by the Department of National Revenue (14). Once again provincial corporate income tax rates were applied to the actual net income of natural resource industries, adjusted to extract agricultural net income, to arrive at the flow of natural resource corporation income taxes to each province. To arrive at the federal taxes paid an estimate was made applying the total per cent for Canada (as explained above) to the adjusted net income figures for each province. This per cent varied from a low of 39.1 to a high of 42.9.

In 1965, as discussed above, D.B.S. (11) took over the publishing of national revenue data. Once again there was a switch in industrial classification but in the area of natural resources it was not serious. The reasons are probably the same as in the switch in 1944. Now, however, each item in each category is enumerated so it becomes possible to extract agriculture and simply take the sum of forestry, fishing and game, mines, quarries, and oil wells. Once again the appropriate corporate tax rates are applied to net income to give the flow of natural resource corporation income tax to each province from 1945 to 1971.

The federal taxes paid on natural resource corporate income by province, however, are not given and once again the total for Canada (which is given) is taken as a per cent of net income in Canada and this per cent is applied to the net income in each province to arrive at federal income tax paid by natural resource industries by province from 1965 to 1971.

To check the accuracy of the provincial taxes paid by corporations, we used a figure giving the sum for Quebec and Ontario published in D.B.S. (11). For example, in 1966 the combined corporate income tax in Quebec and Ontario for natural resource industries is given as $10.5 million. Our estimated figures were $7.4 million in Quebec and $3.2 million in Ontario for a total of $10.6 million. This satisfyingly small discrepancy is even smaller in other years.

No corporate tax statistics were available for New Brunswick in 1944 and 1945. The missing years were estimated by linear interpolation between 1943 and 1946.

In 1971 the same problem occurred for Newfoundland. This time the 1970 per cent of total natural resource net income in Canada derived from Newfoundland was applied to the same total for 1971 to give an estimate. For the federal government, the series in Table 1 is the sum of natural resource revenue and federal corporate income taxes from natural resource industries. Although this does show the flow of comprehensive natural resource revenue to the federal government, it is not strictly correct as tax abatements and credits are later made to the provincial governments after 1941.

In the compilation of series 3, provincial share of corporate income taxes from natural industries, it will be noticed that another series is created as a by-product. This series 4 is the federal income taxes from natural resources by province since 1927.

References

Canada, Department of National Revenue, Taxation Division, *Taxation Statistics: Part Two, Corporations*, 1946-66.

Canada, Dominion Bureau of Statistics (later called Statistics Canada), "Comparative Statistics of Public Finance, 1913, 1921, 1925-39," *Report of the Royal Commission on Dominion - Provincial Relations, Book III, Documentation*, pp. 9-145; and Appendix 1, 1939.

————. "Comparative Statistics of Public Finance, 1933, 1937, 1939, 1941, 1943," *Dominion - Provincial Conference on Reconstruction, Book 2*, pp. 1-129.

————. 11-202, *Canada Year Book*, various years.

————. 61-208, *Corporation Taxation Statistics*, various years.

————. 68-D-21, *Dominion Income Tax, Excess Profits Tax, and Succession Duty Statistics*, various years; also known as "Licences Assessed for Income War Tax in Canada,1932-41."

————. 68 D-22, *Financial Statistics of Provincial Governments of Canada*, 1921-26, 1928, 1929, 1930-37, 1940-49.

————. 68-201, *Principle Taxes and Rates, Federal, Provincial and Selected Municipal Governments*, various years.

————. 68-207, *Financial Statistics of Provincial Governments, Revenue and Expenditure, Actual*, various years.

————. 68-211, *Financial Statistics of the Government of Canada, Revenue and Expenditure, Direct and Indirect Debt, Actual*, various years.

————. 68-506, *The Canadian System of Government Financial Management Statistics and Amendments*.

National Finance Committee, *Comparative Statistics of Provincial Public Finance 1926-36* (Ottawa, 1936).

Perry, J.H., *Taxation in Canada* (Toronto: University of Toronto Press, 1951), pp. 233-54, 365-66.

————. *Taxes, Tariffs and Subsidies: A History of Canadian Fiscal Development* (Toronto: University of Toronto Press, 1955), pp. 258, 642-65, 700.

"Section G: Government Finance," *Historical Statistics of Canada*, M.C. Urquhart and K.A. M. Buckley, eds. (Toronto: Macmillan Co., 1965), pp. 187-221.

Petrie, J.R., *The Taxation of Corporate Income in Canada* (Toronto: University of Toronto Press, 1952), pp. 34ff.

Notes

1. Canada, Dominion Bureau of Statistics, 68-207, *Financial Statistics of Provincial Governments, Revenue and Expenditure, Actual,* various years.

2. Canada, Dominion Bureau of Statistics (later called Statistics Canada), "Comparative Statistics of Public Finance, 1913, 1921, 1925-39," *Report of the Royal Commission on Dominion-Provincial Relations, Book III, Documentation,* pp. 9-145; and Appendix 1, 1939.

3. Canada, Dominion Bureau of Statistics, "Comparative Statistics of Public Finance; 1933, 1937, 1939, 1941, 1943," *Dominion-Provincial Conference on Reconstruction, Book 2,* pp. 1-129.

4. J.H. Perry, *Taxes, Tariffs and Subsidies: A History of Canadian Fiscal Development* (Toronto: University of Toronto Press, 1955), pp. 258, 642-65, 700.

5. Canada, Dominion Bureau of Statistics, 68-D-22, *Financial Statistics of Provincial Governments of Canada,* 1921-26, 1928, 1929, 1930-37, 1940-49.

6. Canada, Dominion Bureau of Statistics, 11-202, *Canada Year Book,* various years.

7. National Finance Committee, *Comparative Statistics of Provincial Public Finance,* 1926-36 (Ottawa, 1936).

8. Canada, Dominion Bureau of Statistics, 68-506, *The Canadian System of Government Financial Management Statistics and Amendments.*

9. Canada, Dominion Bureau of Statistics, 68-211, *Financial Statistics of the Government of Canada, Revenue and Expenditure, Direct and Indirect Debt, Actual,* various years.

10. Canada, Dominion Bureau of Statistics, 68-D-21, *Dominion Income Tax, Excess Profits Tax, and Succession Duty Statistics,* various years; also known as "Income Assessed for Income War Tax in Canada, 1932-41."

11. Canada, Dominion Bureau of Statistics, 61-208, *Corporation Taxation Statistics,* various years.

12. J.H. Perry, *Taxation in Canada* (Toronto: University of Toronto Press, 1951), pp. 233-54, 365-66.

13. J.R. Petrie, *The Taxation of Corporate Income in Canada* (Toronto: University of Toronto Press, 1952), pp. 34ff.

14. Canada, Department of National Revenue, Taxation Division, *Taxation Statistics: Part Two, Corporations,* 1946-66.

15. Canada, Dominion Bureau of Statistics, 68-201, *Principle Taxes and Rates, Federal, Provincial and Selected Municipal Governments,* various years.

The Constitution: A Basis for Bargaining

W.R. LEDERMAN

The right to the revenue from natural resources in Canada clearly involves the federal constitution (the B.N.A. Act) in several important ways. We are a federal country, and so the constitution does have terms that divide and distribute both legislative powers and the ownership of public lands between the provincial and federal levels of government. But automatic and detailed solutions do not emerge by easy logical deduction from the relevant sections of the constitution. Certainly there are several guidelines that do much to shape both the procedure for finding detailed solutions and the nature of the alternative solutions to be expected. In a brief and general way, this is what I shall attempt to explain in what follows.

I have recited the sections of the B.N.A. Act in the Appendix to this paper that deal with the distribution of the ownership of public lands, and the distribution of relevant legislative powers, such as the respective federal and provincial powers of taxation. I will also refer to these sections as part of the text of my discussion of the issues.

The basic point to remember is that any constitution, especially a federal one, is necessarily a complex document. In our federal constitution, each word or phrase used to distribute legislative powers and ownership of public lands to the respective provincial governments and the federal government is in a context of many other such words and phrases. These words are usually words of considerable generality of meaning and overlap one another in their significance. So each must be read in a context that includes the others, and there must be some mutual modification of meanings accordingly. Hence there is a need for sophisticated judicial interpretation of a federal constitution. Judicial review is very important.

I described this process in a previous essay some years ago as follows:

> The federal distribution of legislative powers and responsibilities in Canada is one of the facts of life when we concern ourselves with the many important social, political, economic, or cultural problems of our country. Over the whole range of actual and potential law-making,

our constitution distributes powers and responsibilities by two lists of categories or classes—one list for the federal parliament (primarily section 91 of the B.N.A. Act), the other for each of the provincial legislatures (primarily section 92 of the B.N.A. Act). For instance, the federal list includes regulation of trade and commerce, criminal law, and a general power to make laws in all matters not assigned to the provinces. Examples from the provincial list are property and civil rights in the province, local works and undertakings, and all matters of a merely local or private nature in the province.

These federal and provincial categories of power are expressed, and indeed have to be expressed, in quite general terms. This permits considerable flexibility in constitutional interpretation, but also it brings much overlapping and potential conflict between the various definitions of powers and responsibilities. To put the same point in another way, our community life—social, economic, political, and cultural—is very complex and will not fit neatly into any scheme of categories or classes without considerable overlap and ambiguity occurring. There are inevitable difficulties arising from this that we must live with so long as we have a federal constitution.

Accordingly the courts must continually assess the competing federal and provincial lists of powers against one another in the judicial task of interpreting the constitution. In the course of judicial decisions on the B.N.A. Act, the judges have basically done one of two things. First, they have attempted to define mutually exclusive spheres for federal and provincial powers, with partial success. But, where mutual exclusion did not seem feasible or proper, the courts have implied the existence of concurrent federal and provincial powers in the overlapping area, with the result that either or both authorities have been permitted to legislate provided their statutes did not in some way conflict one with the other in the common area.[1]

So, we have a situation of philosophical competition, so to speak, by the respective federal and provincial words or phrases, to embrace the challenged statute and stamp it as legitimate or valid as an exercise of federal or provincial powers, as the case may be. This means that the federal and provincial words and phrases must be authoritatively construed in relation to one another by the courts, so that there will be the authority of precedent for one of the rational alternatives for reconciling their respective meanings in relation to one another.

Consider, for example, one example of such competition that is very important to the subject of natural resources. I refer to the competition between the federal trade and commerce clause and the provincial property and civil rights clause. As a matter of legal history, a sale of goods is the transfer of property rights to certain commodities from a seller (the owner) to a buyer for a money consideration called the price. The transaction whereby this is accomplished in law is a contract. The right to make contracts and alienate property are classic examples in our legal history of property rights and civil rights. But the competing federal phrase is "trade and commerce." In commodity transactions—tangible movables—where does the one stop and the other start? If you give property and civil rights its fullest possible scope at the expense of the federal trade and commerce power, the latter means virtually nothing. The converse is also true. If every trading and commercial matter from the corner store to General Motors is embraced by the federal trade and commerce clause, there would be little left of the historical commercial meaning of property and civil rights.

In this respect, the courts reached the following compromise, which still stands as our essential constitutional law on the subject. This is a classic example of the mutual modification of definitions of which I have been speaking. The respective provinces have complete and exclusive jurisdiction over trading and commercial transactions that begin and end within a single province. But where tangible goods cross borders, either provincial or international, exclusive federal jurisdiction attaches to the trading and commercial transactions involved. While there are some qualifications to be added—there are some very limited areas of concurrent jurisdiction—the foregoing describes a main division between exclusive provincial legislative power and exclusive federal legislative power that still stands.

In particular, where marketing of products produced in a province is entirely local to that province, only the provincial legislature has power to enact a compulsory marketing scheme which includes, for example, compulsory price-fixing. On the other hand, where commodities that cross borders or are destined to cross borders are concerned, we are talking of interprovincial or international trade. In this latter event, only the federal parliament can enact mandatory marketing legislation that includes, for example, quotas and price-fixing. For the most part then, the federal parliament does have the power to enact into law national marketing schemes or policies—since most commodities involved do cross provincial or international borders, or would have to do so if their owners permitted them to enter into the marketing process. Nevertheless, I should think that complementary marketing legislation would be necessary, enacted by a province, for marketing that was entirely internal to that province from production to consumption.

I have mentioned the matter of ownership. The general scheme of the B.N.A. Act is that ownership of public lands is vested in the respective provincial governments. Insofar as resources from public lands are involved then, the owner is the province within the borders of which those lands are located. Sections 109 and 117 of the B.N.A. Act are generally to this effect. Until 1930, the situation was different in the provinces of Manitoba, Saskatchewan, and Alberta, and also in the Railway Belt and Peace River Block of British Columbia. But, in 1930, by agreements with these provinces, the federal government transferred the ownership of federal public lands generally to the provinces, so as to put them in the same position as that called for by sections 109 and 117 of the B.N.A. Act of 1867. The agreements were given full constitutional effect by amendments to the B.N.A. Act and other relevant British and Canadian statutes. There was an Act of the British Parliament in 1930 validating these agreements.

In the field of energy—certainly gas and oil, and possibly electricity as well—the ownership of the land is obviously important. Of course, all minerals are involved, and also forest products, in the ownership of land; section 92(5) of the B.N.A. Act makes it clear that the respective provinces have "the Management and Sale of the Public Lands belonging to the Province and of the Timber and Wood thereon." I should think that this means two things of significance for present purposes.

(1) As owner of minerals, for example, that are part of public lands, the province can, simply as owner, refuse to sell them for export out of the province. This would not apply to privately owned minerals.

(2) Under the property and civil rights clause, and under the general provincial power over matters of a local and private nature in the province, I consider that the province has the power to enact genuine conservation measures concerning the harvesting or extracting of natural resources from all provincial lands, not just the public lands.

These latter two propositions show that, in interpreting the B.N.A. Act, we not only have to reconcile the provincial property and civil rights clause with the federal trade and commerce clause, but also the provincial ownership of the resources in public lands, and the provincial power to enact conservation measures generally, with the federal trade and commerce power.

Let us now look at the taxing powers under the B.N.A. Act. Under section 91(3), the federal parliament may engage in "the raising of money by any mode or system of taxation." The corresponding provincial power is more limited. The provinces, by section 92(2), have power for "*direct* taxation *within the province* in order to the raising of a revenue for provincial purposes." The result of this is that only the federal parliament can levy import or export taxes because these are classically indirect taxes. Further, there are two special provisions of the B.N.A. Act that limit both provincial and federal taxing authorities. Section 121 forbids interprovincial tariffs. It states: "All Articles of the Growth, Produce or

Manufacture of any one of the Provinces shall, from and after the Union, be admitted free into each of the other Provinces." Secondly, there are strict limits to whether the provinces may tax the federal government and vice versa. Section 125 of the B.N.A. Act states: "No Lands or Property belonging to Canada or any Province shall be liable to Taxation."

A couple of relevant limitations follow from the foregoing. In the first place, mandatory marketing schemes, whether provincial or federal or some combination of the two, must respect the requirement that there shall be no financial provisions that are in effect interprovincial tariffs. This applies to the mandatory pricing provisions of such marketing schemes, or to provincial or federal taxation schemes such as sales taxes. When section 121 says that interprovincial trade shall be free, I take it to mean that neither taxing laws nor the financial provisions of commercial laws may breach this requirement. I emphasize this point because the pricing provisions of a compulsory marketing scheme are commercial law, not tax law. In other words, not every compulsory commercial-financial provision is a tax law, but section 121 catches them both anyway.

But what about straight taxation? Here we come across another problem that is current in this area of revenue from resources. When the Crown in right of the province—the provincial government—leases or grants mineral lands to private persons and reserves royalties, it is simply claiming one of the oldest forms of public revenue there is. Section 109 of the B.N.A. Act makes it clear that the provincial Crown is entitled to royalties respecting provincial lands. A royalty, in the sense in which I am using it here, is a payment to the lessor, in the case of mining leases, whereby the payment due is proportionate to the amount of the mineral that is worked from time to time in the leased land by the lessee. Now, where the lessor is the provincial Crown, the royalty revenues are provincial property. This property cannot be taxed by the federal parliament because of section 125 of the B.N.A. Act. But this means that the provincial government cannot be directly taxed as such by the federal parliament under a federal taxing statute. When the federal parliament says that the *lessee* is not allowed to deduct from federal corporate income tax the royalty payments due to the provincial Crown, what then? Is this really the same thing as the federal parliament attempting to tax the provincial Crown itself for *its income* from royalties? If it is, it offends section 125 of the B.N.A. Act. If it is not, then the unfortunate lessee of the minerals has to pay the royalties to the provincial government, and also pay *income* tax to the federal government without the benefit of the royalties as deductions. I believe this is one of the issues between the province of Alberta and the federal government and Parliament at the present time. The courts have not yet been asked to resolve it, so we do not know whether the present federal disallowance of royalty deductions for federal revenue tax is really a disguised breach of section 125. Something depends too on whether the present royalty scheme of the Alberta government is to be truly characterized as a matter of "royalties" in the classic sense, and thus as within sections 109 and 125 of the B.N.A. Act. If "royalties" are put at an unreasonably high level, no room is left for the federal government to obtain revenues from income tax on resource development companies, if the royalties *must* be allowed as deductions. Conversely, federal income tax could be set so high that the companies had nothing left to pay royalties with, whether or not they were in theory deductible.

This prompts me to make two observations at this point. (1) Where federal and provincial authorities are collectively asking for too much money, it may well be that the federal authorities could insist on being paid in full first. (2) There is no constitutional prohibition against killing geese that lay golden eggs. Federal and provincial governments can be severally or collectively foolish about this—I fear it is true that the power to tax is the power to destroy. The federal and provincial tax collectors have to agree to some kind of a sharing that leaves natural resource enterprises viable and able to produce and flourish within reason. This brings me to my last topic, the necessity for co-operative federalism.

At this point we must realize that there are problems we must learn to live with if we are to have a federal constitution at all. One of these problems is illustrated by what I have just been saying. With respect to the total process of developing and exploiting a given natural resource like oil, there are certain problems of divided jurisdiction that we must learn to live with. Such problems are inevitable in federal countries. For example we have seen that the provinces own the resources in their public lands and can sit on them if they wish. But we have also seen that once natural resources have been severed from the land and have become commodities, then power to regulate the marketing of them is federal, if they are obviously destined (as most of them are) for export out of the province of production.

What is necessary then is that, if there is to be an effective *total* policy for the exploitation of a given natural resource, parts of that policy must be supplied by virtue of statutes of the province of production and other parts of that policy must be supplied by virtue of statutes of the federal parliament. This requires federal-provincial agreement about complementary uses of the respective federal and provincial legislative powers and powers of ownership. This is a political problem, a problem of federal and provincial bargaining. That is the process we are watching with respect to oil from Alberta and Saskatchewan at the present time. Notice that the constitutional provisions I have been outlining do not automatically eventuate in a total solution—a total sensible Canadian oil policy. But they do give an essential definition to the elements of the federal-provincial bargaining process that we call co-operative federalism. Divided jurisdiction, where there is a need for co-operation across the jurisdictional lines, has to be seen as an invitation to practise co-operative federalism—to agree on a properly complementary use of federal and provincial powers and resources.

There are a number of overall policy areas that cross the jurisdictional lines of our present division of legislative powers in our federal constitution. Another example is the abatement of pollution of air, land, and water. In this area, as one example, federal criminal law powers and provincial powers over torts and delicts have to be co-ordinated. Consumer protection is another area involving the provincial commercial powers (property and civil rights), the federal ones (trade and commerce), and the federal criminal law power. So, there is nothing unusual in the necessity for the co-ordinated co-operation of federal and provincial governments passing complementary statutes in order to accomplish a single national oil policy, if one wishes to stay with that example. This necessity and inevitability can be demonstrated philosophically—as a matter of the philosophy of classification systems and the multiple possibilities of cross-classification—but I have done that elsewhere and will refrain from doing it here.[2]

Federal-provincial agreements are therefore necessary, but the autonomy and the identity of the parties for the bargaining process is defined by the constitution itself. The purpose of the bargaining is to agree on wise complementary uses of the respective federal and provincial constitutional powers and resources.

Notes

[1] W.R. Lederman, "The Concurrent Operation of Federal and Provincial Laws in Canada," *McGill Law Journal* 9 (1962-63): 185.

[2] W.R. Lederman, "Cooperative Federalism: Constitutional Revision and Parliamentary Government in Canada," *Queen's Quarterly* 78 (1971): 7, and "Some Forms and Limitations of Cooperative Federalism," *Canadian Bar Review* 45 (1967): 409.

Appendix

EXCERPTS FROM THE B.N.A. ACT

Powers of the [Federal] Parliament.

91. It shall be lawful for the Queen, by and with the Advice and Consent of the Senate and House of Commons to *make Laws for the Peace, Order, and good Government of Canada, in relation to all Matters not coming within the Classes of Subjects by the Act assigned exclusively to the Legislatures of the Provinces*; and for great Certainty, but not so as to restrict the Generality of the foregoing Terms of this Section, it is hereby declared that (notwithstanding anything in this Act) the exclusive Legislative Authority of the Parliament of Canada extends to all Matters coming within the Classes of Subjects next hereinafter enumerated; that is to say,
Legislative Authority of Parliament of Canada

1A.   The Public Debt and Property
2.   The Regulation of Trade and Commerce
3.   The raising of Money by any Mode or System of Taxation.
29.   Such Classes of Subjects as are expressly excepted in the Enumeration of the Classes of Subjects by this Act assigned exclusively to the Legislatures of the Provinces.

And any Matter coming within any of the Classes of Subjects enumerated in this Section shall not be deemed to come within the Class of Matters of a local or private Nature comprised in the Enumeration of the Classes of Subjects by this Act assigned exclusively to the Legislatures of the Provinces.

Exclusive Powers of Provincial Legislatures.

92. In each Province the Legislature may exclusively make Laws in relation to Matters coming within the Classes of Subjects next hereinafter enumerated; that is to say,
Subjects of exclusive Provincial Legislation

2.   Direct Taxation within the Province in order to the raising of a Revenue for Provincial Purposes.
5.   The Management and Sale of the Public Lands belonging to the Province and of the Timber and Wood thereon.
10.   Local Works and Undertakings other than such as are of the following Classes:
a. Lines of Steam or other Ships, Railways, Canals,

Telegraphs, and other Works and Undertakings connecting the Provinces, or extending beyond the Limits of the Province;

b. Lines of Steam Ships between the Province and any British or Foreign Country;

c. Such Works as, although wholly situate within the Province, are before or after their Execution declared by the Parliament of Canada to be for the general Advantage of Canada or for the Advantage of Two or more of the Provinces.

13. Property and Civil Rights in the Province.

16. Generally all Matters of a merely local or private Nature in the Province.

109. All Lands, Mines, Minerals, and Royalties belonging to the several Provinces of Canada, Nova Scotia, and New Brunswick at the Union, and all Sums then due or payable for such Lands, Mines, Minerals, or Royalties, shall belong to the several Provinces of Ontario, Quebec, Nova Scotia, and New Brunswick in which the same are situate or arise, subject to any Trusts existing in respect thereof, and to any Interest other than that of the Province in the same.
Property in
Lands,
Mines, etc.

117. The several Provinces shall retain all their respective Public Property not otherwise disposed of in this Act, subject to the Right of Canada to assume any Lands or Public Property required for Fortifications or for the Defence of the Country.
Provincial
Public
Property

121. All Articles of the Growth, Produce or Manufacture of any one of the Provinces shall, from and after the Union, be admitted free into each of the other Provinces.

125. No Lands or Property belonging to Canada or any Province shall be liable to Taxation.

The Political Context of Resource Development in Canada

DONALD V. SMILEY

Before the 1970's the complexities of the development of natural resources were of primary concern to only a relative handful of specialists. Today these matters are at the centre of so many crucial concerns of the Canadian and world community that no serious student of human affairs can leave them to these few persons whose training and background enable them to discuss resource policy in a sophisticated way. The following remarks are thus those of an amateur fully aware that he is much out of his depth.

I. THE CHANGING PREMISES OF ACTION

Public policies cannot be understood in any adequate way without some grasp of the major premises on which decision-makers act. In respect to resource policies these premises are very different from those of as recently as five years ago. In a highly impressionistic way, I shall try to outline these changes.

a. A growing realization that the planet's resources are limited and that economic growth is not the solution for all human ills. I do not know how profound is the conservation ethic among Canadian politicians, and it is easy to believe that this is something which comes over them in their more inspirational postures and is quickly set aside in favour of the traditional disposition toward growth when important decisions are being made. Yet there is progress on this front. Here and there one encounters the proposition that the conservation ethic distinguishes, or can come to distinguish, the Canadian from the American value system. There is an unprecedented sensitivity to the native peoples and the impact of economic development on their welfare. More crucially perhaps, there is the growing realization that, contrary to past beliefs, Canadian natural resources are not inexhaustible and the judgement that in all likelihood they will be more valuable in the future than now gives sound prudential reasons for conserving them.

b. A growing disposition to treat land and non-renewable resources other than as commodities produced for sale at prices set by the market. There are two contradictory ways to regard land and non-replenishable resources. The first asserts that these are commodities like others whose prices are appropriately set by the operation of market forces. This was in fact the operational assumption of most Canadian public policy until the past two or three years. The private resource industries were able to convince both governments and people that because natural resources were of no value to anyone until discovered and exploited the ancient principle of "finders keepers" should apply. A new view seems now to be in the ascendancy. In his monumental *The Great Transformation*,[1] which offered explanation of economic development in the western world alternative to those of both Marxists and liberals, Karl Polanyi argued that the self-regulating market economy inappropriately treats land—the natural inheritance of a society— along with money and labour as if it were a commodity produced for sale. This formulation has deeply influenced some of the more thoughtful Canadian nationalists. Although he did not proceed directly within the framework of Polanyi's analysis, Donald Creighton came to much the same conclusion in a polemic address in 1971 arguing for the development of Canadian natural resources under Canadian control.[2] He said: "These natural resources are not looked upon as ordinary assets—things Canadians have built or acquired themselves. They are regarded as the original endowment of nature, as the birthright of Canada."[3] In a somewhat similar spirit, Premier Davis of Ontario defended the land speculation tax in the province against certain right-wing elements of his party by reminding them of the common Latin root of "conservation" and "conservatism" and affirming that the controversial measure was designed to tax "people who were trading land as if they were on the stock market."[4] Even more important perhaps, it is of consequence that Canadian economists have recently come to talk of public policies toward resource development in terms of the recapturing of economic rent.[5] Such rent within our normative framework accrues to the owners of assets and the B.N.A. Act unequivocally confers such ownership on the provinces.

c. A declining belief that Canada's economic future will be dominated by the development and export of natural resources in a raw or semi-finished form. It is a truism that Canadian economic development has been dominated by the production and export of a succession of staple products. Perhaps as an extrapolation of this pattern of development into the future, Canadians until very recently looked upon their economy in somewhat physiocratic terms. It may be speculated too that Canadians are a pious people—even those outside Alberta—who have believed that the Creator would not have given them an endowment of such otherwise inhospitable real estate if He did not have plans that they would profit by it. And of course there has been in the background the national dream that we would be able, and very soon, to get our way with the Americans because of this endowment. An emergent Canadian industrial strategy attempts to set the country in new directions. This emergent strategy is most fully and authoritatively formulated in the reports of the Senate Special Committee on Science Policy, several studies published under the auspices of the Science Council of Canada and in parts of the Gray Report on Foreign Direct Investment in Canada. These new requirements are posited in terms of an economy with high capabilities for indigenous technological innovation.[6] In a more specific sense, there is to be a rationalization of the secondary manufacturing sector to make it relatively more important in the Canadian economy and more competitive internationally, measures to encourage the domestic processing of Canadian resources, and a major co-operative effort involving business, government, and the universities towards enhancing the performance and innovative capacity of industry.

   d. A declining confidence in the market as an allocative mechanism. In Canada as in other western nations there is a declining commitment to the market as an allocative mechanism and a growing readiness to tolerate or to demand action by the public authorities when the marketplace yields results deemed on a wide variety of grounds to be unsatisfactory. Nowhere, of course, is this circumstance so dramatically illustrated as in respect to petroleum and petroleum products. Whatever professional economists may say about the "distortions" resulting in the Canadian economy if through governmental action the domestic price for petroleum is made to diverge from the price exacted by the O.P.E.C. cartel, I don't think such advice will have much effect. It may be, too, that the declining commitment to the market mechanism will displace economists from the influential role they have come to play as advisers on Canadian public policy. But that is the subject for another conference.

   e. A declining commitment to continental economic integration. It has become increasingly evident that continental economic integration is no longer an option. This is so more because of American disposition than of Canadian—viz. the refusals of Washington to exempt Canada from the drastic solutions adopted in 1971, "Project Independence" in energy matters and so on. There is in fact every evidence that from now on in the Americans are committed to treating Canada as another foreign nation in respect to resource development and other matters.

II. ENERGY POLICY AND CANADA'S INTERNATIONAL RELATIONS

   Modern countries have formulated the economic requirements of nationhood in quite different ways. What does a jurisdiction have to have to be a nation in other than a juristic sense? a domestic steel industry? atomic energy installations? independent fiscal, monetary, and tariff policies? a strong and growing secondary manufacturing sector? an economy with a capacity for indigenous technological innovation? The events of the fall of 1973 showed the vulnerability of the western nations and Japan to the actions of the petroleum-producing countries and in the wake of this both Canada and the United States have accepted a much higher degree of self-sufficiency in energy as a crucial element of their national economic policies. President Nixon put it bluntly on 15 November 1973: "The United States is a great nation. No great nation must ever be in the position where it is dependent on any other nation, friend or foe, for its energy." The Americans have now combined "Project Independence" with the bicentennial celebrations of the Declaration of Independence.

The critical events of 1973 saw a headlong rush of the O.E.C.D. nations, including Canada, to strike individual bargains with the producing countries. Particularly among the European Common Market nations, the fragility of the structures of economic unity which had been so painfully established were revealed, and it remains in the balance whether under American leadership there will be co-operative procedures developed to deal with the O.P.E.C. countries. Apart from revolutionary régimes which have recently come to power, governments are pre-eminently conservative instruments which seek to protect the human and institutional fabrics of their respective societies against such dislocations as result from the vagaries of the price system, rapid technological change, and actions taken by other governments.

It is as sure as any such thing can be that Canada and the United States will be less integrated in respect to natural resources, specifically fossil-fuel resources, than any of us would have expected as recently as five years ago. Each nation will more than in the past discount price factors in attempting to supply its needs from domestic sources. To the extent that the United States continues to depend on Canadian petroleum and natural gas the Americans will drive very hard bargains to insulate the supply and price of such resources from future changes in Canadian policies.

The increasing involvement of the federal and provincial governments in resource development may well have important effects on Canada's international economic relations. In a dispatch from Washington to the *Globe and Mail* of 28 June 1974, Ross H. Munro reported that within the Treasury Department was circulating a list of seventeen grievances against various aspects of Canadian economic policies. Munro asserted that it was the "increasing intervention of Ottawa in Canada's economy" which constituted the "underlying theme" of these grievances. To the extent that in such matters Canada comes to differ significantly from the United States in our reliance on the market economy, relations between the two countries will be complicated and continental economic integration frustrated. (It may be too that because of its range of international commitments the United States will be disposed to see its resource policies in a very different context than do Canadians.) So far as other nations are concerned, the increasing involvement of Canadian governments in resource matters may lead to closer relations than otherwise. When Donald Macdonald went to Caracas in the fall of 1973 in an attempt to negotiate an arrangement about long-term petroleum supplies, the Venezuelans expressed unwillingness to dictate to private oil companies the conditions under which they would sell their products in Canada but suggested that deals between the two governments, presumably through a Canadian public corporation, might be possible. Similarly, of course, the recent agreement between Canada and the United Kingdom about atomic energy and other such deals that are in the offing are facilitated by this being a field under public control in the countries involved.

III. THE FEDERAL DIMENSION OF CANADIAN RESOURCE POLICIES

So far as federalism is concerned, the context of Canadian policies toward non-renewable resources has three interrelated elements. There is, first, the generalized revolt of the western provinces against their historic economic domination by the central Canadian heartland. Second, there is an Alberta industrial strategy aimed at changing the economic base of that province and its relations with the outside world. And last, there are the implications of federal and provincial resource policies for Ottawa's commitment to narrowing interregional economic disparities in Canada.

Western Canada was from the first and to a considerable extent remains an economic colony of the country's central heartland. The acquisition and subsequent development of a western hinterland was one of the central purposes of Confederation and in the early years of the Dominion and afterward relations between the heartland and the hinterland were regulated according to classic mercantilist principles: a. metropolitan policies required the hinterland to buy the manufactured goods of the heartland; b. capital development in the hinterland was carried out mainly by the activity of public and private institutions centred in the heartland; c. the hinterland and the heartland were physically linked by transportation and communication facilities established and operated for the benefit of the latter; d. in international economic relations, the interests of the hinterland were usually sacrificed to those of the heartland; e. many of the critical aspects of hinterland development were carried out through the instrumentalities of large business organizations protected by heartland policies from foreign or hinterland competition; f. there was a continuing pattern controlling the political authorities of the hinterland in the interests of the heartland through the workings of the national political parties, reservation, and disallowance of provincial legislation, etc.

From the challenge raised by Manitoba against the monopoly clause of the C.P.R. charter in the 1880's there have been western Canadian revolts against that region's place in Confederation—revolts expressed through the various farmers' movements, Progressivism, the Social Credit and C.C.F. parties, and some influential elements of Diefenbaker Conservatism. And these pressures have from time to time been successful in part—witness the cancellation of the C.P.R. monopoly clause, the Crow's Nest Pass differential, Liberal tariff reforms in the 1920's, the establishment of the P.F.R.A., the National Oil Policy of 1961, the recent Liberal commitment to freight rate structures based on costs of service and to removing some of the restrictions on provincial ownership of equity stocks of chartered banks. In his opening speech to the Western Economic Opportunities Conference in July 1973 Prime Minister Trudeau contrasted the "old national policy" based on a "central Canadian 'metropole' with an agricultural and resource 'hinterland' in the West" with current needs for a "new national policy" of "more balanced and diversified regional growth throughout the country." However, as the conference proceeded, the western premiers were able to demonstrate that certain elements of the new national industrial strategy, specifically those of the various industrial incentive programs administered by the Department of Industry, Trade and Commerce, were working to perpetuate or even exaggerate the historic economic dominance of central Canada. What "balanced and diversified regional growth" means in respect to the development of natural resources remains to me unclear, apart from the pressures of the West as well as other parts of Canada toward the further processing of these and other resources in their province or region of origin. Significantly, at the 1973 conference the western premiers were successful in keeping energy and resource matters off the agenda, thereby facilitating a western united front on a group of other issues.

Largely but by no means entirely because of its circumstances in relation to fossil fuels, Alberta has emerged as a province "pas comme les autres." The Alberta situation in terms of Canadian development is a fascinating one, a province with one economic sector based on the older agricultural staples and another on the new staples of petroleum and natural gas. This unique position in the Canadian federation may be outlined briefly:
a. Alberta, like Saskatchewan, is still a new jurisdiction, carved out of the plains in this century. It was the last part of North America to come under agricultural cultivation. Even more crucially, the discovery of

petroleum at Leduc in 1947 decisively altered the nature of the economy in a way not recently experienced by any other province.

b. Alberta is a politically aberrant province in which interests and attitudes which are specifically Albertan have characteristically been channeled almost exclusively through the provincial government and have found little outlet in Ottawa. Not since 1911 has Alberta had a provincial administration of the same political complexion as that in power federally. Since Alberta attained provincial status in 1905 there have been only three changes of government (1921, 1935, 1971) and there has been a characteristic pattern of one-party dominance in contrast with the vigorous inter-party competition of Saskatchewan and British Columbia. With the possible exception of Douglas Harkness as Minister of Agriculture and later Minister of National Defence in the Diefenbaker government, Alberta has not produced an important national politician since R.B. Bennett; since 1957 that part of the province north of Calgary has not been represented in the federal cabinet, with the exception of two months' incumbency in 1963 of Marcel Lambert as Minister of Veterans' Affairs. Although I am here relying on memory and impression, I cannot recall any Albertan who as a non-elected official has had a crucial role in Ottawa in the past generation.

c. Prevailing political attitudes in Alberta are considerably to the right of those which dominate the federal government and the governments of most other provinces. Alberta is closer in time than other parts of Canada to the agricultural frontier, and the "new Alberta" of the past generation has been developed largely through a freewheeling variant of private enterprise.

d. The current revenue structure of the provincial government differs markedly from that of the other provinces in its much heavier relevance on non-tax revenues.

e. Alberta is much more dependent proportionately than other provinces on the exploitation of non-renewable natural resources and it is believed that the supplies of these resources most economical to develop are depleting rapidly.

On the basis of its existing circumstances Alberta has evolved a relatively coherent industrial strategy with these elements: the preservation of provincial autonomy in resource matters against federal influence; the creation of a strong petrochemical industry within the province; the establishment of arrangements by which Albertans are given preferential treatment in terms of employment and investment opportunities in the development of Alberta resources; the dispersal of economic development outside the Edmonton and Calgary metropolitan areas; adjustments in federal transportation and tariff policies to serve Alberta needs.

Ontario has emerged, of course, as the major antagonist of Alberta's policies as I have outlined them. The Ontario industrial complex has been developed on the base of cheap and abundant supplies of energy and is extraordinarily vulnerable to rapid upward shifts in the prices of such energy. Contrary to recent scholarly mythology, Ontario rather than Quebec has been since Confederation the most consistent defender of provincial autonomy and it is a highly unusual position for an Ontario government to be pressing for more aggressive economic policies by Ottawa to control the actions of other provinces.

Something must be said about the federal-provincial aspects of equalization, although the details are left to Professor Courchene. Prior to the events of the last two years the attainment of full interprovincial revenue equalization at the national average was regarded as one of the wonders of the federal world—at least by students of federal finance in such places as the United States and Australia. And this and other equalization policies had resulted in per capita provincial expenditures in the "have-not" provinces being very close to the national average, although the rates of taxation in the less prosperous jurisdictions were higher than elsewhere. As a result of the large revenues now accruing to the oil producing provinces we have now moved away from full revenue equalization and it is at least possible that in the agreements which come into effect in 1977 some new principle of equalization will be found. Whatever this new principle I would hope that we will not in the process lose the progress we have made in ensuring provincial revenues. And, in the long run if not the short, I doubt that Ottawa can discharge this responsibility if it does not recapture a significant proportion of the economic rents accruing to the public treasury from the development of non-renewable natural resources.

IV. INDUSTRY-GOVERNMENT RELATIONS IN NATURAL RESOURCES

In the past two years the relations between governments and the depletable resource industries in Canada have been subjected to rapid change. This change has had two manifestations: a decreasing sensitivity by governments to the interests of private corporations in this field and new and emergent patterns of joint private-public financing and control. There are many salient differences between the circumstances of mining on the one hand and the development of the fossil fuels on the other. Yet, for whatever reasons, recent relations between governments and these two sectors have assumed broadly the same pattern.

M.W. Bucovetsky has made an excellent analysis of how the mining industry in Canada in the period between 1967 and 1971 was for the most part successful in frustrating the implementation of those recommendations of the Carter Report suggesting the elimination of many of the federal tax privileges conferred on the depletable resource industries.[7] In part, the industry was favoured by the underlying physiocratic premises of Canadian ideology and policy to which I have already referred. In large part, too, the geographical dispersion of mining and the result that this activity is dominant in many localities and provinces meant that the industry had "many political pressure points on which local influences [could] be brought to bear." However, the most influential opposition to the aspect of federal tax reform was not the mining industry as such but the provincial governments. These events confirmed the industry as a client of the various provinces and this client relation seems to me reflected in the manifest inability of mining to mount an effective resistance to more recent provincial policies unfavourable to its interests.

In an article published in late 1974, Glyn R. Berry has cogently described the relations between the oil industry and the federal government before and after the energy crisis of 1973.[8] Here is the earlier situation:

When decision-making on energy matters was relatively non-controversial, the companies' targets of influence—MPs, regulatory agencies, federal ministers etc.—seems to have been benevolently responsive, or so the history of government policy would seem to indicate. Consultation with the industry on energy matters was an accepted element in the decision-making process. Both federal and provincial governments, as well as the oil companies themselves, desired a viable Canadian oil industry and the maximum possible increase in exports to the United States. Few groups were arrayed in opposition to the industry, and the public, for the most part, neither knew nor cared about energy problems.[9]

However,

With the advent of the energy crisis. . . all this changed. When the problem of rapidly rising fuel prices was injected into an already inflationary situation, public consternation grew and the majority of provincial governments, as well as some organized groups, pressed for federal action. When the federal government responded, the multifarious efforts of the oil companies were insufficient, in the new crises situation, to preserve their former degree of autonomy, and the emergence of fundamental constitutional issues left the industry clinging to redundant technical arguments. The companies were forced to stand by as spectators while the short-term future of Canadian energy policy emerged from a federal-provincial bargaining process.[10]

If the analyses of Berry and Bucovetsky are broadly accurate, as I believe them to be, any Marxian explanation of the relation between business and government in the resource industries of Canada is unhelpful. In the kingdom of competitive electoral politics the currency of the realm is votes rather than money. Money in considerable amounts is of course a prerequisite of electoral success; apart from the N.D.P. most of this money comes from corporations, and it is alleged that in most of the country the provincial parties have become highly dependent on contributions from the resource industries. Yet more needs to be said, and it is less than obvious that the piper must always call the tune. From what little is on the public record about the raising of party campaign funds from business in Canada it appears that the process is characteristically a shakedown by party bagmen—it is called "tollgating" in Ontario—of businesses heavily dependent on one kind or other of government action or inaction. If this is so, we have here an arbitrary and secret method of taxation with those on whom such levies are made getting few positive benefits if they comply—or more accurately, few benefits not equally available to their compliant competitors—but fearing unfortunate consequences if they don't. Interestingly, business does not seem to have offered resistance to recent federal and provincial legislation making the ways in which campaign expenditures are raised more open. This lack of opposition indicates to me that business does not regard these contributions as a crucial channel of influence over government. In general terms, the advantages lost most dramatically by the resource industries in these relations involve the changing premises of public action which I outlined at the first of this paper rather than through contributions to party expenditures. It seems to me also true that non-socialist Canadian politicians have a very weak ideological commitment to private enterprise or to the market as an allocative mechanism. Such support as they do give arises for the most part from a pragmatic sense of the limitations of governmental action, a hesitation easily overcome when the performance of the private enterprise system is perceived as deficient.

The second change in industry-government relations involves new forms of organization in which the equity stock and control of economic ventures is divided between private industry and the public authorities. These forms, relatively new to Canada but common in western Europe and Japan, would appear to release governments from some of the problems of both public ownership and the public regulation of private industry. Many interesting questions arise. For example, how closely will the actions of governments as shareholders be integrated with other aspects of public policy? But difficulties are likely to be compounded when two or more governments participate in those corporations regulated under the jurisdiction of one of them, as in the Pan-Arctic consortium and the Syncrude organization.

V. THE PROSPECTS FOR RATIONALITY

If the market mechanism is of declining importance in respect to the matters I have been discussing, what are the prospects for a modicum of rationality in the allocative decisions made by the public authorities? Not very favourable. I do not want to indulge in a discussion of the complex nature of rationality or to assert that economists view this entirely within the framework of the workings of the market system. Students of political science and public administration have their own version of rationality which is no more adequate. Faced with the intractabilities of decision within the context of joint action by two or more autonomous yet interdependent political actors, there is a characteristic retreat towards incantations for improved methods of co-ordination. Yet in many circumstances, certainly so in federal-provincial affairs, these actors are determined not to be co-ordinated, and a contemporary student of American government has written what is equally true of Canada: "The quest for coordination is in many respects the twentieth-century equivalent of the philosopher's stone. If only we can find the right formula for coordination we can reconcile the irreconcilable, harmonize competing and wholly divergent interests, overcome irrationalities in our government structures and make hard policy choices to which no one will dissent." [11]

There is no better example of the excesses of rationalist sentimentality than some of the recent official pronouncements in respect to mining policy. In April 1973 the ministers responsible for mineral policies in their respective provincial governments and in the federal government met to establish "a formal mechanism for consultation and cooperation. . . to achieve more effective coordination in mineral policy development." Out of the conference issued a glossy booklet containing a diagrammatic presentation of "mineral policy goals and objectives" with the master objective being to "obtain optimum benefit for Canada from present and future use of minerals" with twelve purportedly more specific aims such as "foster a viable mineral sector," "strengthen knowledge base for national decision-making," and "improve mineral conservation and use." Late in 1974 the results of another meeting led to an even more pretentious compendium of pictures, charts, and vacuous intentions. Yet throughout most of this latter year the federal and provincial governments had been locked in a bitter struggle about the taxation of resource revenues and relations between governments and the mining industry were less constructive than in any previous period.

A high degree of rationality in Canadian resource policy is impossible principally because we live under a federal system in which the most important policy outcomes are determined by bargaining between autonomous though interdependent governments. We need thus to recognize as patently unrealistic such recommendations as the one made by the Science Council of Canada in 1973 to establish a National Resources Management Authority to "develop and coordinate long-range policies for integrated management of resources and environment."

The justifications of federalism over a unitary system are political and the values furthered by federalism have nothing to do with rationalism in public policy. First, federalism is one of several possible devices for constraining political power, particularly executive power. Second, to the extent that within a nation attitudes and interests are not uniformly distributed on a territorial basis, federalism contributes to the responsiveness of government to the popular will.

But even where a single jurisdiction is involved, the prospects for rationality in natural resource and other policies are limited except in those situations where the matter at issue is for whatever reason insulated from the pressure of conflicting political forces. Managerial rationality is possible only after the ends of public action have been determined and the priority of these ends ranked in an operational way. Such is seldom an alternative where important public policies are involved. [12]

In conclusion, and with perhaps undue rudeness to my hosts, I expect that in the resolution of these issues the federal and provincial politicians will use whatever analytical elegancies we can develop as the ammunition of advocacy. These are after all articulate men—many western cabinet ministers and very often the premiers have been to graduate school and my Ottawa informant tells me they are at least as difficult to deal with as their less-educated predecessors. They will in fact welcome whatever help we can give them in documenting their cases about the erosion of the federal tax base, the implications of Ricardian rent or the primacy of Section 109 of the BNA Act as the fundamental element of the compact of Confederation. Yet I am not altogether sure our efforts are fruitless. These political leaders respond not only to specific advice but in a less explicit way to the underlying premises of action influential in their respective communities. So far as the resource development is concerned, those premises are changing rapidly. In such changes the debates among academics are of some consequence.

Notes

1. Karl Polanyi, *The Great Transformation* (Boston: Beacon Press, 1974).

2. "Continentalism and the Birthright of Canada," in Creighton, *Towards the Discovery of Canada* (Toronto: Macmillan, 1972), pp. 286-92.

3. Ibid., p. 287.

4. *Toronto Star*, 24 May 1974.

5. In his introduction to a recent edition of Ricardo's *Principles*, Donald Winch has pointed out the radical uses of this formulation by John Stuart Mill, Henry George, and the Fabians, as well as of course as by Marx. Everyman Paperback (London/New York: Dent/Dutton, 1973), p. xvii.

6. I have attempted to analyze these matters in a recent article, "Canada and the Quest for a National Policy," *Canadian Journal of Political Science* VIII, 1 (March 1975): 40-62.

7. "The Mining Industry and the Great Tax Reform Debate," in A. Paul Pross, ed., *Pressure Group Behaviour in Canadian Politics* (Toronto: McGraw-Hill Ryerson, 1974), pp. 87-114.

8. G.R. Berry, "The Oil Industry and the Energy Crisis," *Canadian Public Administration* 17 (Winter 1974): 600-35.

9. Ibid., p. 634.

10. Ibid.

11. Harold Seidman, *Politics, Position and Power: The Dynamics of Federal Organization* (New York: Oxford University Press, 1970), p. 164.

12. See the thoughtful criticism of the current excesses of administrative rationalism in Ottawa in "Conclusions and Observations" by G. Bruce Doern and V. Seymour Wilson in Doern and Wilson, eds., *Issues in Canadian Public Policy* (Toronto: Macmillan, 1974), pp. 337-45.

Equalization Payments and Energy Royalties

THOMAS J. COURCHENE

I. INTRODUCTION

To the majority of our trading partners the notion that Canada is in the throes of an energy crisis must seem ironical, to say the least. Nonetheless, the whopping increase in the price of oil has had and will continue to have a profound impact on the economic and political fibre of our nation. Not surprisingly, there is more than one issue fueling Canada's energy crisis. Indeed, it is instructive to anatomize the crisis into at least four separate but obviously interrelated components: a. The allocational and distributional issues relating to the pricing of oil and natural gas; b. The distribution of the windfall gains or rents between the energy producers and the public sector; c. The distribution of the public sector energy revenues between Ottawa and the producing provinces; and d. The distribution of some portion of these public sector revenues to the non-energy-producing provinces (i.e., the impact on equalization payments).

The purpose of this paper is to direct attention to the fourth component, namely the impact of the massive increases in the price of oil and soon-to-come equivalently large increases in the price of natural gas on the system of equalization payments to Canada's "have-not" provinces. To the extent that it is possible, the analysis will ignore the first two ingredients of the energy crisis. However, in addressing the equalization payments issue it will not be possible to ignore the third component—the allocation of public sector energy revenue between Ottawa and the producing provinces—because it is a critical input into the current equalization legislation.

While the energy crisis has already generated a substantial literature within Canada, most of this discussion, at least by economists, has focussed on items a. and b., above. And perhaps appropriately so since it is these issues that subsume the critical allocational aspects of the controversy. Hence it is perhaps not surprising that Gainer and Powrie can claim that "the fact of the matter is that the federal-provincial scramble for a cut of the windfall oil revenues has largely eclipsed the more important issue regarding the appropriate treatment of the producing industry in the kinds of supply and pricing circumstances recently exhibited within the international oil industry."[1] But I am not convinced that this "federal-provincial scramble" must play second fiddle to resource allocation considerations. As will be detailed below, the potential implications of rising energy prices on both Ottawa's financial position and on equalization are rather astounding.[2] Indeed, it is probably accurate to suggest that unless and until the financial issues involving Ottawa and the provinces are sorted out, not much progress will be made on more economic issues of optimal pricing and utilization of energy. Furthermore, the particular decisions taken with respect to energy and equalization may well usher in a new era of political and economic federalism.

The outline of the paper is as follows. Part II focuses on the implications of rising energy prices on the equalization scheme and Part III presents several alternative proposals for solving the issues raised in Part II. In more detail, section A of Part II outlines the salient features of Canada's present legislation with respect to equalization payments. Basically, the purpose of this section will be to provide the needed background for the remainder of the paper. Since there exist several good references on the manner in which Canada distributes these equalization payments to the poorer provinces, the analysis will be relatively brief.[3] Parts B and C pull together the results from appendices to this paper. The purpose of Appendix A is to focus on the impact of rising oil prices on equalization payments. Data on equalization payments are presented for 1973-74 and then the payments are recalculated for various alternative prices for oil, namely $6.50 per barrel, $8.00 per barrel, and $12.50 per barrel, the latter reflecting the current international price. All of these calculations are based on the counterfactual notion that the present system of equalization is to remain unchanged. Appendix B essentially repeats the previous analysis for natural gas royalties. The sensitivity analysis once again allows for various prices of natural gas including an "oil equivalent" price that is consistent with the world price of oil being in the $12.50 range. Apart from the obvious implication that the equalization payments arising from increases in Canadian domestic energy prices to anywhere near the world price level are absolutely staggering, the analysis is also directed toward the very interesting funding implications associated with these rising transfers to the have-not provinces. To anticipate these results, there was no way that Ottawa could afford to allow the present equalization structure to remain intact and at the same time permit "appropriate" increases in energy prices. Part II concludes with a brief outline of the policies that Canada resorted to in order to avoid these implications.

Part III of the paper focusses on alternative solutions to the energy equalization issue, namely those by Musgrave, Helliwell, Gainer and Powrie, and finally, Ottawa's proposal as reflected in speeches by former

Finance Minister John Turner. These proposals differ not only in their financial implications, but as well in the manner in which they view the role of equalization payments. Because Ottawa's proposals are most likely to become embodied in future legislation, considerable attention will be directed to the Turner proposal. A short conclusion completes the paper.

II. ENERGY AND EQUALIZATION: ANATOMY OF A CRISIS

A. *The Present System of Equalization Payments*

The equalization formula. The current legislation in respect of equalization payments stems from the Federal-Provincial Fiscal Arrangements Act of 1967. Originally designed to remain in force for five years, the legislation, with only slight modification, was extended for a second five-year period in 1972. The precise formula for equalizing revenues over each of the twenty-odd revenue sources that come under the purview of the agreement can be expressed as follows:

$$E_{ij} = TR_i [P_j/P_c - B_{ij}/B_{ic}] \tag{1}$$

where E_{ij} = the equalization payment to province j arising from revenue source i.

TR_i = total revenue from revenue source i.

P_j = population of province j.

P_c = population of Canada.

B_{ij} = tax base in province j for revenue source i.

B_{ic} = total tax base in Canada for revenue source i.

for prices between $.32 and $.76

$$\text{production} \times \text{price} \times \frac{[922 + 50 \text{ [price} - 32]]}{\text{price}}$$

for prices over $.72:

$$\text{production} \times \text{price} \times \frac{[2722 + 50 \text{ [price} - 72]]}{\text{price}}$$

$$[(\text{oil price} + \$.70) \div 5.8] - \$.35 = \text{“heat equivalent to oil”}$$
$$\text{gas price}$$

In words, for a particular revenue source, if a province's proportion of Canada's population exceeds its proportion of the aggregate revenue source base, then it is entitled to an equalization payment. For example, suppose total revenue from a particular revenue source was 1 billion dollars. Suppose further that Nova Scotia's proportion of this tax base was 2.65%. Compared to its share of Canada's population (i.e., 3.65% in 1973-74), Nova Scotia would have a so-called "fiscal capacity deficiency" of 1%. Accordingly, her equalization payment deriving from this revenue source would be 1% of 1 billion, or 10 million dollars. These equalization payments are calculated for each of the revenue sources and the resulting entitlements are then summed. If the total is positive, the resulting figure is the amount of the province's equalization payment. If the total is negative, then the province is deemed to be a have province and it receives no equalization.

Estimates for 1973-74. Tables 1 and 2 contain the data necessary to calculate equalization payments and they also present estimates of equalization payments for 1973-74. Table 1 displays the fiscal capacity deficiency (+) or excess (-) by province and by revenue source. This is simply the difference, for each revenue source, between the province's share of Canada's population and its share of the revenue source. Data on provincial population shares appear in the notes to the table. Obviously, if a province has no tax base for a particular revenue source, the fiscal capacity deficiency equals its share of the population. This is often the case for energy revenue sources and it is the principal reason why the equalization implications of rising oil prices are so staggering. For example, Quebec has no revenue source for the energy categories (i.e., rows 11 through 14), and hence, its fiscal capacity deficiency in Table 1 for these four categories equals its share of the population, namely 27.596182%.

Table 2 presents the equalization payments by revenue source and by province. The last column of the table contains the estimates for the total revenues from each revenue source, i.e., the TR_i figure in equation (1). The figures for each cell in Table 2 are calculated by multiplying the total revenue estimate of the fiscal capacity excess or deficiency from the corresponding cell in Table 1. The sum of all equalization entitlements appears in row 21. Equalization payments (row 22) equal entitlements whenever entitlements are positive. For Ontario, Alberta, and British Columbia these entitlements are negative and, therefore, equalization payments are set equal to zero.

Funding the scheme. It is crucial to recognize that equalization payments come out of Ottawa's general revenues and *not* out of provincial coffers. The

TABLE 1

PROVINCIAL REVENUE EQUALIZATION PAYMENTS FOR 1973-74 THIRD INTERIM ESTIMATE - JANUARY 1974
FISCAL CAPACITY DEFICIENCY OR EXCESS (PERCENTAGES)

		Nfld.	PEI	NS	NB	Que.
1.	Personal income taxes	1.311757	0.299386	1.223089	1.274461	3,396157
2.	Corporation income taxes	1.351293	0.335073	1.841353	1.669930	3.076486
3.	General and miscellaneous sales taxes, tobacco					
	taxes, and amusement taxes	0.567603	0.170517	0.684547	0.500663	4.047639
4.	Motive fuel taxes	0.896546	0.040903	0.504261	0.121354	1.517538
5.	Motor vehicle licensing revenues	0.896546	0.040903	0.504261	0.121354	1.517538
6.	Alcoholic beverage revenues including profits of					
	provincial liquor boards	0.739721	0.012319	0.217616	0.729153	6.019075
7.	Hospital and medical care insurance premiums	0.939705	0.213448	0.719743	0.692536	2.105308
8.	Succession duties and gift taxes	2.146164	0.344659	1.499522	1.938285	0.920229
9.	Race track taxes	2.410890	0.162724	2.130491	2.142184	-1.237489
10.	Forestry revenues	-0.002352	0.521686	3.130226	-0.614482	7.724301
11.	Oil royalties	2.453992	0.521686	3.652039	2.957454	27.596182
12.	Natural gas royalties	2.453992	0.521686	3.652039	2.958058	27.596182
13.	Sales of Crown leases and reservations on oil and					
	natural gas lands	2.453992	0.521686	3.652039	2.958058	27.596182
14.	Oil and gas revenues other than those described in					
	lines 11, 12, and 13	2.453882	0.178871	3.652039	2.958058	27.596182
15.	Metallic and non-metallic mineral revenues	-7.767605	0.521686	2.688407	1.111206	4.230638
16.	Water power rentals	-3.694578	0.521686	3.208803	1.296266	-16.111449
17.	Miscellaneous provincial taxes	1.178954	0.256470	1.285521	1.232796	3.041263
18.	Miscellaneous provincial revenues	1.178954	0.256470	1.285521	1.232796	3.041263
19.	Payments by the government of Canada					
	pursuant to					
	A. the Public Utilities Income Tax Transfer Act	1.178954	0.256470	1.285521	1.232796	3.041263
	B. Part V of the Federal-Provincial Fiscal					
	Arrangements Act, 1972	-0.247842	0.521686	-6.286848	-1.866645	16.724519
20.	School purpose taxes	1.178954	0.256470	1.285521	1.232796	3.041263

Table 1 (cont'd)

		Ont.	Man.	Sask.	Alta.	BC
1.	Personal income taxes	-8.750923	0.861371	1.573089	0.367925	-1.609477
2.	Corporation income taxes	-10.240385	1.030900	1.994204	-1.354113	0.295259
3.	General and miscellaneous sales taxes, tobacco taxes, and amusement taxes	-3.074073	0.250286	0.762266	-1.134659	-2.774798
4.	Motive fuel taxes	-2.537104	0.026880	0.102189	-0.863870	0.181016
5.	Motor vehicle licensing revenues	-2.537104	0.026880	0.102189	-0.863870	0.181016
6.	Alcoholic beverage revenues including profits of provincial liquor boards	-3.029504	-0.529052	-0.001584	-1.134226	-3.079173
7.	Hospital and medical care insurance premiums	-5.145258	0.250623	0.870685	0.277426	0.994495
8.	Succession duties and gift taxes	-12.606448	1.661721	1.818284	2.720554	-0.442976
9.	Race track taxes	-15.999583	2.374372	3.511538	0.232811	4.258796
10.	Forestry revenues	22.834986	2.905210	1.752071	2.735861	40.987507
11.	Oil royalties	35.899050	4.371671	-4.324518	-80.360172	7.232616
12.	Natural gas royalties	35.692505	4.527736	3.313884	-82.751525	2.035362
13.	Sales of Crown leases and reservations on oil and natural gas lands	36.024908	4.527736	-1.373936	-64.887572	-11.473083
14.	Oil and gas revenues other than those described in lines 11, 12, and 13	35.682093	4.459172	-1.383678	-78.765403	3.168675
15.	Metallic and non-metallic mineral revenues	2.027233	-2.816453	-3.310460	7.469203	-0.099388
16.	Water power rentals	12.861895	-1.312617	2.362317	6.758481	-5.890804
17.	Miscellaneous provincial taxes	-7.910253	0.600752	1.283994	-0.668979	-0.300517
18.	Miscellaneous provincial revenues	-7.810253	0.600752	1.283994	-0.668979	-0.300517
19.	Payments by the government of Canada pursuant to					
	A. the Public Utilities Income Tax Transfer Act	-7.910253	0.600752	1.283994	-0.668979	-0.300517
	B. Part V of the Federal-Provincial Fiscal Arrangements Act, 1972	4.117543	-5.314658	1.032780	-8.828417	0.147901
20.	School purpose taxes	-7.910253	0.600752	1.283994	-0.668979	-0.300517

Notes: Figures in the table are the differences between the proportion of the province's population and its proportion of the relevant revenue base, i.e., this is the percentage in the square brackets of equation (1).

For 1973-74, the provincial shares of population were as follows: Nfld. (2.453992); PEI (0.521686); NS (3.652039); NB (2.958058); Que. (27.596182); Ont. (36.024908); Man. (4.527736); Sask. (4.120569); Alta. (7.639901); BC (10.504929).

Source: Department of Finance, Ottawa.

TABLE 2

PROVINCIAL REVENUE EQUALIZATION PAYMENTS TO THE PROVINCES UNDER THE FEDERAL-PROVINCIAL FISCAL ARRANGEMENTS ACT, 1972 AND REGULATIONS THEREUNDER, THIRD INTERIM ESTIMATE FOR THE FISCAL YEAR 1973-74, MADE IN JANUARY 1974 (IN THOUSANDS OF DOLLARS)

ENTITLEMENTS	Nfld.	PEI	NS	NB	Que.	Ont.
1. Personal income taxes	48,707	11,116	45,414	47,322	126,102	-324,929
2. Corporation income taxes	16,193	4,015	22,065	20,011	36,866	-122,712
3. General and miscellaneous sales taxes, tobacco taxes, and amusement taxes	18,346	5,511	22,126	16,182	130,828	-99,357
4. Motive fuel taxes	12,234	558	6,881	1,656	20,708	-34,621
5. Motor Vehicle licensing revenues	4,225	193	2,376	572	7,152	-11,956
6. Alcoholic beverages revenues including profits of provincial liquor boards	5,995	100	1,764	5,909	48,781	-24,552
7. Hospital and medical care insurance premiums	6,364	1,445	4,874	4,690	14,257	-34,843
8. Succession duties and gift taxes	3,498	562	2,444	3,159	1,500	-41,097
9. Race track taxes	1,203	81	1,063	1,069	618	-7,984
10. Forestry revenues	-7	1,611	9,664	1,897	23,847	70,498
11. Oil royalties	8,347	1,774	12,421	10,059	93,860	122,103
12. Natural gas royalties	1,746	371	2,598	2,105	19,634	25,392
13. Sales of Crown leases and reservations on oil and natural gas lands	2,010	427	2,991	2,423	22,600	32,778
14. Oil and gas revenues, other than those described in lines 11, 12 and 13	3,513	256	5,228	4,234	39,504	51,076
15. Metallic and non-metallic mineral revenues	-5,259	353	1,820	752	2,864	-1,374
16. Water power rentals	-1,012	143	879	355	-4,411	3,521
17. Miscellaneous provincial taxes	5,211	1,134	5,682	5,449	13,442	-34,956
18. Miscellaneous provincial revenues	6,201	1,349	6,762	6,485	15,997	-41,606
19. Payments by the government of Canada pursuant to						
A. the Public Utilities Income Tax Transfer Act	253	55	276	265	654	-1,698
B. Part V of the Federal-Provincial Fiscal Arrangements Act, 1972	-7	15	-175	-52	466	-114
20. School purpose taxes	19,420	4,225	21,175	20,307	50,096	-51,193
21. Total Entitlements	157,181	35,294	178,328	151,055	664,129	-524,231
22. Equalization Payments	157,181	35,294	178,328	151,055	664,129	0

Table 2 (cont'd)

ENTITLEMENTS	Man.	Sask.	Alta.	BC	Estimate of Total Revenue *
1. Personal income taxes	31,983	58,410	14,109	-59,780	3,713,038
2. Corporation income taxes	12,353	23,897	-16,177	3,599	1,198,320
3. General and miscellaneous sales taxes, tobacco taxes, and amusement taxes	8,090	24,638	36,524	-89,532	3,232,212
4. Motive fuel taxes	367	1,394	-11,735	2,456	1,364,600
5. Motor Vehicle licensing revenues	127	482	-4,052	848	471,260
6. Alcoholic beverages revenues including profits of provincial liquor boards	-4,288	-13	-9,157	-24,961	810,436
7. Hospital and medical care insurance premiums	1,697	5,896	1,896	-6,704	677,204
8. Succession duties and gift taxes	2,709	2,964	-8,867	-1,434	326,003
9. Race track taxes	1,185	1,752	115	2,126	49,906
10. Forestry revenues	8,969	5,409	8,459	-126,580	308,733
11. Oil royalties	14,869	-14,709	-273,321	24,590	340,121
12. Natural gas royalties	3,221	2,358	-58,872	1,451	71,146
13. Sales of Crown leases and reservations on oil and natural gas lands	3,708	-1,125	-59,049	10,437	91,000
14. Oil and gas revenues, other than those described in lines 11, 12 and 13	6,383	-1,981	-112,760	4,537	143,151
15. Metallic and non-metallic mineral revenues	-1,907	-2,241	5,057	-67	67,703
16. Water power rentals	-359	647	1,850	-1,612	27,381
17. Miscellaneous provincial taxes	2,655	5,675			
18. Miscellaneous provincial revenues	3,160	6,754	-2,961	-1,325	441,993
19. Payments by the government of Canada pursuant to					
A. the Public Utilities Income Tax Transfer Act	129	276	-3,524	-1,578	526,003
B. Part V of the Federal-Provincial Fiscal Arrangements Act, 1972	-148	29	-142	-64	21,500
20. School purpose taxes	9,896	21,150	-245	4	2,787
21. Total Entitlements	104,799	141,662	479,460	-265,471	15,359,640
22. Equalization Payments	104,799	141,622	0	0	0

Notes: *This is the total revenue from each of the relevant revenue sources, i.e. the TR:term in equation (1). The figures in the cells are obtained by multiplying total revenue by the corresponding cell number of Table 1.

first column of Table 3 presents data relating to the proportion of equalization payments going to each of the provinces (based on row 22 of Table 2). The second column of the table contains a very rough estimate of how Ottawa finances this equalization transfer. Specifically, it contains the share of Ottawa's revenue from each province, based on the data relating to personal and corporate income tax bases across the provinces. Unfortunately, these data refer to the situation in the late 1960's and really need to be updated and, as well, corrected for the geographical distribution of the remainder of Ottawa's revenue. Nonetheless, they will suffice for the present purpose. Ontario gets no equalization payments, but Ontario's residents pay approximately 46% of all the qualization payments. On the other hand, Quebec receives just over 45% of all equalization and its residents account for just under 25% of the cost of funding the programme. Estimates by province of the "net benefits" of the equalization programme appear in the last column of Table 3.

One of the principal dilemmas posed by rising energy prices is that while Alberta's royalty revenues soar, Ottawa's ability to extract a greater proportion of funding of the resulting increases in equalization from the residents of Alberta may be quite limited: Ontario will still have to bear the lion's share of funding the programme. It is within this context that the Ottawa-Alberta controversy over the deductibility or non-deductibility of royalty payments for purposes of calculating corporation income taxes must be viewed. If royalties were fully deductible, Ottawa would be forced into the embarrassing position of watching Alberta's revenues rise substantially and equalization payments increase, but not being able to get

TABLE 3

NET BENEFITS FROM EQUALIZATION

	Share of 1973-74 Equalization Received by Province* (%)	Share of Federal Revenue to Finance Equalization **	Net Benefits
Nfld	10.972	1.092	9.88
P.E.I.	2.463	0.185	2.278
N.S.	12.449	2.011	10.438
N.B.	10.545	1.466	9.079
Que.	46.363	23.618	22.745
Ont.	0.00	45.581	- 45.581
Man.	7.316	3.952	3.364
Sask.	9.889	2.866	7.023
Alta.	0.00	7.557	- 7.557
B.C.	0.00	11.676	- 11.676

Notes: * Based on the figures in row 22 of table 2.

** Estimated provincial share of personal and corporate income taxes (from Table 5 of Courchene and Beavis, *op. cit.*)

Alberta's residents to pay much more than 6.6% (from Table 3) of the costs of these increased transfers. More on this crucial issue in section C below.

B. *Equalization Impact of Rising Energy Prices*

With this background on the system of payments, attention can now be directed to a statistical analysis of the impact of varying energy prices on the magnitude and distribution of equalization payments to Canada's have-not provinces. The analysis contained in the appendices assumes that the present system of payments will be maintained. Clearly, this is an inappropriate assumption since the oil crisis has already forced Ottawa to alter the equalization formula, and further modifications are about to be legislated. Nonetheless, it is instructive to present the analysis on the basis of the pre-oil price increase legislation because it will serve to heighten the dramatic implications that the recent energy price increases posed for the financing of the Canadian federation.

The implications of rising oil prices on equalization payments are presented in Appendix A, while the potential impacts of corresponding increases in natural gas prices are detailed in Appendix B. Table 4 summarizes these simulation results, presenting the estimated increases in equalization payments as a result of combinations of oil and gas price increases. Rather than attempt to exhaust all permutations, the table restricts itself to three combinations. With oil at $6.50 per barrel and gas at 45 cents/MCF domestic and $1.50/MCF exported, equalization payments increase by approximately $1 billion. Under the second scenario (oil at $8.00 per barrel and natural gas at 90 cents and $1.50/MCF for the domestic and export markets respectively) these payments jump to well over $2 billion. Finally, at world prices (scenario 3), Ottawa must transfer just over $4 billion to have not provinces. Once again there is no need to spend much time evaluating these numbers. Even if the estimates are considerably off, the numbers are still bound to be astoundingly high.

C. *Funding Inequities*

At this juncture it is appropriate to return to the important issue of how these potential equalization payments are to be financed. The first column of Table 5 reproduces the Table 3 estimate of the provincial distribution of revenues used to finance these equalization transfers. Column 2 presents data from 1973-74 on each province's proportion of total provincial revenues from its own sources (excluding equalization payments and such things as conditional grants from Ottawa). Even in 1973-74 a considerable discrepancy is apparent: Ontario has only 39.92% of total provincial own-source revenues but its residents must bear about 46% of the total funding

TABLE 4

ENERGY AND EQUALIZATION: POTENTIAL COSTS

		Scenario	Additional Equalization Payments beyond 1973-74 Level ($'000)
1	oil:	$6.50/barrel	
	gas:	$ .45/MCF (domestic) 1.50/MCF (exported)	1,017,321
2	oil:	$8.00/barrel	
	gas:	$ .90/MCF (domestic) 1.50/MCF (exported)	2,329,941
3	oil:	$12.50/barrel	
	gas:	$1.93/MCF (both markets)	4,059,921

Source: Adaptation of Tables AI and BI.

bill for equalization. Now let us introduce the energy price increases. At the world price for both oil and gas (the last column of Table 5), Alberta's own revenues *exceed* Ontario's—the latter has 28.08% of total revenue and the former has 29.94%. However, the fantastic rise in equalization payments associated with the energy price being at the world price is still likely to be borne by provincial residents in proportions that remain fairly close to column 1 of Table 5.

This must present a serious dilemma for Ottawa: with equalization payments running rampant as a result of tremendous inflows into Alberta's treasury, Ottawa may not be able to get Alberta to contribute its "fair" share toward financing these equalization payments. The source of the problem is, of course, the fact that the revenue base that is generating all the equalization payments is *not* one that is under Ottawa's control. Under the previous equalization schemes where revenues among provinces were equalized only with respect to those revenues that were shared by Ottawa and the provinces (i.e., personal income taxes, corporate income taxes, and estate taxes) such a situation could not develop. If equalization payments increased, this must have been due to increases in these three tax sources and the relative burden of financing would automatically be shifted to the provinces that had become relatively richer. Not so now, as Table 5 clearly indicates.

D. Ottawa's Reaction to Rising Energy Prices

Up to this point, the analysis has been carried on at the hypothetical level. Equalization payments of the magnitudes portrayed in Table 4 simply will

TABLE 5

POTENTIAL DIVERGENCE BETWEEN PROVINCES'
OWN REVENUES AND SHARES OF FEDERAL TAX BASE

	September 1973-74		Scenario 1	Scenario 2	Scenario 3
	Share of Federal Tax Base*	Share of Provinces' Own Revenues	Share of Provinces' Own Revenues	Share of Provinces' Own Revenues	Share of Provinces' Own Revenues
Newfoundland	1.092	1.38	1.22	1.10	0.99
Prince Edward Island	0.185	0.29	0.26	0.23	0.21
Nova Scotia	2.011	2.52	2.22	2.03	1.80
New Brunswick	1.466	2.05	1.81	1.64	1.47
Quebec	23.618	26.10	22.96	20.90	18.65
Ontario	45.581	39.92	34.49	31.40	28.02
Manitoba	3.952	3.57	3.14	2.86	2.55
Saskatchewan	2.866	3.64	4.54	4.73	5.56
Alberta	7.557	8.99	17.35	23.44	29.94
British Columbia	11.676	12.21	12.00	11.60	11.20

Note: *taken from Table 3.

not occur because Ottawa has taken action to prevent such a situation. Given this, it might appear that the statistical exercise has merely been a flight of fancy. However, I assert that the implications for both equalization payments and the likely distortion between own provincial revenues and provincial contributions to funding the scheme that are so obvious in Tables 4 and 5 literally forced Ottawa's hand and led to her intervention. This intervention took several forms. First of all, the domestic price was set well below the foreign or world price. Secondly, Ottawa levied a tax on exported oil to fill in the gap between the domestic price and the world price. This action served two purposes. If Ottawa decided to revert these export revenues back to Alberta, they would not be eligible for equalization since they would be a direct transfer from Ottawa to Alberta and outside the twenty revenue categories that now enter the equalization programme. But Ottawa actually used this money derived from oil exports to the U.S.A. to subsidize oil imports to eastern Canada in order to maintain a uniform domestic price across the country. Over the past fifteen months the figures indicate that this programme has cost Ottawa some $1.5 billion. I am not sure just how much of this amount has been recouped from Canada's tax on oil exports to the U.S.A.[4]

Two other initiatives must also be mentioned. First of all, at the time of the agreement in the spring of 1974, to raise the domestic price to $6.50 per barrel Ottawa agreed that to the extent that the resulting increases in royalties were entered into the capital sector of the budgets of Saskatchewan and Alberta rather than brought into general revenues, they would not be eligible for equalization. This action had two principal effects. First of all it served to reduce equalization payments. Secondly, it allowed Saskatchewan to collect the increased oil royalties without incurring a dollar-for-dollar reduction in equalization payments.

The second initiative was and is far more controversial. Royalties paid to the provinces will no longer be deductible for corporation income tax purposes. More will be said about this provision in Part III. For the present, it is appropriate to note that this action was probably motivated by the implications so very apparent in Table 5. If oil and gas royalties remained deductible, it is quite possible that despite the fact that Alberta could well receive revenues in excess of those accruing to Ontario, its residents would not pay anything near Ontario's contribution to funding the equalization program (compare columns 5 and 1 of Table 5).

As mentioned above, in December 1974 Finance Minister John Turner announced further important alternations to the equalization formula. Prior to evaluating this latest Ottawa initiative it seems appropriate to survey some of the various alternative proposals for equalization payments.

III. ALTERNATIVE PROPOSALS FOR EQUALIZATION AND ENERGY

A. *The Musgrave Proposal*

The seminal article on equalization in a federal nation was R.A. Musgrave's "Approaches to a Fiscal Theory of Political Federalism". Even though the Canadian equalization scheme does not quite coincide with any of Musgrave's seven alternative plans, it is useful to compare the difference between the manner in which Musgrave proposes to fund his plans and the manner in which the Canadian plan is funded. Specifically, under the Musgrave proposals once the levels of equalization payments are decided upon, they are financed by a tax levied in the province's own revenues. This is very different from the Canadian scheme where Ottawa bears the responsibility of financing equalization out of its general revenues.

As an example of how this scheme would work I shall outline its implications in terms of the above experiments. Under the 1973-74 provisions, equalization payments amounted to $1.432 billion and own provincial revenues totalled $15.360 billion (i.e., the figure in the last column and last row of Table 2). This level of equalization could be financed by a 9.33% tax on provincial own revenues. Actual provincial dollar shares can be obtained by multiplying total equalization ($1.432 billion) by the provincial percentage in column 2 of Table 5.

For the three combined scenarios outlined in Table 4 the corresponding figures are

	SCENARIO I	SCENARIO II	SCENARIO III
Total own provincial revenues	$17.461 billion	$19.186 billion	$21.442 billion
Total equalization payments	$ 2.450 billion	$ 3,762 billion	$ 5,491 billion
Proportional tax required to fund the scheme	14.03%	19.61%	25.61%

Consider the results for Scenario III. Total provincial revenues from provinces' own sources equal 21.442 billion dollars and equalization payments equal 5.492 billion (i.e., the 1973-74 level, $1.432 billion, plus the increase for this combined experiment which appears in Table 4). The dollar shares by province would be in proportion to the provincial shares of aggregate own revenues, i.e., column 5 of Table 5. Accordingly, Alberta would provide 29.94% of all the funds required to finance the equalization programme. The break-even tax rate would be approximately 25%, levied on provincial own revenues.

While it may be very unlikely that Canada would adopt a programme that would be funded entirely from the provincial coffers, the plan does have a certain degree of equity in the sense that the rich provinces bear the cost of equalization in direct proportion to their revenue position. Naturally such a scheme could be modified to take account of considerations such as the degree of tax effort across the provinces.

Were this scheme in operation in Canada, I dare say that Ottawa would be far less concerned with whether or not royalty payments were deductible, since Ottawa would not bear the resulting equalization cost. If Alberta wants to levy high royalties, she has to be prepared to share them with her sister provinces.

B. The Gainer-Powrie Proposal

The lead article in the first issue of Canada's new journal, *Canadian Public Policy/Analyse de Politique* by professors Gainer and Powrie deals with the public revenues from Canadian crude production.[6] Towards the end of this article they propose a method of sharing oil royalties between Ottawa and the provinces. Specifically, the authors argue that

> claims against any flow of rent should be the same whether it accrues to a government or to a private company.... If all royalties in Alberta went to private individuals, they would be subject to personal income tax. Federal marginal rates of personal income tax range between 20 and 30 per cent on most taxpayers, although the general level of marginal rates in Alberta would be raised if potential maximum royalty revenues were distributed to persons because they would amount to several thousand dollars per taxpayer. If corporations received all the royalties, they would be subject to a federal marginal rate of nearly 40 per cent. If royalties were regarded as capital gains both the personal and corporate rates would be halved. Obviously there is much room for negotiation about what the federal share of royalty income should be deemed to be under our principle that the federal share should be the same as it would have been were the resources privately owned. We have chosen the figure of 30 per cent as a reasonable suggestion and for use in an arithmetic illustration. (Our illustration refers to oil revenue only. In principle our suggestion is that the federal government should share in all provincial natural resource revenues, but we have not at this stage worked out the impact of this general application.)[7]

The illustration they refer to is not reproduced here. Essentially, they perform a simulation similar to the ones I did in Table AI (and in particular, Experiment III).[8] Compared to a situation in which Ottawa would not get a share of oil royalties, they calculate that the federal burden of equalization payments would be reduced by about a billion dollars when the 70:30 sharing is in effect. Compared to the 1973-74 figures, equalization payments would still be increased by about $1.2 billion. However, as a result of its 30% cut, Ottawa's revenues increase by $1.3 billion. Hence, there is no net burden on the federal treasury as a result of the increase in equalization payments.

This proposal differs from the modified Musgrave proposal in that Ottawa still bears the responsibility for funding the equalization scheme. However, it is similar in the sense that Alberta, and the oil-producing provinces in general, do bear a major share of funding the increased payments.

C. *The Helliwell Proposal*

In a recent paper in the *International Journal of the Canadian Institute of Public Affairs*, U.B.C.'s John Helliwell presented the bare bones of a proposal to revise the methods used for transferring revenues from the richer provinces to the poorer provinces.[9] Since his discussion of the proposal is very brief, it is convenient to present it in full:

> At present, additional current resource revenues accruing to a have-not province lead to an almost equivalent offsetting reduction in the equalization payments from the federal government. On the other hand, extra resource revenues to a rich province like Alberta lead to extra payments from the federal government to the have-not provinces, unless the resource revenues are "deemed" to be capital payments to keep them out of the average revenues used to define the size of the equalization payments. These problems would be much reduced by converting the system into a more balanced interprovincial revenue-sharing fund. For example, there could be two key levels of provincial government expenditure per capita that governed payments into and out of the fund. The lower level of expenditure would be sufficient to provide an absolute minimum of provincial services, and any provinces with revenues below that would get the difference made up entirely from the fund. The higher level would be a "slightly more than bare bones" minimum, and provinces with revenues below that amount would recover a percentage of the gap from the fund. All provinces with revenues above the second expenditure level would pay into the fund a fraction of all revenues above that level. The "marginal tax

rate" would be set high enough to keep the fund solvent, on average if not in each year. Such a system could contribute much more than does the present equalization payments system to the problems of adjusting to large and unevenly distributed changes in revenues from extractive industries. [10]

While I am not altogether clear on precisely what Helliwell has in mind, it appears that he is arguing for a Musgrave-type funding scheme in the sense that the provinces rather than Ottawa are responsible for the financing, but with a few important exceptions. First of all, Helliwell wants to ensure that if have-not provinces experience substantial revenue increases from their own revenue sources they should not lose equalization payments on a dollar-for-dollar basis. In a subsequent paper, when referring to this proposal, he asserts that "one of the aims would be to make the marginal tax rate (used for the equalization fund) on resource revenues equal for rich and poor provinces." [11] For example, suppose the agreed-upon marginal rate is 25 per cent (actually this rate would be set at a rate to keep the fund solvent). An increase in resource revenues accruing to a have province would call for a 25 per cent transfer of monies into the fund. Likewise, if a poor province came into extra resource revenues, they too could keep 75 per cent of the increase. In other words, this system is quite similar to a negative income tax scheme where the tax-back rate is the same above and below the break-even (or equalization) level.

The second and corollary notion introduced by Helliwell is that equalization payments should be geared to raise all provinces up to some *absolute* standard, rather than the current provisions which adopt the principle that all provinces should have revenues at least equal to the *national average* of the provinces. Obviously these "two key levels of provincial government expenditure per capita" that Helliwell considers would probably rise over time. Nonetheless, this would represent a major conceptual change from the present system. Interestingly enough, Finance Minister Turner's proposals also incorporated this very concept. And to the Ottawa proposal I now turn.

D. The Ottawa Proposal

At the federal-provincial meeting of the minister of finance and provincial treasurers in December 1974, Finance Minister Turner made public Ottawa's position with respect to equalizing energy revenues for the remainder of the present five-year extension of the Federal-Provincial Fiscal Arrangements Act. In Turner's own words:

The proposal provides that in calculating equalization of provincial revenues from oil and natural gas we would distinguish between "basic" revenues, that is revenues that are not attributable to the international oil disturbance, and "additional" revenues, that is, revenues which are attributable to the international oil disturbance. "Basic" revenues would be equalized in full and "additional" revenues would be equalized to the extent of one-third.... "Basic" revenues for any given year would be defined in terms of actual revenues in 1973-74 escalated by a volume index that would take account of any increases in the volume of production of oil or gas between 1973 and such given year. "Additional" revenues for the given year would then be actual revenues minus "basic" revenues. In order to protect the equalization-receiving provinces against the possibility that production volume would fall below 1973 levels, a floor would be built into the definition of basic revenues. The effect of this arrangement would be to permit the equalization-receiving provinces to benefit from increases in production volume and to protect them against decreases in volume. [12]

In addition, Ottawa will continue to impose and collect the revenues from the export tax on oil and the non-deductibility of oil and gas royalties for purposes of corporate income tax calculations will be maintained.

This package is most interesting and it may well have a profound effect on federal-provincial relations. It is worth focussing further on the various components of the package.

Abandoning full equalization. By only allowing one-third of energy royalties above the 1973-74 levels to enter the equalization formula, Ottawa has clearly abandoned the *full* equalization concept that underlay the 1967 Federal-Provincial Fiscal Arrangements Act. Mr. Turner is really quite straightforward on this issue:

When the present comprehensive system of equalization was introduced in 1967 its purpose as stated at that time... was to ensure that all provinces would be able to provide their citizens with a reasonably comparable level of basic services, without resorting to unduly burdensome levels of taxation.... I believe that goal has been effectively achieved in Canada today. A simple test of this assumption is to be found in a comparison of the per capita expenditures of two groups of provinces—those which receive equalization and those which do not. For 1973-74... the expenditures of the above-average provinces were $1,256 per capita. For the below-average provinces they were $1,234 per capita. The spread between the two groups was only about 2 per cent. This very small difference is striking proof of the success of the equalization programme. [13]

What the finance minister appeared to be saying was that the spirit of the equalization scheme would not be violated by decreasing the equalization flows accruing from oil royalties. The point might be put as follows: Will it cost the have-not provinces more to provide the basic level of services just because Alberta now has greater revenues? The answer, of course, depends on how one defines "basic level of services," and in turn it essentially boils down to the issue of whether or not equalization payments are designed to enable the provinces to provide an *absolute* or *relative* (to other provinces) level of services. As stated above, Ottawa now favours the former interpretation.

In future years, however, the provincial per capita expenditures referred to in the above quote will likely show substantially greater division. Even under the present formula, revenues are equalized only to the national average, so that Alberta's per capita revenue will grow substantially relative to that of other provinces. However, if only one-third of the large oil and gas revenues are to be equalized, considerable further deviation in these provincial per capita expenditures is likely to materialize. In the unlikely event that Alberta decides not to increase her per capita expenditures, the disparity will then arise on the tax-effort side, which amounts to essentially the same thing.

Equalizing on the cost side. As long as the domestic price remains below the world price, Turner may well have had another reason for abandoning the full equalization concept. Ottawa's revenues from the export tax are used to maintain a constant price for oil (excluding transportation costs) across the country. As mentioned above, maintaining a fixed oil price the 11 months preceding June 1974 cost Ottawa about $1.5 billion. And it turns out that all the provinces benefiting from this were have-not provinces. Conceptually, this can also be viewed as an equalization payment—one that adjusts for *fiscal need*. Douglas Clark has defined the fiscal need concept of equalization as the "measure by which the *cost* to that province of providing a given standard of public services exceeds the *revenues* that would derive from applying a given rate of taxation to its own base." [14] Hence equalization to take account of fiscal need requires both an expenditure component and a revenue component. [15] It is possible to view Ottawa's guarantee of maintaining a uniform petroleum price as compensating those provinces whose expenditure needs were greater, in the sense that without the federal guarantee they would be forced to spend a large amount of their own funds to generate the price of oil prevailing in

Ontario and the West. In this light, Ottawa may be excused for bringing only one-third of "additional" revenues in the formula. Implicitly, they are bringing some of the remainder in the formula via the maintenance of a single domestic price for oil.

Non-deductibility of royalties. Earlier, I indicated that one rationale for non-deductibility of oil royalties was that this would enable Ottawa to capture some of Alberta's potential revenues and apply them against the increases in federal costs that equalization will generate. Ottawa does not justify the non-deductibility on these grounds. Rather, it argues that the federal government has the right to set corporate tax rates and if it allowed deductibility the federal government would be in the "position of having its effective rate of tax in every province determined by the tax policies of the provincial government."[16] After all, provincial income tax surcharges are not deductible from federal income tax.

However, Finance Minister Turner went on to say that

> so far as we are concerned, the deductibility or non-deductibility of provincial royalties involves a very practical problem, not a constitutional, legal, or philosophical problem. Had we been able to achieve the same financial result for the federal government by other means, we would have been more than content.[17]

This statement is surely consistent with the point raised above, namely that the potential costs that energy would impose on Ottawa via increased equalization payments required that Ottawa obtain some fair share of revenue from the energy producing provinces. As far as the reference to obtaining money from some other means, the Musgrave and the Gainer-Powrie proposals represent alternatives to non-deductibility.

E. *More Recent Ottawa Initiatives*

In his June 1975 budget, Finance Minister Turner introduced further proposals regarding oil and gas. With respect to oil, the price was increased from $6.50 at the wellhead to $8.00. The natural gas increase went from roughly 45¢ to 80¢ with an indication of still more increases in the future. Finally, a 10-cent-a-gallon surcharge on pumped gas was enacted with exemptions for commercial users available on a refund basis. Once again several features of this package merit attention. The increases in gas and oil correspond fairly closely to Scenario II of Table 4. The resulting increase in equalization payments will be less than one-third of the $2,329 million listed in the table in part because the price of gas for the Table 4 calculation is assumed to be 90¢ rather than 80¢ and, in part, because Ontario will not become a have-not province as quickly now that the one-third equalization proposal that is being applied as far as oil and gas royalties are concerned. Nonetheless, the increased equalization cost will still be substantial. Indeed, Ottawa's December 1974 proposals regarding equalization and energy were probably a necessary condition for even these price increases to occur.

Secondly, the move to a higher world price does reduce Ottawa's cost of maintaining a uniform petroleum price across Canada. With oil imports now exceeding oil exports, the cost of the uniform oil price is a direct function of the divergence between the world price and maintained domestic price. An increase in the domestic price to $8.00 reduces the cost of the subsidy programme and, hence, allows Ottawa to transfer these savings to the increased equalization costs. Note that a move to the world price level would eliminate the subsidy payments. There are undoubtedly a great many reasons why Canada is not willing to allow the domestic price to rise to the world level. The thesis of this paper is that one of the more important reasons is the financial burden it would place on Ottawa because of increased equalization payments, even allowing for the fact that only one-third of increased royalties will be eligible for equalization.

Finally, the 10¢ surcharge on pumped gas can be interpreted as a measure to subsidize producers at the expense of consumers. Because of its relatively low oil price, Canada has not reduced relative oil consumption per capita in line with many or perhaps most of the western industrialized nations. If Ottawa wants to bring Canadian oil prices more in line with those elsewhere in the world, a 10¢ surcharge has the distinct advantage of allowing the Canadian price to rise in a manner that does not put her in a financial straightjacket. Indeed, the opposite is the case: Ottawa stands to collect substantial revenue from this surcharge which in turn can be used to pay for its other actions on the oil and gas front.

IV. TOWARDS A NEW EQUALIZATION SCHEME

I began this paper by suggesting that unless and until the financial issues arising from the energy crisis involving Ottawa and the provinces are sorted out, little progress is likely to be made on the more important issues of optimal pricing and utilization of energy. Ottawa has already proposed a series of measures with respect to energy that reflect the binding nature of this financial constraint in the area of energy policy. But most of these measures are either temporary or expire in 1977, the year when the Federal-Provincial Fiscal Arrangements Act is to be revised. Furthermore, Ottawa's initiatives have also altered substantially the conceptual framework underlying the current equalization system. It would not surprise me if we have seen the last of "full" equalization as embodied in the current formula. If this is the case then the time has surely arrived for a complete review of Canada's system of transferring funds to the have-not provinces. Indeed, it may well be that this can only be done within the more general context of a complete rethinking and reworking of the financial basis of Confederation. In the narrower framework of revamping the equalization scheme, each of the three alternative proposals to that offered by Ottawa merits serious attention. In addition, I would also like to raise one issue that has always concerned me about the present equalization scheme. If a province wishes to increase its revenues by levying a tax on one of its revenue bases, the present system may tend to distort its selection of the tax base. For example, if Quebec desires to raise $12 million by increasing its income tax rates, it will also *increase* its equalization payments by about one-half million dollars. However, if it raises the same revenue from a revenue source for which it is a have province (e.g., water power rentals) its equalization payments will *fall* by over $2 million. [18] It would appear desirable to devise an equalization system that treats all increases in revenue in an identical manner, regardless of the source.

Notes

* It is a pleasure to acknowledge the substantial research input into this paper provided by Paul Boothe. Work on the paper was financed by a Canada Council grant.

1. Paper first circulated. Professor Gainer's subsequent thoughts on this matter may be found in Harry F. Campbell, W.D. Gainer, and Anthony Scott, "Resource Rent: How Much and For Whom?" See this volume.

2. It must be emphasized that Gainer and Powrie are fully aware of these implications. See W.D. Gainer and T.L. Powrie, "Public Revenue from Canadian Crude Petroleum Production," *Canadian Public Policy/Analyse de Politiques* I, 1 (Winter 1975): 1-12.

3. For example, Douglas H. Clark, *Fiscal Need and Revenue Equalization* (Toronto: Canadian Tax Foundation 1969); George E. Carter, *Canadian Conditional Grants since World War II* (Toronto: Canadian Tax Foundation 1971), chapter 3; Thomas J. Courchene and David A. Beavis, "Federal-Provincial Tax Equalization: An Evaluation," *Canadian Journal of Economics* VI, 4 (November 1972): 483-502.

4. In a recent pamphlet, Judith Maxwell notes that for much of 1975 net oil imports were averaging about 150,000 barrels per day, so that Ottawa's revenue shortfall was substantial. See Judith Maxwell, *Developing New Energy Sources: The Syncrude Case* (Montreal: C.D. Howe Research Institute, 1975), p. 1.

5. R.A. Musgrave, "Approaches to a Fiscal Theory of Political Federalism," *Public Finance: Needs, Sources, Utilization* (Princeton: Princeton University Press, 1961), pp. 71-123.

6. Gainer and Powrie, "Public Revenue from Canadian Crude Petroleum Production."

7. Ibid., pp. 10-11.

8. It is interesting to note that Gainer and Powrie estimate that at a price of $11.50 per barrel, royalties from oil would equal $4.278 billion. Considering all the assumptions that have to be made in generating these numbers, my estimate of royalties of $4.031 billion at the world price level is comfortably close to theirs.

9. J.F. Helliwell, "Extractive Resources in the World Economy," *International Journal* (of the Canadian Institute of International Affairs) XXIX (Autumn 1974): 591-609.

10. Ibid., p. 603.

11. J.F. Helliwell, "Overlapping Federal and Provincial Claims on Mineral Revenues," paper prepared for a conference on "Mineral Leasing as an Instrument of Public Policy," sponsored by the B.C. Institute for Economic Policy Analysis, Victoria (September 1974), p. 30.

12. John N. Turner, "Statement on Taxation of the Resource Industries," paper presented to the federal-provincial meeting of ministers of finance and provincial treasurers, December 1974, p. 1.

13. Ibid., pp. 1-2.

14. Clark, *Fiscal Needs and Revenue Equalization*, p. 18.

15. The reader will note that the definition of equalization that we have been applying throughout this paper has referred only to the revenue component, i.e., provincial revenues were equalized to bring them up to the national average, irrespective of the particular expenditure needs of the province.

16. John N. Turner, "Statement on Taxation of the Resource Industries," p. 3.

17. Ibid., p. 2.

18. See Courchene and Beavis, "Federal-Provincial Tax Equalization: An Evaluation," p. 495. These figures relate to the fiscal year 1968-69.

Appendix A

A TAXONOMY OF ALTERNATIVE OIL SCENARIOS

Table A1 presents the implications on equalization payments of three alternative prices for oil—$6.50, $8.00, and $12.50 per barrel. The $6.50 price was that which prevailed from April 1974 until very recently. The $8.00 price is reasonably representative of the June 1975 Canadian domestic price while the $12.50 price represents the June 1975 world price for crude oil. Details relating to the manner in which these estimates were constructed are contained in Appendix C. It is hardly necessary to point out that the numbers which appear in this table, and the following table as well, are rough-and-ready calculations. Anyone who has bothered to delve even slightly beneath the surface of the oil industry will appreciate that a whole host of heroic assumptions underlie the numbers in the table. However, for the purpose intended—to get a handle on the magnitude of potential equalization payments stemming from the rising energy prices—these numbers are probably in the ball park.

Row 1 of the Table A1 contains the provincial population shares, reproduced from the notes beneath Table 1. Row 2 presents provincial shares of the value of crude oil production from crown lands for 1974. These shares were utilized rather than the shares implicit in row 11 of Table 1, principally because there was a considerable shift in the production to crude oil, especially in Saskatchewan, that was subject to royalty payments. Row 3 contains the fiscal capacity deficiency (+) or excess (-) for each province. Note that for most of the provinces the fiscal capacity deficiency is identical to their proportion of Canada's population, since they have no crude oil production. Row 4 reproduces from Table 2 the equalization credits or debits arising from crude oil (row 11 of Table 2).

The next three sets of two rows present royalty revenues and equalization flows by province for the three alternative oil prices. I assume that the only oil revenue category that is affected by the price increase is that of oil royalties (i.e., category 11 of tables 1 and 2). While categories 13 and 14, as listed in Tables 1 and 2, also relate to oil, the analysis assumes that they remain unchanged throughout. The procedure underlying the experiments is (a) to assume that the 1974 production level holds regardless of the price; (b) to apply a royalty rate, which varies across provinces (see Appendix C); (c) to calculate oil royalties by province and present total revenues under the "total" column in Table A1; (d) to multiply this total revenue figure by the appropriate fiscal capacity deficiency or excess to obtain rows 6, 8, and 10; and (e) to calculate the aggregate increase in equalization payments, i.e., the last column of the table. This last calculation takes account not only of the existing level of equalization arising from oil royalties (row 4) but as well takes account of the province's overall equalization entitlement. For example, in the $6.50 experiment, B.C. obtains an equalization credit of $98 million. However, this does not add to overall equalization payments, since B.C. would still remain a have province and not be eligible for a fiscal transfer. Finally, the analysis assumes that no other revenue source changes. This is quite unreasonable since it is only natural for increases of the magnitude incorporated in the table to have some considerable impact on such

TABLE AI

OIL AND EQUALIZATION: ALTERNATIVE PRICE SCENARIOS

	Nfld.	PEI	NS	NB	Que.	Ont.	Man.
1 Population share	2.5	.5	3.7	3.0	27.6	36.0	4.5
2 Share of revenue base	0.0	0.0	0.0	0.0	0.0	0.0	0.2
3 Fiscal capacity deficiency (+) or excess (−)	+2.5	+.5	+3.7	+3.0	+27.6	+36.0	+4.3
4 Equalization credit from oil royalties (1973–74)('000)	8,347	1,774	12,421	10,059	93,860	122,103	14,869
Experiment I [P = $6.50/barrel]							
5 Provincial oil royalties ('000)	0.0	0.0	0.0	0.0	0.0	0.0	0.0*
6 Equalization payments from oil ('000)	35,000	7,000	51,800	42,000	386,400	504,000	60,200
Experiment II [P = $8.00/barrel]							
7 Provincial oil royalties	0.0	0.0	0.0	0.0	0.0	0.0	0.0*
8 Equalization payments from oil	65,650	13,130	97,162	78,780	724,776	945,360	112,918
Experiment III [PD = $12.50/barrel]							
9 Provincial oil royalties	0.0	0.0	0.0	0.0	0.0	0.0	0.0*
10 Equalization payments from oil	96,000	20,000	148,000	120,000	1,104,000	1,440,000	172,000
Experiment IV [P = $6.50/barrel] (Transfer of Alberta oil resources to Quebec)							
11 Equalization payments from oil	35,000	7,000	51,800	42,000	0	504,000	60,200

Table A1 (cont'd)

	Sask.	Alta.	BC	Total	Increase in Aggregate Equalization Payments[a]
1 Population share	4.1	7.6	10.5	100.0	
2 Share of revenue base	11.2	85.0	3.5	100.0	
3 Fiscal capacity deficiency (+) or excess (−)	−7.1	−77.4	+7.0		
4 Equalization credit from oil royalties (1973-74)('000)	−14,909	−273,321	24,590		
Experiment I [P = $6.50/barrel]					
5 Provincial oil royalties ('000)	253,888	1,071,482	60,736	1,386,106	
6 Equalization payments from oil ('000)	0	0	98,000	1,184,400	357,366[b]
Experiment II [P = $8.00/barrel]					
7 Provincial oil royalties	378,659	2,150,480	97,117	2,626,308	
8 Equalization payments from oil	0	0	158,200	2,195,960	1,078,554[c]
Experiment III [P = $12.50/barrel]					
9 Provincial oil royalties	519,642	3,360,012	151,840	4,031,494	
10 Equalization payments from oil	0	0	280,000	3,380,000	2,041,143[c]
Experiment IV [P = $6.50/barrel] (Transfer of Alberta oil resources to Quebec)					
11 Equalization payments from oil	0	106,400	98,000	904,440	421,105[d]

Notes: * Manitoba does have some oil, but the amount is negligible in comparison with the other producing regions. Hence it is omitted.

[a] The figures in this column differ from those in the total column because while some provinces, notable BC and Ontario, receive equalization credit for oil, over all the revenue sources they still remain rich enough not to qualify for any payments.

[b] Total column minus the Ontario and BC entries.

[c] Ontario becomes a have-not province once equalization payments for oil exceed $646 million. This $646 million is deducted from the total figure. British Columbia becomes a have-not province once equalization payments to BC for oil exceed $290 million. Since this does not occur in any of the experiments, BC receives no equalization payments and its equalization credit in lines 8 and 10 are deducted from the total to obtain the figure in the final column.

[d] Equals the total column minus the credits for Ontario and BC since they would still remain have provinces overall. The Alberta entry is also deducted from the total column.

things as personal incomes, retail sales, corporation revenues, etc., all of which would in turn feed back on equalization payments. Nonetheless, these secondary effects are ignored.

THE RESULTS OF THE EXPERIMENTS

At a $6.50 price, total oil royalties amount to $1,386 million (second last column, row 5) compared with $344 million in 1973-74 (last column, row 11, Table 2). Total equalization arising from these royalties is $1.184 billion. However, the increase in equalization payments over 1973-74 is only $357 million, principally because Ontario and B.C. still remain "have" provinces and are not eligible to receive these transfers.

At $8.00 per barrel, total provincial royalties are nearly double those accruing at the $6.50 price. This occurs because I have allowed the royalty rate to increase with the price level. That it should increase is entirely reasonable; the exact amount of the increase is another matter (the reader can consult Appendix C for details). Equalization arising out of oil nearly doubles as well but the increase in actual equalization payments that is due the have-not provinces is more than tripled—from $.357 billion to $1.079 billion. This occurs because Ontario now becomes a have-not province. More specifically, from Table 2, Ontario has a *negative* entitlement of $524 million dollars (row 21). If one takes account of the positive influence that the 1973-74 oil royalty credit makes to Ontario (i.e., $122 million, row 11, Table 2), then Ontario becomes a have-not province once it receives an oil royalty equalization entitlement of $646 million (i.e., 524 + 122). From row 8 of Table A1, the evidence indicates that Ontario receives $945 million in entitlements. Hence, under an $8.00 price per barrel of crude oil, Ontario would receive approximately $300 million in equalization payments.

At $12.50 per barrel, equalization payments skyrocket: Ottawa would have to distribute over $2 billion more to the have-not provinces. And of this amount, Ontario, now a have-not province, would get about $800 million! Alberta would receive substantially more than $3 billion in oil royalties. To put this figure in perspective, it is instructive to note that in 1973-74 Alberta's total revenues from the 20 categories (including oil) enumerated in Tables 1 and 2 were approximately $1.4 billion.

LUCKY PIERRE

Canada's equalization formula worked very well prior to the oil price increase. However, if there is a set of circumstances that will lead to dramatic increases in equalization, it would be the following: (a) a substantial increase in revenue, concentrated in one province; (b) this province should be a have province already, and (c) it should have the smallest population of the have provinces. Only Alberta meets requirements (b) and (c) and it clearly satisfies criterion (a). Hence, from a purely financial point of view, this is the worst set of circumstances that could have befallen Ottawa. To see this, suppose that Ontario, rather than the three western provinces, had all the oil. Once the remaining provinces become have-not provinces, every extra dollar that Ontario would collect in royalties would cost Ottawa 64 cents because the rest of the provinces account for 64 per cent of Canada's population. However, since Alberta has only 7.6 per cent of Canada's population, Ottawa faces the prospect of paying 92.4 cents in equalization payments every time Alberta gets an extra dollar of oil royalties. This does not quite happen, even in Experiment 3 because B.C. and Saskatchewan maintain rich-province status. Nonetheless, at the $12.50 price per barrel, every additional dollar that flows into Alberta's coffers costs Ottawa 77.8 cents in increased equalization payments. [1,2]

OIL IN QUEBEC

To delve further into the realm of fantasy, let us imagine that it is Quebec rather than Alberta that has the oil resources. Or, more generally, suppose that Quebec acquired a revenue source equivalent to Alberta's position with respect to oil. Experiment 4 in Table A1 performs just this transfer. It interchanges the Alberta and Quebec shares of the revenue base and produces results for the $6.50 price per barrel of crude oil. As a result, equalization payments *fall* by over $421 million compared to the $357 million increase in Experiment 1. The reason for this is that the bulk of Quebec's increase in royalty revenue in Experiment 4 is offset by a corresponding fall in its equalization payments from Ottawa.

Appendix B

EQUALIZING NATURAL GAS ROYALTIES

It is only very recently that public awareness concerning the price of energy is moving toward the inclusion of the implications for the price of natural gas and the implications for equalization payments of these price increases. The principal purpose of this section is to demonstrate that gas royalties have implications for equalization payments that are every bit as drastic as those associated with oil royalties.

Table B1 contains estimates of gas royalties and the resulting equalization flows for alternative prices of natural gas. Calculations of the natural gas royalties are considerably more complex than those for oil. First of all, gas can be marketed in a gaseous or liquid form (e.g., pentane, butane). Hence we show two separate revenue source bases (rows 2 and 3) even though for equalization purposes they represent a single category. Secondly, Saskatchewan does produce some natural gas but it is my understanding that it collects very little in the way of royalty payments, so that we simply ignore Saskatchewan's gas royalties. On the other hand, B.C.'s revenues from gas accrue to the British Columbia Petroleum Corporation and really do not enter the equalization formula unless they are remitted to the B.C. government as part of their general revenues. Finally, the export price of gas is substantially higher than the domestic price. This is true for oil as well, but it does not affect the oil

TABLE B1

GAS ROYALTIES AND EQUALIZATION PAYMENTS

	Nfld.	PEI	NS	NB	Que.	Ont.	Man.
(1) Population share	2.5	0.5	3.7	3.0	27.6	36.0	4.5
(2) Share of gas revenue base (1)	0.0	0.0	0.0	0.0	0.0	.38	0.0
(3) Share of gas liquid revenue base (2)	0.0	0.0	0.0	0.0	0.0	0.0	0.0
(4) Fiscal capacity deficiency (+) (1)	+2.5	.5	3.7	3.0	27.6	35.62	4.5
(5) or excess (-) (2)	2.5	.5	3.7	3.0	27.6	36.0	4.5
(6) Equalization payments from gas royalties (73-74)('000)	1,746	371	2,598	2,105	19,634	25,392	3,221
Experiment 1							
(Pgas = $ .45 MCF domestic Pliquids = $5.75 /barrel)							
(7) Provincial gas royalties	0.0	0.0	0.0	0.0	0.0	3,557	0.0
(8) Equalization payments from gas	28,200	5,500	41,200	33,500	298,900	399,600	50,300
Experiment 2							
(Pgas = $ .90 MCF domestic Pliquids = $5.75 /barrel)							
(9) Provincial gas royalties	0.0	0.0	0.0	0.0	0.0	5,560	0.0
(10) Equalization payments from gas	41,200	8,200	61,000	49,400	440,200	588,200	74,200
Experiment 3							
(Pgas = $1.93 MCF domestic Pliquids = $12.50 /barrel)							
(11) Provincial gas royalties	0.0	0.0	0.0	0.0	0.0	7,807	0.0
(12) Equalization payments from gas	62,600	12,500	92,600	75,000	668,300	894,500	112,700

Table B1 (cont'd.)

	Sask.	Alta.	BC	Total	Increase in Aggregate Equalization Payments**
(1) Population share	4.1	7.6	10.5	100.0	
(2) Share of gas revenue base (1)	1.12	90.89	7.52	100.0	
(3) Share of gas liquid revenue base (2)	0.0	97.96	2.04	100.0	
(4) Fiscal capacity deficiency (+) (1)	2.98	-83.38	2.98		
(5) or excess (-) (2)	0.0	-90.36	8.46		
(6) Equalization payments from gas royalties (73-74)('000)	2,358	-58,872	1,451		
Experiment 1					
(Pgas = $ .45 MCF domestic Pliquids = $5.75 /barrel)					
(7) Provincial gas royalties	0.0*	931,653	184,951	1,116,604	
(8) Equalization payments from gas	35,200	0.0	46,900	936,000	659,955
Experiment 2					
(Pgas = $ .90 MCF domestic Pliquids = $5.75 /barrel)					
(9) Provincial gas royalties	0.0*	1,318,636	286,203	1,610,399	
(10) Equalization payments from gas	61,400	0.0	62,700	1,986,700	1,094,865
Experiment 3					
(Pgas = $1.93 MCF domestic Pliquids = $12.50 /barrel)					
(11) Provincial gas royalties	0.0*	2,048,593	405,980	2,462,380	
(12) Equalization payments from gas	79,700	0.0	107,700	2,105,600	1,768,755

Notes:*Saskatchewan is assumed to collect no royalties from natural gas.
** Additional equalization payments, assuming that the $6.50 price for oil prevails, i.e., Experiment 1, Table 4.

royalty calculations because Ottawa collects the export tax, which essentially makes up the difference between the domestic and export price. Not so with gas. There is no export tax and Ottawa has indicated that it will not impose one. Therefore it is reasonable to expect that the producing provinces will want to capture a larger proportion (or perhaps even all) of the extra rent deriving from production destined for sales in the U.S. market than from production for the domestic market. If anything, we have probably underestimated the royalties from gas for export in Table B1. The reader is referred to Appendix C for details underlying the calculation of the numbers in the table.

RESULTS OF THE SIMULATIONS

Experiment 1 assumes (a) that the domestic gas price is 45 cents per thousand cubic feet (MCF), (b) that the export price is $1.50/MCF, and (c) that gas liquids are priced at $5.50 per barrel. One-half of the gas is assumed to be destined for the export market. As a point of reference when calculating the gas royalties and equalization payments, *the analysis assumes that Experiment 1 for oil prevails*. At a 45-cent/MCF price, royalties total $1.117 billion and equalization entitlements total just under $1 billion. However, equalization payments increase very substantially— $.689 billion. This occurs because Ontario becomes a have-not province in Experiment 1, under the assumption that the price of oil is at $6.50 per barrel.

Experiment 2 sets the price of gas at 90 cents/MCF. The justification for this price is that it approximates the "energy equivalent" price of gas coinciding with the $6.50 per barrel price of oil. The export price of gas is set at $1.95. Experiment 3 is designed to price gas at the "energy equivalent" to the world price of oil. Both the export and domestic prices are identical for this simulation. Total gas royalties rise to nearly $2.5 billion with Alberta gaining over $2 billion. Equalization payments increase by $1.768 billion over those paid out under the $6.50 per barrel price of crude oil. There is no need to dwell further on the results in this table. The essential point is that rising prices for natural gas have the potential for generating astounding further increases in equalization payments.

Appendix C

CALCULATION PROCEDURES FOR OIL AND GAS ROYALTIES

A. Procedures Underlying Table A1

In Alberta, approximately 83 per cent of all oil is extracted from Crown lands. Oil from non-Crown lands in Alberta is subject to only negligible provincial royalties. For this reason 83 per cent of Alberta's total oil production in 1973-74 was used to calculate provincial oil royalties and resulting equalization payments.

In all cases, equalization payments are calculated as the product of fiscal capacity deficiency and total oil revenues. In cases where there is a fiscal capacity excess, equalization payments are set at zero.

The increases in aggregate equalization payments (last column) are less than the total increases in equalization payments due to oil because some provinces receiving oil equalization payments remain overall have provinces, and therefore do not benefit from increased oil equalization.

Line 2: Weights do not correspond directly to provincial share of Canadian volume of production. These weights, used by the federal government, are based on value of production.

Lines 5, 6: This experiment assumes the price of oil to be $6.50 per barrel for Alberta and British Columbia, $6.08 per barrel to Saskatchewan. Royalty rates for Alberta are assumed to be 22 per cent of first $3.80 and 65 per cent of the remainder of the price. Saskatchewan royalty rates are assumed to be 15.8 per cent of the first $3.08 and 100 per cent of the remainder of the price. The royalty rate for British Columbia is assumed to be 50 per cent of the price.

Lines 7, 8: In Experiment 2, the volume of production for the three provinces is assumed to remain at the Experiment 1 levels. The price of oil rises to $8.00 per barrel in all three provinces and the royalty rate is 65 per cent of the price in the three cases.

Lines 8, 9: In Experiment 3, the volume of production is again assumed to remain at the Experiment 1 levels. The price is allowed to rise to an approximation of the world price at $12.50 per barrel. The royalty rate is again 65 per cent of the price, and the prices and the royalty rates are equal for all three provinces.

Line 11: Experiment 4 has the same assumptions as Experiment 1 with one major exception. It is assumed that all present Alberta oil resources are transferred to Quebec, with the subsequent changes in the pattern of equalization payments.

B. Procedures Underlying Table B1

In Alberta, approximately 80 per cent of total gas and gas liquids are extracted from Crown land. Non-Crown land gas and gas liquids production are subject to only negligible provincial royalties, hence, in the calculation of provincial royalties and subsequently equalization payments, 80 per cent of Alberta's natural gas and gas liquids production were used.

Increases in aggregate equalization payments (far right column) are somewhat less than total equalization payments for gas (as shown in column 11) because some provinces remain have provinces overall and therefore cannot take advantage of increased gas equalization entitlements.

Lines 2, 3: Share of gas and gas liquids do not correspond directly to provincial share of total Canadian volume of production. Rather, these weights, used by the federal government in the calculation of equalization payments, are based on value of production, as in Table A1.

Lines 7, 8: It is assumed that 50 per cent of all natural gas is exported, with the domestic price set at $.45/MCF and the export price $1.50/MCF. The price of gas liquids is assumed to be $5.75 per barrel. Saskatchewan collects no royalties and the royalty rates throughout for Ontario, Alberta, and British Columbia are assumed to be calculated in the following manner:

for prices between $.32 and $.72:
$$[9.22 + .50 (price - 32)]/price$$

and for prices above $.72:
$$[29.22 + .50 (price - 72)]/price.$$

A characteristic of this formula is that royalty rates rise with rising gas prices. These methods of royalty calculation apply for gas and gas liquids. I would imagine that royalties on exported gas could well be higher than the rate generated by this formula.

Lines 9, 10: In Experiment 2, the value of natural gas is set to its "heat equivalence" with respect to oil. "Heat equivalence" is determined in the following manner:

$$[(oil price + $.70) \div 5.8] - $.35 = \text{"heat equivalent to oil"} \text{ gas price}$$

where the $.70 and $.35 are the transportation costs for oil and gas respectively since the basing point is Toronto. As in Experiment 1, it is assumed that 50 per cent of all natural gas is exported. With oil priced at $6.50 per barrel, the "heat equivalent" domestic gas price is $.90/MCF. The "heat equivalent" export gas price is determined by adding ($1.50-$.45) to the domestic price. The price of gas liquids is again set to $5.75 per barrel and royalty rates are determined by the formula given in Experiment 1. As with oil, the volume of production is assumed to be constant throughout.

Lines 11, 12: In Experiment 3, the value of natural gas is again set to its "heat equivalence" oil price. The price of oil is assumed to have risen to world price levels or $12.50 per barrel. There is, of course, no difference in this case between domestic and export prices. The new natural gas price is $1.93/MCF. Volume of production remains constant and royalty rates are calculated as in Experiment 1. The price of gas liquids is now set to $12.50 per barrel.

Notes

1. I.e., Alberta, Saskatchewan, and B.C. account for 22.2 per cent of Canada's population, the remaining provinces accounting for 77.8 per cent.
2. At the limit, if P.E.I. had all the oil and everyone else became have-not provinces, Ottawa would shell out 99.5 cents for every dollar accruing to P.E.I.

Note on Equalization and Resource Rents

DOUGLAS H. CLARK

This brief note on the purpose and workings of the equalization programme was sparked by the contributions of A.D. Scott and T.J. Courchene. Courchene's paper demonstrates, once again, his excellent understanding of the workings of Canada's complex equalization formula. It, and Scott's paper as well, raise some fundamental questions about the purpose of the federal government's programme of fiscal equalization, and it might be helpful if I were to make some comments on this matter. This I do in a personal context and not as a representative of the Department of Finance of Canada.

The present equalization programme began in 1967. Its intended purpose was stated at a federal-provincial conference the previous year by the then Minister of Finance and has been reiterated by successive ministers of Finance since that time. As formulated by Mitchell Sharp in 1966, the purpose was set out as follows:

> Where circumstances—whether natural or man-made—have chan-
> nelled a larger than average share of the nation's wealth into certain
> sections of the country, there should be a redistribution of that wealth
> so that all provinces are able to provide to their citizens a reasonably
> comparable level of basic services, without resorting to unduly burden-
> some levels of taxation.[1]

The 1967 equalization formula was designed to carry out this purpose, taking into account a comprehensive list of provincial revenues from own sources. The revenues subject to equalization were classified into groups, known as "revenue sources," each with a separate measure of fiscal capacity, or revenue-raising capacity. Of the sixteen original revenue groups, no fewer than seven related to natural resources, i.e., oil royalties, natural gas royalties, sale of Crown leases and reservations on oil and gas lands, other oil and gas revenues, revenues from metallic and non-metallic minerals, forestry revenues, and revenues from water power rentals. These seven sources covered all of the special levies that the provinces imposed in respect of natural resources. There was, therefore, a clear intention to measure differences between provinces in respect of resource revenues or, more basically, in respect of resource rents. However, this attempt to take account of resource rents was not a central part of the equalization programme since, at that time, resource revenues accounted for only about 8 per cent of the total revenues equalized and for only about 20 per cent of the total equalization paid. When the formula was renewed in 1972-73, these shares had fallen to 6 per cent and 16 per cent respectively.

The 1967 equalization formula has, in general, worked very well in respect of non-resource revenues, but a number of problems have arisen in respect of natural resource revenues. I might refer to two of these. Firstly, precise measurement of the relative revenue-raising capacities of the ten provinces with respect to natural resource revenues really requires the federal government to estimate the amount of pure rent in each province for each category of natural resources; such measures are not available and it has been necessary to make use of proxies whose quality appears to be somewhat less satisfactory than the measures used for equalizing non-resource revenues. Secondly, the international oil disturbance of 1973-74 and its aftermath brought about a situation where enormous increases in equalization could occur—as Professor Courchene has demonstrated—followed by the prospect of substantial year-to-year instability in payments. Indeed it could readily happen that disparities in resource rents would account for well over one-half of total equalization and hence dominate the entire programme. The foregoing induced the federal government to introduce legislation—in the form of the July 1975 amendment to the Federal-Provincial Fiscal Arrangements Act—to limit the amount of equalization payable in respect of windfall revenues of the provinces from oil and gas.

This brings me back to fundamentals. Equalization is concerned with the financing of public services and with trying to make it possible for citizens of relatively poor provinces to enjoy such services at levels that are reasonable in relation to those provided in the ten provinces as a whole, without having to submit to unduly high levels of taxation. However, it is quite a step to go from this basic premise to the position that resource rents of no matter what size must be subject to equalization in full. To make this assertion is to get carried away by the mathematics of the formula and to lose sight of the more substantive problem to which equalization is directed, namely the financing of some basic level of public services in all provinces.

The difficulty here is that a sudden, sharp increase in resource rents is likely to be accompanied by a substantial increase in interprovincial fiscal disparities, but not by a parallel increase in the relative cost of providing public services in the lower income provinces.[2] Similarly, a sudden, sharp narrowing in resource rents is likely to be accompanied by a substantial decrease in interprovincial disparities, but not by a parallel decrease in the relative cost of providing public services in the lower income provinces. What I am saying is that, having regard to the fundamental purpose of the equalization programme, it would be unfortunate to have it overly dependent upon fluctuations in the level of resource rents. This would create undesirable financial uncertainties—both for the federal government which pays equalization, and for the below average provinces which receive it—and would result in a tendency for federal support to these provinces to lose its close relationship to their basic needs.

In conclusion, equalization does have a significant role to play in allocating, among provinces, that portion of resource rents which goes to the provincial government sector. With any given formula, this role is carried out automatically. However, the present equalization formula was not devised to deal with the situation where resource rents are very large and, having regard to the basic purpose of equalization, it would appear undesirable to look to the equalization programme as a means of maintaining some given distributional pattern of resource rents within the public sector in all circumstances.

If the foregoing conclusion is accepted but it is nevertheless considered desirable for resource rents to be more evenly distributed amongst the provinces, then other measures in addition to equalization will have to be adopted, presumably by the central government. The history of resource rent allocations in Canada and other federations, and even in unitary states such as the United Kingdom, suggests that this will be no easy task and that resource-rich regions, rightly or wrongly, will tend to end up with very substantial shares of the total rents emanating from their territories. History also suggests that, if the latter is true, such regions can, over a period of years, expect to experience significant population inflows from other regions less well endowed with resources, thereby lessening interregional disparities in ratios of resources to people.

In the final analysis, therefore, the adjustment of people to resources—which, I think, is one manner of describing what was discussed at the conference on natural resource revenues—is likely to take place in two basic ways: one, by a redistribution of rents among provinces, and the other by a redistribution of people among provinces. To the extent that the adjustment takes place through a reallocation of rents, pressures bringing about a redistribution of people will be diminished. To the extent that the adjustment does not take place through rents, the population pressures will increase.

If any of you care to examine Canadian statistics concerning the population shares of the "have" and "have-not" provinces, you will find that the basic historical trends are remarkably strong and persistent. There has, however, been a recent change in thinking about the long-term benefits of population increases. It might serve a useful purpose, therefore, to ask the resource-rich provinces whether they have thought about resource rent allocations in these terms and also whether demographic considerations make any difference to their views concerning the sharing of resource rents.

Notes

1. Federal-Provincial Tax Structure Committee, Proceedings of the Meeting of 14 and 15 September 1966, p. 15, extract from statement by the Honourable M.W. Sharp, Minister of Finance of the Government of Canada.

2. The large increase in resource rents from oil and gas from 1973 to 1974 could be cited as an example. It is true that this must have resulted in large percentage increases in expenditures by equalizing-receiving provinces for fuel oil and motive fuels but such expenditures would be of minor significance in terms of total budgets and, in any case, would have to be met by the high income provinces as well.

Natural Resource Revenue Sharing: A Dissenting View

ANDREW R. THOMPSON

Anthony Scott asks: "Who should get natural resource revenues?"

The form of the question puzzles me, and a reading of the papers prepared by Professor Scott and by Professor Moore[1] confirms the puzzlement. The word "get" is the puzzler. Does it simply mean "who is to be the beneficiary of natural resource revenues?" or does it mean "who is to have responsibility and authority to manage natural resources for profit?"

I think Professor Moore is asking and answering only the first question, and his message seems to be that natural resource revenues must be shared by all Canadians. I know of no one in Canada who disagrees with this conclusion. But I have a suspicion that Professor Moore means something else. Maybe he is really saying that the federal government of Canada alone should manage natural resources and divide the revenues among Canadians. If that is his conclusion, I do not believe that his deductive logic supports it. This logic seems to run as follows: Canada is a community because it clearly recognizes a need to provide equal welfare to its citizens; therefore, the economic rent from natural resources, which belongs to the community, should be shared by all members of the community.

This syllogism says nothing about which government should control and manage natural resources. Professor Moore is surely not saying that there is only one community within Canada. It is true that scientists sought the ultimate particle first in the molecule and then in the atom. But each in turn revealed subsets of particles and subsets beyond these. In much the same way, communities are composed of subsets. Possibly the individual human being can be regarded as the ultimate community particle, but even here you would get arguments that artificial entities should be included—unborn persons and even inanimate objects such as heirlooms and trees.

The very concept of tax revenue equalization in Canada assumes multiple communities (provinces) that are not equally endowed with tax base. You cannot deduce a need for central control and management of natural resources from a principle that it is desirable to equalize benefits available to the diversely endowed communities that make up the nation.

I believe that in his paper Professor Scott was probing beyond sharing of natural resource revenues (though I may be guilty of reading implications about resource management that were not there) when he discussed risk aversion and time preferences. It may be that we are at a point where the two disciplines of law and economics intersect without either being aware of the fact. It may be that the economists' discussion of economic rent and who is to receive it includes by implication all the components which I, as a lawyer, conceptualize in other terms.

As a teacher of real property law, I have for many years invited students to analyze ownership rights under three headings: Who has the power of alienation? Who has the right to manage (sometimes referred to as the executive right)? Who has the right to use and enjoyment?

Each of these headings can be related to Professor Scott's analysis. Exercise of the rights of alienation and of management establish the time preferences and the form in which rents are to be realized. They can also, of course, signify much more of relevance to the lawyer. For example, when the lawyer knows who has the right to alienate, he will be able to advise as to the legal formalities required to effect a binding transfer of property rights. In fact, the need for a distinction between the functions of alienation and of management may puzzle the economist because he would be more likely to consider alienation as merely one way of exercising management powers. The lawyer makes the distinction simply because some property rights can be owned and alienated which do not include any right to manage physical or tangible property. An illustration is a right to receive income as beneficiary of a trust where the beneficiary has full rights of alienation of his interest but has no right to manage the trust property.

The heading "right to use and enjoyment" comes closest to the question of who is to receive natural resource revenues. A holder of the right to use and enjoyment may also enjoy the rights of alienation and management, as in the case of a freehold property owner, but he may also be in the position of the beneficiary of the trust income. Any lawyer is aware that the basic right of the beneficiary is merely to receive a periodic accounting and payment of his due. Otherwise, the beneficiary can interfere with management by the trustee, who has the executive or management power, only in very limited circumstances where a dereliction of duty can be assigned.

It is with such an analytical framework in mind that I pursue the question whether this symposium is discussing purely natural resource revenue sharing or whether natural resource management and control is at the heart of the matter.

Nor is the question merely an academic quibble. The provincial politician clearly has control in mind as much as revenues when he confronts the federal government over natural resources. The questions which concern him are who can develop what natural resources where, who can determine price, and who can determine what revenue share will belong to the resource developer and what share will accrue to the province? While he does not assert that these questions are exclusively his to answer, he will not, on the other hand, yield an exclusive position on them to his federal counterpart. Undoubtedly, the provincial politician claims more to say about some of these questions than about others. He will most certainly expect to designate who the developer of provincially owned natural resources will be. He will be anxious to control rates of exploitation because of the impacts such rates have on physical and social infrastructure in the province, not to mention the overall performance of the provincial economy. In the case of markets outside the province, he expects a heavy federal hand, and if the commodity is a vital one he may also tolerate federal intrusions into price regulation. Finally he knows that revenue sharing is a matter that can only be resolved on a co-operative basis with Ottawa and the other provincial governments.

Turning to the subject of economic rent, would I be correct in suggesting that it is the peculiar form of Canadian federalism that has transformed the term from an academic construct to current jargon in the politics of Canadian natural resources? In the jurisdictional mix of the Canadian confederation, the federal government is perceived as the income tax collector with the role of taxing labour and capital returns from the exploitation of natural resources in accordance with levels generally pertaining in the country for the taxation of labour and capital.[2] If there is a surplus above normal returns, it is by definition an economic rent which should accrue to the owner of the resource. Where the tax collector also is the resource owner, there is no need to identify the economic rent separately from normal returns on capital and labour because all is taxable to yield the government's share of revenues. But because in Canada the public resource owner is the province and not the federal government, we have an entity only too ready and willing to identify and claim the economic rent. Because the western provinces had exacted undertakings from resource developers to pay "such royalties as may be established from time to time by the Lieutenant-Governor in Council [the provincial cabinet]," they had the legal means to "fine tune" royalty rates so as to capture economic rent.

One of the principal arguments in favour of provincial ownership of natural resources during the recent dispute with the federal government has been that, compared with the complicated income tax system with its appendage of incentives, concessions, and loopholes, the provincial royalty systems provide much sharper and defter instruments for collecting the government's share of revenues. Certainly the complaints of resource developers have borne out a conclusion that provincial royalties cut sharper than do federal income taxes. A principal reason for recommending the establishment of the British Columbia Petroleum Corporation to act as a broker in the sale of the province's natural gas[3] was to wrest control of the industry from a producing company and a transmission company which were subsidiaries controlled by the same foreign parent corporation. But an equally important reason was the need to find a system as flexible and pointed as royalties to capture the economic rent. The fine tuning was to be accomplished by the Corporation establishing producer prices at an acceptable level and reselling at newly established export prices, with the mark-up over processing and transmission costs being received by the Corporation as an agent for the province.

It will be argued that there is no inherent reason why it should be easier for the province to "fine tune" the collection of economic rent through its royalty system or an arrangement like the British Columbia Petroleum Corporation than it is for the federal government under the income tax provisions. I do not agree. The basic difference is that the income tax provisions must, for reasons of equity, apply equally to all corporations in any particular kind of business. This necessity for equal treatment is perceived as a necessary requirement of a taxation system. On the other hand, it is not so imperative for a province to apply entirely uniform royalty rates and, because its position derives from its ownership of the natural resource, the province is free to negotiate particular terms and conditions. In addition, a province is a smaller geographic entity than Canada as a whole, and therefore it can design royalty systems which are more responsive to the particular situation in the province than would be the case if the system had to be designed to meet the needs of the industry in the country as a whole.

There is another side to this question of the relative efficiency of various systems for collecting a government's share of resource revenues. Resource industry advocates argue that taxation of net profits is the only fair way to extract the government's share of revenues because net income taxation recognizes the differences in costs of extraction of various resource properties (and offers less inducement to high grading). This argument is more applicable in the case of mining than in the case of the oil and gas industry because it is more likely in mining that a developer will pay his royalties or taxes on only one or two mining properties, so that the extent to which the costs of extraction from these properties vary from the norm is highly critical, whereas in the case of oil and gas properties each developer will usually have a mixed portfolio of high cost and low cost properties with the average of extraction costs running close to the average for the entire industry.

While this argument in favour of net profits taxation is supportable on tests of fairness in the case of the mining industry, it fails to take account of the reality that income taxation of natural resource revenues in Canada has been an unsatisfactory method of realizing economic rent for the public, the resource owner. Certainly, when the action of the O.P.E.C. countries suddenly escalated the value of crude oil at the wellhead, it was clear that the existing federal income tax laws would not capture much of this windfall for the public, the resource owner, and past experience (the Carter Commission of recent years) indicated that it was not practical to attempt a major revision of the income tax laws so as to increase the returns to government from crude oil profits. In the outcome, the western provinces, by changing their royalty rates, effectively gained a substantial share of the windfall profits for public treasuries. The federal government had to stake out a claim to these increased revenues by the indelicate procedure of making provincial royalties non-deductible items for the purposes of calculating the income tax of oil and gas companies. But all that is past history.

Returning to my main point, which is to question where the issues concerning management and control of natural resources fit into an analysis of resource revenue sharing, I refer to an article entitled "Petroleum Land Policies—Alaska and Northern Canada"[4] in which I pursued the different interests which would dominate petroleum resource policies depending on whether resources were under federal ownership and management or under provincial or state ownership and management. I identified four categories of such interests, being local regional interests, revenues, sovereignty and national security issues, and resource and economic planning. Economists who are used to rigorous quantitative analysis will be offended by the broad and sweeping generalizations made in the article without much verification or substantiation. Lawyers are uncomfortable, too, when they cannot cite clear and authoritative precedents. But I recall making no apology for these sweeping generalizations at the time of writing because until then none of the disciplines which might address these issues in more scientific terms had given them attention. Now that you, the economists, are focussing the analytical techniques of your discipline on the question of revenue sharing, I hope that you will explain how your conclusions relate to the solution of these other questions of resource management policy.

For example, Professor Scott connects time preference with the rate of development of resources, but he does not consider the effects of the different time preferences which will inevitably result if resource management is dominated by multiple provincial jurisdictions rather than a single federal jurisdiction. Would there be any substantial difference between the time preference of the federal government, on one hand, and the time preference of a provincial government, on the other hand? What are the implications of these different time preferences? Suppose that the federal government is anxious to hasten the pace of natural resource development to stimulate overall economic growth for the country whereas a particular province may wish to husband its resources and avoid overstimulation of its regional economy. If the impacts of varying time preferences can be quantified, the choices between alternatives, which must remain in the political realm, will be that much easier.

Professor Scott begins by saying that he is shaking off the bondage of present institutions of government in Canada so that his analysis will reveal valid underlying principles concerning resource revenue sharing. Lawyers, too, are great respecters of first principles, but we believe that the test of their validity is how firmly they are rooted in real life situations and experiences. That is why I have shifted the argument from the question of economic rent in the abstract to questions of control over natural resource development. And by now, I will have revealed why I entitled my paper "A Dissenting View." In my experience, most economists conclude the issue of federal versus provincial ownership and management of natural resources in favour of the federal government. Maybe that reflects their faith in economies of scale. But I am a believer that "small is beautiful," and, as a firm defender of the provincial position, I will not be surprised to find myself a member of a small minority.

Notes

1. Paper first circulated. Professor Moore subsequently submitted a totally revised paper.
2. Generally speaking, the provinces permit the federal tax authorities to collect a share of income taxes for the provinces in addition to the income tax collected for federal purposes.
3. See *Report on Matters Concerning the Natural Gas Industry in British Columbia*, British Columbia Energy Commission, 14 September 1973.
4. *U.B.C. Law Review* (1969): 227-43.

Resource Rent: How Much and for Whom?

HARRY F. CAMPBELL, W.D. GAINER, ANTHONY SCOTT

I. INTRODUCTION

This paper is intended to serve as an introduction to the discussion of government claims on resource rent. First, it provides a brief summary of the current controversy over the division of natural resource revenues in Canada. This summary concludes with the observation that all resource rents could be regarded as private rents for analytical purposes if the agency of one government could be taxed by another government. Secondly, the paper turns to an analysis of the rent accruing to the private or public owners of exhaustible resources. The approach is first to present a simple analogy between the familiar concept of agricultural rent and the less familiar concept of mineral rent, and then to discuss the more complex problems posed by mineral exploration and risk, and the taxation of mineral rent. The concluding section of the paper suggests that the existence of competing government claims to resource rent may result in a mineral tax structure which reduces the total amount of rent available to be shared among public and private landlords.

II. SOME BACKGROUND CONTROVERSY

The substantial increases in world oil prices initiated in late 1973 have occasioned much controversy over the appropriate "divisioning," via taxation or other means, of the changeable revenues arising from the exploitation of a natural resource over time. It is true that much of the heat in the controversy has resulted from the size and abruptness of "administered" changes in world wide prices alone. Nevertheless, it makes timely a re-examination of the whole theory of rent and of production in the particular context of natural resource exploitation, a timeliness increased by the growing importance of raw resource materials in international trade and in the import structures of many of the industrialized countries of the world. Much of the public debate has centred on questions about an appropriate divisioning of oil rents passed among three principal groups—

consumers directly via controlled price, various levels of government via taxation and a variety of resource charges, and the producing industry via the degree of forebearance exercised in the combined use of all of the above measures by governments.

With respect to the sub-controversy as to which level of government should have priority access to any windfall spoils deemed by these governments to be surplus to the industry, one of the present authors has already commented elsewhere on this matter.[1] This earlier contribution suggested that whether the greatly enlarged opportunity revenues available to oil producers are viewed as properly belonging to producer entrepreneurs and risk capitalists as profits and capital earnings, or to private or public landlords as revenues from charges designed to appropriate rents should make no difference. Such net revenues should, in either case, have no special claim to exemption from the present omnibus rules of income taxation which seek to encompass all forms of earnings and capital gains (whether explicitly or merely as a residual).

Thus it is the view here that revenues generated from various price or income related charges levied against producers by private or public landlords for the rights to the use or sale of a natural asset are in the nature of realized capital gains appropriated by the landlord; or, stated differently, such charges amount to a price established or negotiated by a private or public landlord for the sale or use of a natural resource by another party. The revenues so generated represent that portion of the resource rent which the landlord has seen fit to recover; the total rent being all such net income accruing in the process of exploitation in excess of all necessary internal and external factor costs involved in finding, caring for, and marketing the natural asset by all parties involved. Now if the public or private landlord does not have the wit nor the market power to appropriate such realized capital gains on his own land, those same gains will nevertheless accrue to other interests involved in the process of exploitation. If not appropriated by the landlord, they will then appear elsewhere as unearned increments to sales values, usually as supra-opportunity "profits" in the absence of leases. No matter in whose hands they end up, and whatever the accounting designation of such gains, their functional description remains that of economic rent, as distinct from either entrepreneurial profit or return to capital.

Likewise, from the point of view of dividing the revenues from direct taxation between federal and provincial governments, distinguishing between "economic rent" and functional sources of income usually has not been critical, as a practical matter. For instance, surplus income (or capital gains) arising as rents has ordinarily been subject to the same rules of shared federal/provincial income taxation whether the rents have first been appropriated into the hands of (private) resource owners, or have been left with the (private) lessee, and there subject to omnibus income taxation. In the case of such private lessees or lessors the size and form of private resource owners' charges is of little concern to either level of government. Whether these be by fixed or variable royalty, by leasehold bidding, by rental charges, or any combination of these, such private net receipts are subject to shared federal/provincial taxation in a predictable fashion.

The whole situation becomes quite different, and controversial, if the resource owner or landlord is another government or government agency and has undertaken to levy resource charges against lessees. In this case, resource revenues (or indeed any kind of government revenue, lands, or properties) are expressly exempted from taxation by any other government under certain past interpretations of section 125 of the B.N.A. Act, and possibly of sections 102 and 126 of that Act as well. [2] Given this wide-ranging constitutional provision, all provincial government resource rental charges (and even taxes, fees for service, or general commercial profits) would therefore appear to be exempt from taxation, unlike the same rental charges or royalties if paid to private resource owners in their effort to capture surplus income or capital gains which would otherwise remain with the tenant.

This is an anomaly. If it were not for this differential treatment of public and private gains enshrined in the B.N.A. Act, it would be easier to argue that each province, under an ideal sharing arrangement, should be free to establish its own rental schedule. That is, it could levy whatever amount and form of charges seemed prudent for the use of the resources in the province's public domain in order to appropriate, as trustee for its local residents, a desired level of changeable resource rent over time. Having once appropriated any part of the rents arising from the use of the public domain, such provincial rental receipts would be subject to the ordinary and agreed rules of shared federal/provincial direct taxation as though the receipts had accrued directly to a private owner of resource rights. This kind of sharing arrangement appears to be excluded by the present "incest" clause of the B.N.A. Act under which members of a government family in Canada are restrained from "doing it to each other."

However, it may be possible for the government to negotiate around this obstacle. For instance, the provincial revenues derived from natural resources (in excess of cost of service) could be deemed annually as taxable receipts in the hands of every income tax reporting resident of the province. This could be arranged according to the number of such taxpayers and the size of the designated provincial net resource receipts. Each taxpayer could then be subject under the personal income tax act to the federal portion of the joint income tax (or to the provincial portion as well if the province should have a particular bookkeeping penchant for self-abuse) on such deemed net receipts. Alternatively, following the example of the B.C. Petroleum Corporation, the provincial Crown could simply agree to pay a federal corporation tax on certain deemed profits. Finally, reversing a tradition already well established in Canada, provincial governments might agree to a system of annual block grants to the federal government based on agreed formulae for estimating the federal portion of income tax revenues foregone.

But whatever the possibilities for further negotiation, in the meantime the federal/provincial scramble for a cut in the windfall oil revenues has largely eclipsed an important but even more elusive issue: what is the appropriate tax treatment of the producing industry irrespective of whether the resources are in the private or the public domain? In this paper we assume that the objective of governments with a claim to natural resource revenues is to collect their share of rent without disturbing the pattern of resource exploitation which would be freely chosen by the private industry. For the sake of simplicity we assume that this choice of level and timing of extraction would be socially optimal. In the course of our analysis of the concept of resource rent we argue that many forms of taxation designed to appropriate rent for the public sector will result in a departure from this optimal pattern. The main focus of our discussion, however, is on the identification of resource rent under different circumstances.

III. AN ANALYSIS OF RESOURCE RENT

Introduction

In this section of our paper we describe a series of sets of circumstances in which "rent" can appear. The Ricardian tradition, based on analysis of farm land, has always insisted that increasing demand and scarcity will lead to rising rents (and so rising incomes for landlords). But we show here that when resources are exhaustible, rents and rental incomes may fall over time. While this conclusion is contrary to Ricardo's generalization, it is not mysterious. If the need to have recourse to low grade or remote deposits means that society's mining costs rise faster than prices per ton of final mineral product, rent per ton, and per acre, is bound to be squeezed.

This is only one of the questions addressed. To throw light on it we develop increasingly more complex cases starting from a simple agricultural example and working through to situations where resources are depleted and risk also appears.

Renewable Resources

In this section we review the situations that can arise on farmland which we assume is inexhaustible (i.e., renewable). Starting with a homogeneous-land, one-crop, many-farm economy, we trace changes in rent that emerge when land becomes heterogeneous, and different crops compete for the land. The demand curve for land is the value of the marginal product of land given exogenously-set prices for each crop and for all factors except land.

Assume initially that units of land are homogeneous and that there is only one use for land, for example in corn production. Then, assuming a competitive product market, the demand curve for land is the value of marginal product schedule of land in corn production. If land is not scarce, *OA* units of land will be employed, and each acre will earn a zero rent. If,

FIGURE 1

SCARCITY RENT

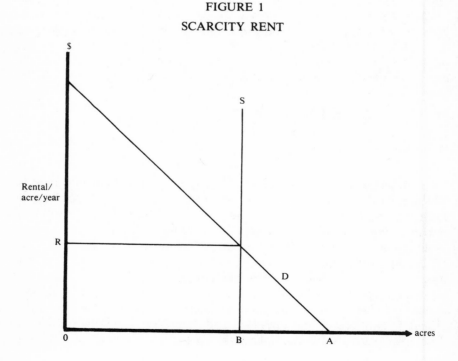

however, land is scarce, as indicated by the supply curve in Figure 1, each of the *OB* acres will earn an annual rent of *OR* per acre. This annual rent can be described as a "scarcity rent."

Assume now that land has more than one use, for example in corn production or in wheat production. In Figure 2, D_c is the demand curve for land in corn production and D_{w_1} and D_{w_2} are alternative demand schedules for land in wheat production: D_{w_2} is the value of marginal product schedule corresponding to a high price of wheat, D_{w_1} is that corresponding to a low price of wheat.

FIGURE 2

RENT WITH TWO USES

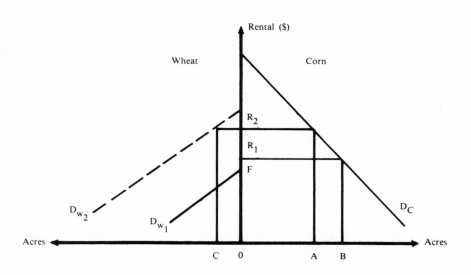

If the low price of wheat is established (in a world wheat market, for example) none of the area's land will be used in wheat production: *OB* corn acres will earn a scarcity rental of OR_1 per acre. If, however, the high price of wheat obtains, then the fixed amount of land, $OB = OA + OC$, will be rationed between wheat and corn production by means of an annual scarcity rent of OR_2 per acre.

In another terminology, in the first situation, OR_1 was the rent of land from the point of view of the landlord, made up of *OF* rent from the point of view of wheat production (also known as a transfer payment or opportunity cost of land) plus FR_1 rent from the point of view of corn production (the surplus over the transfer payment or opportunity cost). We shall not make this distinction here.[3]

This argument about the use of scarcity rent to ration land among uses can be extended to cover the case of many uses of land, for example, residential, commercial, various types of crop, grazing, and recreation. Note that our partial-equilibrium analysis allows uses to be excluded from this area altogether; presumably all other products are produced on lands elsewhere.

Assume now that land is not homogeneous. The simplest example is plots of land which are all of the same quality but which are different distances from the centre of population where the product of land is sold. Suppose also that there is only one use for land and that the demand curves are

FIGURE 3

RICARDIAN RENTS

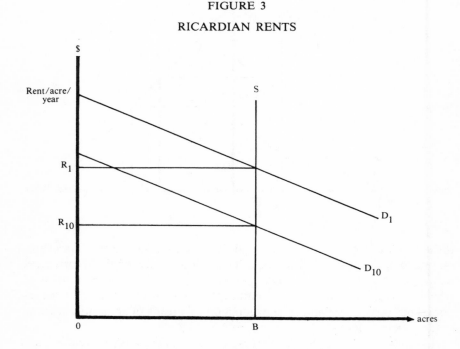

arrayed as in Figure 3 where the subscript indicates the distance the land is from the centre of population. The vertical distance between D_1 and D_{10}, for instance, is the uniform marginal physical productivity of a given plot of land multiplied by the difference between farmgate price received in the different locations (that is, multiplied by the difference between the freight rates for 10 miles and 1 mile transport of corn). If we assume that the supply of land at each distance is OB then the intersections with the supply curve S will give the annual rentals OR_1 and OR_{10} paid to land at each distance. The rents OR_{10} and OR_1 now reflect two factors—the scarcity of land in the entire area and its non-homogeneity. The difference between the rents does not reflect differential scarcity, since there are OB acres in each location. The rent OR_{10} might be thought of as a basic scarcity rent, while the excess of OR_1 over OR_{10} is a "Ricardian" rent reflecting the lower transport costs. More generally, the rent of any piece of land reflects both its "Ricardian" differential and the scarcity of each type of land. This analysis would also apply to other characteristics of land such as fertility, drainage, sunshine, precipitation, workability, and so on.

Non-Renewable Resources

Once the assumption of exhaustibility is introduced account must be taken of the time path of extraction. In this section we consider (a) the development of a known stock of a homogeneous resource; (b) the development of a known stock of a non-homogeneous resource; and (c) exploration for and development of a resource. We assume initially that resource owners sell rights to extract on a competitive market, that there is a perfect futures market for the resource, and that extraction is instantaneous. Since we are considering alternative long-run equilibrium situations the subjects of quasi-rents and windfall gains do not enter the discussion. Subsequently, in part (d) of the section, we discuss the effects on the mineral rights market of the imposition of royalties designed to collect resource rent for the public sector. In part (e) we consider a situation in which the price of mineral rights is determined exogenously, and we conclude the section with part (f) which contains a brief discussion of risk.

a. Just as in the case of agriculture, mineral landlords are assumed to sell production rights. In the mineral industry, however, they sell rights to extract units of a known material from homogeneous, exhaustible mines. The extractive industry's aggregate demand curve for these rights is, as with agriculture, the sum of the marginal value product curves of the individual extractive firms. This derived demand depends upon the market demand for the final product, the production function in the extractive industry, and the cost of other factors. On the supply side, landlords attempt to maximize the present value of the stream of revenues from the sale of rights; in Figure 4 the constant aggregate demand curve[4] for mineral rights is intersected by a series of aggregate supply curves representing the quantities of rights placed on the market, in each period, by landlords. These quantities decrease because it will pay landlords not to hold their initial stocks of rights unless their unit value (denoted by λ in Figure 4) is increased at the rate of interest: they will hold them only until the rate of increase of their value falls to the rate of interest, r. The number of rights that landlords decide to sell each year will determine the price and an annual decrease in this quantity offered will cause λ to rise over time.

FIGURE 4
THE MINERAL RIGHTS MARKET

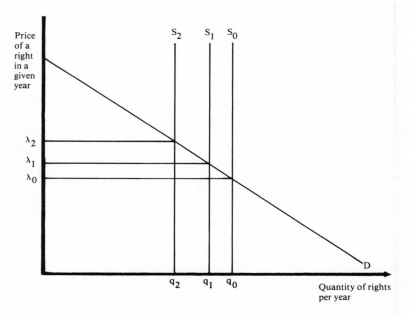

If λ tended to rise more quickly than the interest rate, landlords would tend to hold stocks rather than sell them. If λ tended to rise more slowly than the interest rate, landlords would tend to unload additional quantities of mineral rights. Thus the quantity of rights supplied will decrease at a rate sufficient to set the price of a right at time t at $\lambda_0 e^{rt}$, where λ is the price of a right at time zero and r is the interest rate.

The stream of scarcity rents accruing to all landlords is given by the successive rectangles $\lambda_0 q_0, \lambda_1 q_1, \lambda_2 q_2, \ldots, \lambda_T q_T$, in Figure 4. These rents are analogous to the agricultural rents described in Figure 1. The present value of this stream of rents is

$$_0\int^T \lambda(t)q(t)e^{-rt}dt = \lambda 0\bar{q}$$

where $\bar{q}$ is the total stock of the resource. In Figure 4 the present value of the rents from the resource is given by

$$\lambda_0 [q_0 + q_1 + q_2 + \ldots q_T].$$

Note that, although λ_t will rise steadily, $\lambda_t q_t$ need not increase over time. Landlords may or may not become an impoverished class as their minerals disappear.

b. Stocks of a mineral resource may be non-homogeneous with respect to a number of characteristics—location, grade of ore, depth of deposit, etc. Differences in these characteristics affect either the price received at the mine, or the cost incurred, by firms in extracting and marketing their produce. Taken together, they may be summarized as the "quality" of the deposit.

The main consequences of non-homogeneity for rents is that the extractive industry's demand curve for rights shifts steadily inward. This is because landlords, seeking to maximize the present value of their lands, will offer high quality deposits earlier than low quality deposits (see Herfindahl and Kneese [1974, 119-32]). Consequently, the extractive industry's costs of production will increase over time. (Individual mines may increase, or may decrease, their annual rates of production; in either case their average extractive costs will rise.) Thus it can be predicted that the extractive *industry*'s average costs will increase, and this will be manifested in a steady leftward shift of the industry's demand curve for the landlords' mineral rights. In Figure 5 successive demand curves correspond to rights to extract successively higher cost resources.

The price of extractive rights now rises over time but at a rate lower than the rate of interest.[5] The stream of Ricardian rents accruing to landlords is given by

$$\lambda_0 q_0, \lambda_1 q_1, \lambda_2 q_2, \lambda_T q_T.$$

FIGURE 5

NON-HOMOGENEOUS MINERAL RIGHTS MARKET

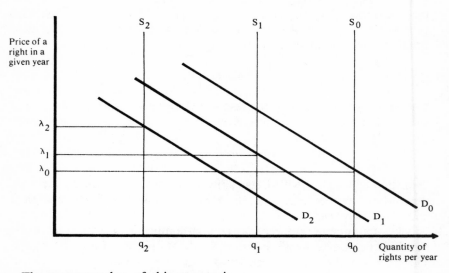

The present value of this stream is

$$_0\!\int^t \lambda(t)q(t)e^{-rt}dt.$$

If λ_t rises at a rate $(r\text{-}g)$, where r is the interest rate and g is the rate of increase in the average cost of extraction due to the decline of resource quality, the present value can be expressed as

$$_0\!\int^T \lambda_{(0)}e^{(r-g)t}q(t)e^{-rt}dt$$

which is

$$\lambda_0\,_0\!\int^T e^{-gt}q(t)\,dt.$$

If we assume that the quality of the mineral deposits sold in the initial period in the non-homogeneous case is the same as the constant quality in the homogeneous case, and also that total quantity is the same, in both cases, then initial values of λ, (λ_0) are the same in both cases. Under these circumstances, the present value of the stream of Ricardian rents would be lower than the present value of the stream of scarcity rents since, obviously,

$$_0\!\int^T e^{-gt} q(t)\, dt < \bar{q}.$$

Two important points should be noted. First, the presence of rising average costs over time now makes it even more likely than in the homogeneous case that $\lambda_t q_t$ will fall over time. For those who are familiar with Ricardian models in agriculture, where increasing scarcity leads to rising rents, this is an unfamiliar result: the working of the mineral rights market leads to increasing scarcity in terms of successively lower quantities of rights offered for sale at successively higher prices, coupled, perhaps, with decreasing annual rents.

Second, because the annual "rents" are interdependent, taxation may not be neutral. In any year, $\lambda_t q_t$ has a certain value only so long as the values of λ in earlier and later years have the same value, plus or minus an interest discount or premium. Hence, if a tax collector is not expected to take the same proportion of the rent every year, the landlord will offer his rights at times or in sequences that are not the same as when rents are uniformly taxed or untaxed. This too is unlike agricultural taxation. We return to this question in a subsequent section of the paper.

c. An advantage of the exposition so far is that by a simple extension, it can be used to analyze the impact of exploration costs on rent. In order to introduce these costs while sequestering the influence of risk and uncertainty, we begin by assuming as before that although each landlord knows the total stock of homogeneous resources to which he can sell rights, he must incur exploration expenses in order to describe to the buyer the exact location of each deposit. This assumption permits us to regard exploration costs as analogous to an agricultural landlord's development investments (e.g., road maintenance) that facilitate his tenant's use of farm land.

In the simplest case, exploration costs would be a constant sum per unit of mineral deposit offered for sale. The final effect of introducing this assumption into our model is to cause the market price of mineral rights in the initial period to rise.[6] The price paid (for mineral rights) by extractors would thereafter rise at a rate less than the rate of interest, while the price of rights (net of the fixed unit exploration cost) would rise at the interest rate as before. Corresponding to the higher initial and subsequent prices of mineral rights would be smaller annual quantities of rights marketed, and, hence, a longer optimal period of extraction.

A more realistic assumption about the nature of the exploration process is that the landlord chooses the appropriate level of exploration in each period. We can assume that fixed capacity in the exploration industry causes unit exploration costs to be an increasing function of the quantity of the resource found and marketed at any time. The market price in the initial period is now higher than the initial market price in the model without exploration costs. The market price of rights rises at a rate less than the rate of interest if the supply price of exploration services is a linear function of the quantity of rights marketed, and at an even lower rate if the supply price is an increasing function of the quantity of rights marketed. In either case the price of rights net of the supply price of exploration services rises at the interest rate. This situation is diagrammed in Figure 6. In Figure 6, D represents the demand curve for mineral rights, and SE is the supply function for exploration services. The price of rights net of the price of exploration services $(\lambda_{(t)} - S_{(t)})$ is growing at the interest rate. The annual mineral rent[7] accruing to the landlord is given by $(\lambda_{(t)} - SE_{(t)}) q(t)$.

FIGURE 6

THE MINERAL RIGHTS MARKET WITH
EXPLORATION COSTS

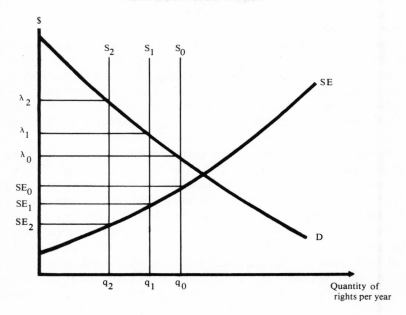

The result of the previous paragraph was obtained by reasoning that as the rate at which rights are marketed falls, the marginal exploration cost associated with marketing rights also falls. This involves assuming that resources are homogeneous with respect to finding costs and that increasing marginal finding costs are caused only by capacity limitations in the exploration industry.

We can introduce non-homogeneity by assuming that while deposits are of equal quality, as defined earlier, they are of varying size, and that larger deposits are less costly to locate than smaller deposits. Assuming for the moment that there are no capacity limitations in the exploration industry, the marginal cost of finding each unit of the industry's resource stock can be arrayed in order on a "supply curve." In Figure 7, the *SE* curve for each succeeding year is shown to be a higher segment of the "supply curve" for the stock. Since marginal finding costs are assumed to rise with cumulative resource finds, then successive time periods will be associated with higher and higher supply prices of *successful* exploration effort. As before, the rate of increase of the price of mineral rights net of marginal finding costs will be equal to the interest rate. The analyses of Figures 6 and 7 may be integrated by regarding the exploration cost function of Figure 6 as a short-run, and that of Figure 7 as a long-run cost function.

d. We may now consider the effect of a royalty. Consider first a fixed sum per unit of mineral payable at the time of extraction. The analysis follows that of a fixed unit exploration expenditure. It follows, from the argument of subsection (c), that a royalty of this type is not neutral in its effect on the market in resource rights. The imposition of a royalty upon a hitherto untaxed resource will result in a higher initial price of rights and a longer period of extraction. Since the landlord finds it profitable to alter the pattern of resource exploitation over time, it follows that, in the phraseology of the tax incidence literature, he is not bearing all of the burden of the tax. A similar result would follow from a royalty on the mineral. If, on the other hand, the resource rent tax were assessed as a constant proportion of the market value of the resource *right*, it would have no effect upon prices or the time path of exploitation. The landlord would bear all of the burden of the tax. These results are in contrast to the analysis of a tax on agricultural resource rent. Taxing rent on the basis of either acreage or value results in the landlord bearing all of the burden of the tax.

e. We now suppose that the price of minerals is determined in a foreign rather than a local market. In order to analyze this case we abandon the assumption that resource owners face a downward sloping derived

FIGURE 7

THE MINERAL RIGHTS MARKET WITH
NON-HOMOGENEOUS DEPOSITS WITH RESPECT
TO EXPLORATION COSTS

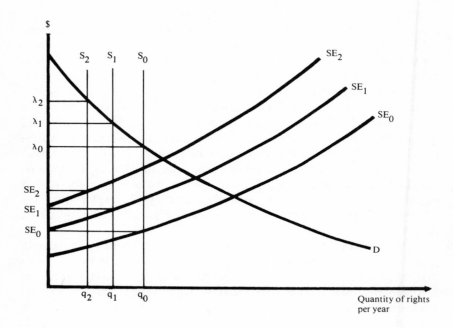

demand curve for mineral rights, and assume for the moment that the price of mineral rights is exogenously determined. This assumption might accord more closely with the Canadian situation, in which the price of rights to mineral properties is determined on world markets in minerals, and by exploration and extractive costs. If mineral deposits are assumed to be homogeneous with respect to extractive and exploration costs, and if the current price of rights and costs of exploration and extraction are expected to continue, all rights will either be sold in the initial period of the rights market, or be abandoned as worthless. If we assume that exploration is subject to increasing costs, as in part (c), this prediction no longer holds. Figure 8 illustrates the market in mineral rights with rising marginal finding costs. In Figure 8, the annual mineral rent accruing to owners of mineral resources[8] is $(\lambda - SE_{(t)})q(t)$.

FIGURE 8

THE MINERAL RIGHTS MARKET WITH
PRICE DETERMINED EXOGENOUSLY

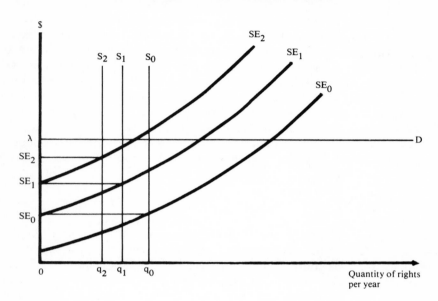

The assumption that landlords expect the current price of mineral rights to continue does not, however, accord with our observation. Canadian landowners and extractors can form expectations about diminishing annual quantities of mineral rights, $q_{(t)}$, offered for sale on a global basis, and an increasing world price of rights, $\lambda_{(t)}$, just as well as if their mineral holdings were located in the main consuming areas. Thus the results of subsections (a) to (d) still apply.

f. We now conclude our discussion of mineral rents with a few comments on the role of risk. Our analysis has been conducted on the assumption that all resource rent accrues to the sellers of rights to extract; extractive firms are assumed to earn only the market rate of return on invested capital. Risk can be introduced into the analysis by assuming that owners of mineral rights are not able to predict with certainty the outcome of exploration activity.

If the cost of discovering each mineral deposit is a random variable, then the rate of return on exploration activity is also a random variable. Assuming risk aversion on the part of investors, the cost of using capital to explore for minerals will be higher than in less risky uses. This higher cost will be reflected in the exploration cost function. If the price of mineral rights is constant as in Figure 8, the rent accruing to the resource owner is reduced as a result of the introduction of exploration risk.

The analysis of the various figures has assumed that the price of mineral rights is constant and known with certainty. While the current price of mineral rights may reasonably be supposed to be known with certainty, it is unrealistic to assume that landlords are certain as to future prices; the possibility of windfall gains or losses as a result of price fluctuations exists. In this kind of situation the resource owner might be assumed to attempt to maximize the expected present value of his holdings, or to adopt some more complicated type of strategy. A government, or governments, wishing to share in mineral rent must similarly adopt a strategy or tax structure which results in the appropriate amount of public risk-bearing.

IV. CONCLUSION

Our analysis of the question "How much mineral rent?" was based on the familiar model of the determination of the annual rent to a renewable resource, such as farm land. Into this model were introduced the variouscomplications associated with mineral rent determination, such as exhaustibility, exploration, and uncertainty. In the course of the analysis, it was suggested that the total amount of mineral rent accruing to the various resource owners might not be independent of the methods used to apportion that rent among them. It was argued, for example, that certain kinds of mineral royalty schemes, designed to effect a sharing of resource rent between private and public landlords, might reduce the total amount of rent generated in the course of exploiting the resource. A similar outcome may result from a situation of competing government claims on resource rent, such as that described in Part II of the paper, in which each claimant attempts to maximize its own resource revenues without sufficient regard to the effects of its policies on collective resource rent receipts. In such a situation the questions of "How much mineral rent?" and "For whom?" are not independent of one another.

Notes

1. See Gainer and Powrie (1975).

2. See, for instance, La Forest (1967, 150-54).

3. See Joan Robinson (1936, ch. 8).

4. It may be helpful to illustrate some points in our argument by referring to an analysis of resource rent presented by W.D. Schulze (1974). The demand curve for rights can be obtained by integrating Schulze's equation (2.16). The demand curve is $n(t)q = (\lambda(t)-\lambda(T))/P'$, where $n(t)$ is the number of extractive firms, q is the firm output which minimizes the costs of extraction, $\lambda(t)$ and $\lambda(T)$ are prices of mineral rights at time t and T, and $P' = (dP/dnq)$, the derivative of the inverse demand curve for the mineral. Setting P' equal to a constant gives the demand curve in Figure 4. Note that the output of each extractive firm is a constant, and that changes in the quantity of the mineral supplied result solely from changes in the number of firms.

5. See Schulze (1974), equation (4.19): the rate of increase in the price of mineral rights is the interest rate less the rate of increase in the average cost of production resulting from the change in the quality of the mineral resource over time.

6. This result is obtained by subtracting exploration costs ($=\beta \times (t)$, where β is unit exploration costs) from the present value of mineral rights given by equation (2.11) in Schulze (1974). The price of mineral rights at time t is now $\lambda_t = \lambda e^{Pt} + \beta$, where λ assumes a value appropriate to this particular problem. Since the rate of price increase is now less than the interest rate, and the price of resource rights in the terminal period is unaltered (because the demand curve for resource rights is unchanged), the initial price of rights must be higher, and the time lapse between the initial and terminal periods longer, to ensure resource exhaustion in the terminal period.

7. It can be seen from Figure 6 that a producer's surplus of $[SE_{(t)}q_{(t)} - {}_0\int^{q(t)}SE_{(t)}dq]$ also accrues to suppliers of exploration effort. Some of this surplus may be taxable within the jurisdiction in which exploration occurs.

8. See note 7.

References

Gainer, W.D. and T.L. Powrie, "Public Revenue from Canadian Crude Petroleum Production," *Canadian Public Policy* I, 1 (1975): 1-12.

Herfindahl, O.C. and A.V. Kneese, *Economic Theory of Natural Resources* (Columbus: Charles E. Merrill Publishing Co., 1974), pp. x, 405.

La Forest, G.V., *The Allocation of Taxing Power under the Canadian Constitution* (Toronto: Canadian Tax Foundation, 1967), p. 185.

Robinson, J., *Economics of Imperfect Competition* (London: Macmillan 1936), pp. xii, 352

Schulze, W.D., "The Optimal Use of Non-Renewable Resources: The Theory of Extraction," *Journal of Environmental Economics and Management* I (1974): 53-73.

Static Redistributive and Welfare Effects
of an Export Tax

T.L. POWRIE

I. INTRODUCTION

In many of the papers in this volume, it is assumed that the distributive
question is the sharing of tax revenue between provincial and federal
governments. In the case of crude oil, this assumption may be very
misleading. In the first place, an export tax such as that implemented by the
federal government is not simply a source of revenue. Its chief and
presumably its desired effect is to make crude cheaper to Canadian
consumers. It has other effects, however; like a subsidy, it increases
domestic consumption, and, like a royalty, it reduces the total amount of
crude discovered and produced. Thus it must also affect net imports,
revenue obtainable from other provincial and federal taxes, provincial
royalties, and foreign dividends.

The purpose of this paper is to apply a standard textbook description of
the redistributive and welfare effects of an export tax—a negative tariff—to
a numerical model that is loosely descriptive of the Canadian market for
crude oil. This standard textbook description is extended to take some
account of the effect of the tax on provincial royalties and on income taxes,
transportation costs, investment, and depletion.

Most Canadian incomes, and government revenues, fall when the export
tax revenue rises; only oil consumers benefit. However, some of the loss is
borne by foreign owners. Recognition of this transfer makes it possible to
estimate an "optimum export tax" under which, because of foreign
ownership, total national income to Canadians in all categories would be
greater than if there were no export tax. But this is not the best of all worlds.
Canadian national income would be greater still if there were no export tax
and if profits tax rates were raised to capture (among other effects) part of
the income going to foreign shareholders.

While these calculations cannot point to unique policy conclusions about
the division of taxing powers, they do illustrate more than other
calculations offered in this volume the extent of the substitutability between
consumers' welfare and the two levels of government revenue. Second, they
illustrate how revenue transfers among these parties can change total

national income to all parties. Thirdly, they suggest that the ideal division of revenue between the two forms of government must take account of the base (or form) of each government's chosen taxes. Export taxes and royalties are both shown here to be inferior to profit-related production levies and income taxes.

II. A SIMPLE NUMERICAL MODEL

The standard textbook diagram[1], but for the case of an export tax rather than a tariff, is presented in Figure 1. Domestic supply of and demand for some commodity are shown on the diagram. A perfectly elastic export demand is implied, at the world price P_w. In the absence of impediments, the world price P_w will prevail domestically, and domestic production will be Od, of which Oa is consumed domestically and ad is exported.

If an export tax of f is introduced, the domestic price is forced down to P_w-f. Production falls to Oc, domestic consumption rises to Ob, and for both reasons exports fall to bc.

Economic rent accruing to producers is reduced as a result of the export tax by the sum of areas 1, 2, 3, and 4. Of this loss to producers, area 1 represents a transfer to consumers' surplus, and area 3 represents a transfer to government revenue in the form of export tax receipts. Areas 2 and 4 are losses to producers not offset by gains to anyone else; they are deadweight losses of economic welfare. Area 2 is a loss from misallocation of consumers' budgets because consumers are buying more of the commodity than is economically efficient given the opportunity-price of P_w in the export market. Area 4 is a loss from misallocation of resources in national production because producers are producing less of this commodity than is economically efficient at its opportunity price.

Now to apply this model to a simple approximation of the Canadian market for crude oil. The first adaptation is to take account of the fact that crude oil is an exhaustible natural resource for which a conventional supply curve, which implies a continuing flow of output from renewable resources, is not appropriate. What we need is a supply curve that describes the exhaustion of a stock. The next several paragraphs give the derivation of a simple version of such a supply curve.

The supply curve required is

$$J_q = J_q(P) \tag{1}$$

where P is price and

$$J_q = q_o + q_1/(1+i) + ... + q_n/(1+i)^n \tag{2}$$

FIGURE 1

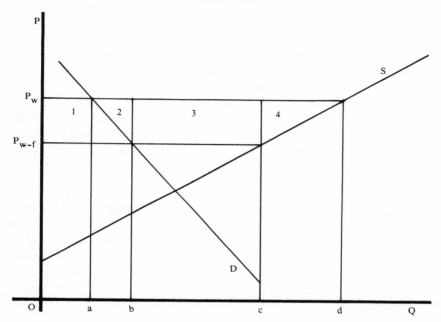

where J means "discounted present amount of" when it is prefixed to any other symbol, q means "quantity produced," i is the discount rate, and the subscripts o and n refer to years. In short, we want a supply curve relating "discounted present quantity supplied" to price.

Let the total cost of producing, that is, lifting oil in year j be

$$TCL_j = cq_j^2 \tag{3}$$

where c is a constant.

For simplicity, we assume that all exploration and discovery of proved reserves of oil occurs in year zero. The quantity discovered is Q. Let the total cost of exploration and discovery be

$$TCE = eQ^2 \tag{4}$$

where e is a constant.

The discounted present value of the oil industry is

$$JV = V_o + V_1/(1+i) + \dots + V_n/(1+i)^n \tag{5}$$

where

$$V_j = -eQ_j^2 + Pq_j - cq_j^2 \tag{6}$$

(Remember that Q_j exists only when $j = o$.)

In order to find the form of the required supply equation (1), one must find the set of solutions for Q, q_o, ..., q_n in terms of P that will maximize JV. Then substitute these solutions for q_o, ..., q_n into the expanded form of equation (1) to get the required function for Jq in terms of P.

The procedure that was used for the solution was, briefly, as follows:

First, set $\delta V_j/\delta q_j = \delta V_{j+1}/\delta q_{j+1}(1+i)$.

Second, apply the constraint that $q_o + ... + q_n = Q$.

Third, solve the $n + 1$ equations that arise from the first two steps for q_o, ..., q_n in terms of Q, P, and the various parameters.

Fourth, substitute these expressions for q_o, ..., q_n into the expanded form of equation (5). In the resulting equation, find $\delta JV/\delta Q$, set it equal to zero, and solve for Q in terms of P and other parameters.

Fifth, substitute this solution for Q into the third step solutions for q_o, ..., q_n in order to get solutions for the latter in terms of P and the parameters only.

Finally, place these solutions for q_o, ..., q_n into the expanded form of equation (1) to get the explicit form of the supply function.

In order to avoid lengthy algebra, we are using a numerical illustration of the model, in which:

$n = 9$ (which means a ten-year planning period from year 0 through year 9),

$i = 0.1$ (a 10% per year discount rate),

$c = 0.001,581,744,4$

$e = 0.000,133,201,23$.

These peculiar values for c and e were chosen because they serve to yield the following numerically simple explicit form of the supply curve:

$$J_q = 1000P \tag{7}$$

Also,

$$Q = 1349.66P \tag{8}$$

So much for the supply curve.

For comparability with this kind of supply curve, the demand curve must be expressed in terms of "discounted present quantity demanded" as a function of price, or

$$JD = D_o + D_1/(1+i) + \ldots + D_n/(1+i)^n = JD(P) \qquad (9)$$

(Note that D is domestic demand for *domestic* oil only; Dm will separately mean demand for imported oil.) To find $JD(P)$, we must first find the function for D_j. The function for D_j is constructed from the following assumptions:

—The domestic Canadian market for oil is evenly distributed along a line 2500 miles long between the oilfields of Alberta and the east coast.

—There is on every mile of that line a demand for d units ("barrels") of oil. This demand is perfectly inelastic with respect to price.

—But, although residents of each mile insist on d barrels of oil regardless of price, they will always buy the cheaper of foreign or domestic oil. Therefore, although their total demand for oil is perfectly price-inelastic, D_j, their demand for domestic oil may be highly price-elastic because of the close substitutability of imported oil.

—Foreign oil can be landed on the east coast at $P_m = \$9.50$ per barrel.

—It costs $t = \$0.0004$ per barrel per mile to transport any oil within Canada.

From these assumptions, it follows that the delivered price of foreign oil to a Canadian customer is $\$9.50 + \$0.0004m_c$, where m_c is the number of miles the customer is from the east coast. The delivered price of Alberta oil to that customer is

$$P_a + \$.0004(2500 - m_c),$$

where P_a is the Alberta wellhead price. The domestic demand for domestic oil will be zero if P_a is above $\$9.50 + \$(2500 \times .0004)$, or $\$10.50$, because all Canadians including Albertans would buy imports. As P_a falls below $\$10.50$, domestic demand for domestic oil will increase, through import displacement, until the entire Canadian market is served by domestic oil when P_a reaches $\$9.50 - \$(2500 \times .0004)$, or $\$8.50$. Equation (10) summarizes all of this:

$$D_j = d(9.50 + 2500t)/2t - dP_a/2t, \text{ max. } 2500d \qquad (10)$$

Then, with $i = 0.1$ and $n = 9$, and with D_j assumed to be the same for all j from 0 to n,

$$JD = 6.759,024D_j \qquad (11)$$

which, with $t = .0004$ and $d = .236,720,56$ gives

$$JD = 21,000 - 2,000P_a, \text{ maximum } 4,000 \tag{12}$$

Equation (12) is the requisite demand curve in terms of discounted present quantity demanded of domestic oil.

III. SUMMARY OF MODEL

Our basic model thus is:

Supply of domestic oil

$$J_q = 1000(1-r_1)P_a \tag{13}$$

where r_1 is the percentage rate of price-related royalties so $(1-r_1)P_a$ is the wellhead price net of such royalties.

Domestic demand for domestic oil

$$JD = 21,000 - 2,000P_a, \text{ max. } 4,000 \tag{12}$$

Domestic wellhead price

$$P_a = P_x - tm_x - f$$
$$= \$10 - f \tag{14}$$

where $P_x = \$10.30$ is the given price of exports at the border,

$t = \$.0004$ is transport cost per barrel per mile,

$m_x = 750$ is the number of miles from wellhead to export border point, and

f is any export tax in dollars per barrel.

Discounted present volume of imports

$$JDm = 4,000 - JD$$
$$= 2,000 P_a - 17,000 \tag{15}$$

Discounted present volume of exports

$$JDX = Jq - JD$$
$$= 3{,}000\,P_a - 1{,}000\,r_1 P_a - 21{,}000 \quad (16)$$

The solutions to this basic model are:

$$Jq = 1000(1-r_1)(10-f) \quad (17)$$

$$JD = 1000 + 2000f \quad (18)$$

$$JDm = 3000 - 2000f \quad (19)$$

$$JDx = 9000 - 3000f - 1000r_1(10-f) \quad (20)$$

A number of other variables may be considered, in extension of the basic model:

Number of miles of domestic market served by imports

$$m_m = Dm_j/d = (2500^d - D_j)/d$$

$$= 1875 - 1250f \quad (21)$$

Cost of domestic transport of imported oil

$$Tm_j = m_m(m_m+1)\,dt/2$$

$$JTm = 1125.6 - 1500.4f + 500f^2 \quad (22)$$

Number of miles of domestic market served by domestic oil

$$m_d = D_j/d$$
$$= 625 + 1250f \quad (23)$$

Cost of transport of domestic oil to domestic market

$$Td_j = m_d(m_d+1)\,dt/2$$

$$JTd = 125.6 + 500.4f + 500f^2 \quad (24)$$

Total cost of domestic transport to serve domestic market

$$T_j = Tm_j + Td_j$$

$$JT = 1250.8 - 1000f + 1000f^2 \tag{25}$$

Total cost of transport of exports from wellhead to border

$$Tx_j = 750tDx_j$$

$$JTx = 2700 - 900f - 300r_1(10-f) \tag{26}$$

Total value of exports at border

$$X_j = P_xDx_j$$

$$JX = 92,700 - 30,900f - 10,300r_1(10-f) \tag{27}$$

Total value of imports at border

$$M_j = P_mDm_j$$

$$JM = 28,500 - 19,000f \tag{28}$$

Trade balance in crude oil

$$X_j - M_j = P_xDx_j - P_mDm_j$$

$$JX - JM = 64,200 - 11,900f - 10,300r_1(10-f) \tag{29}$$

Total delivered cost of crude oil to Canadian consumers

$$S_j = P_aD_j + P_mDm_j + T_j$$

$$JS = 39,750.8 - 1000f - 1000f^2 \tag{30}$$

Total government revenue from export tax

$$F_j = fDx_j$$

$$JF = 9000f - 3000f^2 - 1000r_1f(10-f) \tag{31}$$

Total domestic wellhead revenue gross of royalties

$$W_j = P_a q_j$$

$$JW = 1000(1-r_1)(10-f)^2 \tag{32}$$

Total government revenue from price-related royalties

$$R_{1j} = r_1 W_j$$

$$JR_1 = 1000 r_1 (1-r_1)(10-f)^2 \tag{33}$$

Total cost of exploration and discovery

$$TCE = eQ^2$$

The solution for Q in our numerical model is $Q = 1349.66 P_a(1-r_1)$. Since all exploration occurs in year zero, TCE does not need to be discounted. So,

$$TCE = 242.638(10-f)^2(1-r_1)^2 \tag{34}$$

Total cost of lifting or producing oil

$$TCL_j = cq_j^2$$

In our numerical model, the set of solutions for q_j is such that

$$JTCL = 257.362(10-f)^2(1-r_1)^2 \tag{35}$$

Total government revenue from profit-related royalties

$$R_{2j} = r_2(W_j - TCE_j - TCL_j - R_{1j})$$

$$JR_2 = r_2(JW - TCE - JTCL - JR_1)$$

$$= 500 r_2 (10-f)^2(1-r_1)^2 \tag{36}$$

Note that r_2 is the royalty rate, applied to any excess of receipts over costs, with full allowance for exploration cost.

Total government revenue from corporate income tax at rate g

$$G_j = g(W_j - TCE_j - TCL_j - R_{1j} - R_{2j})$$

$$JG = 500g(1-r_2)(10-f)^2(1-r_1)^2 \qquad (37)$$

Net revenue to shareholders after costs, royalties, and taxes

$$I_j = W_j - TCE_j - TCL_j - R_{1j} - R_{2j} - G_j$$

$$JI = 500(1-g)(1-r_2)(10-f)^2(1-r_1)^2 \qquad (38)$$

Net revenue to non-resident shareholders in oil industry

$$I_{fj} = i_f I_j$$

$$JI_f = i_f JI \qquad (39)$$

Net revenue to resident shareholders

$$I_{dj} = (1-i_f) I_j$$

$$JI_d = (1-i_f) JI \qquad (40)$$

Note that i_f is the proportion of foreign ownership in the industry. We will use 0.8 as its numerical value.

IV. NUMERICAL RESULTS

Table 1 presents the solutions for this model, for the numerical example in which

$$r_1 = 0 \qquad \text{(no price-related royalty)},$$
$$r_2 = 0.5 \qquad \text{(50\% profit tax in lieu of royalty)},$$
$$g = 0.3 \qquad \text{(30\% corporate profit tax on profit after royalty)},$$
$$i_f = 0.8 \qquad \text{(80\% foreign ownership)},$$
$$f = 0 \qquad \text{(no export tax)}.$$

Total discoveries, Q, are 13,496.63 "barrels," and their production, q, is spread over the ten-year planning period but of course concentrated in earlier years. Domestic consumption of domestic oil, D, is constant from year to year, so exports, Dx, must decline as production declines. Imports, Dm,

TABLE 1

SOLUTIONS TO NUMERICAL MODEL WHEN EXPORT TAX, f, IS ZERO
(AND $r_1 = 0$, $r_2 = 0.5$, $g = 0.3$, $i_f = 0.8$)

y	J_y	Y_0	Y_1	Y_9
P_a	—	10.00	10.00	10.00
Q	13,496.63	13,496.63	—	—
q	10,000.00	2,024.49	1,910.84	481.09
D	1,000.00	147.95	147.95	147.95
Dm	3,000.00	443.85	443.85	443.85
Dx	9,000.00	1,876.54	1,762.89	333.14
m_m	—	1,875.00	1,875.00	1,875.00
Tm	1,125.60	166.53	166.53	166.53
m_d	—	625.00	625.00	625.00
Td	125.20	18.52	18.52	18.52
T	1,250.80	185.05	185.05	185.05
Tx	2,700.00	562.96	528.87	99.94
x	92,700.00	19,328.36	18,157.77	3,431.34
M	28,500.00	4,216.58	4,216.58	4,216.58
X-M	64,200.00	15,111.78	13,941.19	-785.24
S	39,750.80	5,881.13	5,881.13	5,881.13
F	0	0	0	0
W	100,000.00	20,244.94	19,108.37	4,810.88
R_1	0	0	0	0
TCE	24,263.80	24,263.80	—	—
TCL	25,736.20	6,482.90	5,775.42	366.09
R_2	25,000.00	-5,250.88	6,666.48	2,222.40
G	7,500.00	-1,575.26	1,999.94	666.72
I_f	14,000.00	-2,940.49	3,733.23	1,244.54
I_d	3,500.00	-735.12	933.31	311.14

also are constant from year to year, so the trade balance $X-M$, worsens year by year. Wellhead revenue, W, shrinks from year to year as production declines, as do the royalties R_2, taxes G, and shareholders' net revenues I_f and I_d that arise from it. (Note that royalties, taxes, and shreholders' net revenue are all negative in year 0, because the full burden of exploration costs is carried in that year, and negative net cash flows are assumed to be shared, by some fiscal device, between the private and the public sectors in the same proportions as are positive net cash flows.)

Table 2 shows the *changes* that result to the above solutions if, while other things remain constant, an export tax, f, of $0.50 is introduced.

In Table 2, because the wellhead price is reduced by the export tax, total discoveries and each year's production are all reduced, by 5 per cent in this example.

D, domestic consumption of domestic oil, is doubled by the effects of the export tax. The tax, by reducing the domestic wellhead price, makes

TABLE 2

CHANGES IN SOLUTION TO NUMERICAL MODEL WHEN EXPORT TAX
OF $0.50 IS INTRODUCED (AND $r_1 = 0$, $r_2 = 0.5$, g @ 0.3, $i_f = 0.8$)

y	J_y	Y_0	Y_1	Y_9
P_a	—	-0.50	0.50	-0.50
Q	-674.83	-674.83	—	—
q	-500.00	-101.22	-95.54	-24.05
D	+1,000.00	+147.95	+147.95	+147.95
Dm	-1,000.00	-147.95	-147.95	-147.95
Dx	-1,500.00	-249.18	-243.49	-172.00
m_m	—	-625.00	-625.00	-625.00
Tm	-625.20	-92.50	-92.50	-92.50
m_d	—	+625.00	+625.00	+625.00
Td	+375.20	+55.51	+55.51	+55.51
T	-250.00	-36.99	-36.99	-36.99
Tx	-450.00	-124.59	-73.05	-51.60
X	-15,450.00	-2,566.50	-2,507.96	-1,771.65
M	-9,500.00	-1,405.53	-1,405.53	-1,405.53
X-M	-5,950.00	-1,160.97	-1,102.43	-366.12
S	-750.00	-110.96	-110.96	-110.96
F	+3,750.00	+813.68	+759.70	+80.57
W	-9,750.00	-1,973.92	-1,863.04	-469.04
R_1	0	0	0	0
TCE	-2,365.72	-2,365.72	—	—
TCL	-2,509.28	-632.08	-563.10	-35.70
R_2	-2,437.50	+511.94	-649.97	-216.67
G	-731.25	+153.58	-194.99	-65.00
I_f	-1,365.00	+286.69	-363.98	-121.34
I_d	-341.25	+71.67	91.00	-30.33

domestic oil displace imports along an additional 625 miles of the domestic market. Imports, *Dm*, are correspondingly reduced. Exports, *Dx*, are reduced both because domestic production is smaller and because more of it is used domestically.

T, total transport cost to service the domestic market, is reduced, indeed, minimized, by the effects of the $0.50 export tax. Imported and domestic oil now meet exactly half-way along the line between the east coast and the Alberta wellhead, and that arrangement minimizes transport cost given our assumption that the market is evenly distributed along that line.

With exports reduced more than are imports as a result of the export tax, the value of the trade balance on oil, *X-M*, is reduced.

S, the total delivered cost of oil to Canadian consumers, is reduced both because the wellhead price of domestic oil is reduced and because total transport cost is lowered. Export tax revenue, *F*, appears, but in diminishing amounts as exports shrink from year to year.

Wellhead revenue is reduced, and this reduction is shared in our assumed proportions among costs, royalties, taxes, and shareholders' net revenue.

V. AN OPTIMAL EXPORT TAX

So, Table 2 compared with Table 1 indicates various effects, in our model of an export tax. One may also use the model to deal with the question, "What is the optimal level of an export tax, if the objective is to maximize national income?"

The presence of foreign ownership in this model makes it possible that the deadweight losses of economic welfare caused by an export tax may be more than offset by transfers, also caused by the export tax, from foreign shareholders to domestic beneficiaries. The adaptation of the ideas in Figure 1 to contain this possibility may be set out as follows:

In Figure 1:

> Loss of producer's surplus = sum of areas 1, 2, 3, 4.
> Gains to other sectors = areas 1 + 3
> Net loss = areas 2 + 4

In present analysis:

> Loss of producer's surplus = sum of areas 1, 2, 3, 4.
> = (loss to domestic incomes) +
> (loss to foreign incomes)
> = (loss of $JR + JG + JI_d$) + (loss of JI_f)
>
> Gains to other sectors = areas 1 + 3
> = (saving to Canadian consumers) +
> (export tax receipts)

> Net gain or loss to national income = (saving to Canadian
> consumers) + (export
> tax receipts) − (loss
> of $JR + JG + JI_d$) = ΔY

So, algebraically, our question is, what level of f would maximize ΔY? Algebraically, we seek the value of f that will maximize the value of

$$J[(S_o - S_f) + F - (R_0 - R_f) - (G_0 - G_f) - (I_{do} - I_{df})]$$

where S is delivered cost of oil to Canadian consumers

F is export tax revenue
R is royalty revenue
G is government revenue from corporate income tax

I_d is net income to resident shareholders in the oil industry, and the subscripts 0 and f mean without or with export tax.

The optimal level of f, in this context, turns out to be:

$$\frac{10(1-r_1)[i_f(1-g)(1-r_1)(1-r_2) - r_1]}{4 - 2r_1 + (1-r_1)[i_f(1-g)(1-r_1)(1-r_2) - r_1 - 1]}$$

If $i_f = 0$, that is if there is no foreign ownership, the optimal value of f is zero if r_1 equals zero, r_1 being the percentage rate of royalty applied to the wellhead value of production.

If $i_f = 0$, and r_1 is positive but less than one, the optimal value of f is negative. That is (as an example of the "theory of the second best"), an export subsidy would tend to offset some of the adverse effects of a price-related royalty system.

If foreign ownership is present, then the optimal f will be positive if (from the numerator of the formula)

$$i_f(1-g)(1-r_1)(1-r_2) > r_1$$

$$i_f > r_1/(1-g)(1-r_1)(1-r_2).$$

This condition would be met whenever $r_1 = 0$ and $i_f < 0$. In the case where $r_1 = 0$, $r_2 = 0.5$, $g = 0.3$, and $i_f = 0.8$, optimal f is \$0.85366 per barrel. With this level of f, the gain to Canadian real national income is, compared with the situation where $f = 0$:

	$JS_o - JS_f$	(area 1 of Figure 1)	= \$1,582.39
plus	JF	(area 3)	= 5,496.73
less	$JR_o - JR_f$		= -4,086.11
less	$JG_o - JG_f$		= -1,225.83
less	$JI_{do} - JI_{df}$		= -572.06
	Total, ΔY		= + \$1,195.12

This gain comes from the portion of the transfer from the income of foreign shareholders that is not offset by deadweight losses from the export tax:

$I_{fo} - I_{ff}$	$= \$2,288.22$
less misallocation of consumption (area 2)	$= -\ \ 728.73$
less misallocation of production (area 4)	$= -\ \ 364.37$
Total	$\$1,195.12$

Note that "misallocation of consumption" here means too much domestic consumption of domestic oil instead of imports. The optimal export tax causes domestic oil to serve an additional 1,067 miles of the domestic market, or an additional 1,707 barrels of "discounted present quantity." Total transport cost of imported and domestic oil to Canadians is actually reduced as a result, by \$124.93. But this saving is outweighed by a loss of \$853.66 involved in sacrificing 1,707 barrels of discounted present exports, worth \$9.50 per barrel. The net loss is \$728.73 or area 2.

VI. CONCLUDING COMPARISONS

An optimum export tax is not, of course, a first-best way to maximize national income. Either a higher rate of profit-related royalties r_2 , or a higher rate of corporate profit tax g, would achieve the transfer from foreign shareholders without the adverse side-effects of an export tax. Since profit-related royalties and corporate profit tax are equally efficient instruments in this sense, and since the federal and provincial governments in Canada both have access to at least one of these instruments, one cannot argue to exclude either level of government from this revenue source on the grounds that it lacks the authority to exploit it efficiently.

The question of how this revenue should be divided among levels of government could be primarily a question of equity among regions, not one of economic efficiency. At present, of course, both levels of government are using inefficient instruments: the province, price-related royalties r_1; and the federal government, an export tax f.

In conclusion, one must be explicit about a limitation of the present model. The price of oil in the model is given, determined in the export market. Therefore there must be exports in every year of the planning period in order for the export market to fulfill its role in price determination. A somewhat more complicated version of the model would be required to cover the possibility that exports may cease and that the domestic wellhead price would then be determined by other forces.

Notes

* I wish to acknowledge indebtedness to Frank Roseman for showing me the ideas of a supply of "discounted quantity" and of a demand deriving its price elasticity entirely from spatial competition and transport costs.

1. See, for example, Caves and Jones, *World Trade and Payments* (Boston: Little, Brown 1973), p. 274.

Taxes, Royalties, and Equity Participation as Alternative Methods of Dividing Resource Revenues: The Syncrude Example

JOHN HELLIWELL

GERRY MAY

I. INTRODUCTION

Some of the papers for this conference deal with the rights and wrongs of competing federal and provincial taxation and royalty claims on resource revenues. In this paper we shall take a different tack and shall compare various tax and royalty arrangements with the use of direct equity investment as a means of spreading the risks and returns from resource development among the three main types of participants—the federal government, provincial governments, and private producers. The obvious example to use as a basis for our study is Syncrude, the $2 billion Athabaska oil sands mine and processing plant in which the federal government, the Alberta government, and the Ontario government have recently become, respectively, 15 per cent, 10 per cent, and 5 per cent equity shareholders by means of initial capital commitments totalling $600 million.

Although the Syncrude project will be the main focus of our attention, we hope to use it to illustrate some issues of more general application. In Section II we shall lay some theoretical groundwork by interpreting the choice of resource revenue sharing arrangements as a problem in the economic theory of principal and agent, complicated by the existence of two principals (the two levels of government with overlapping claims on the resource base), each of which is inclined to take a fling as agent, and a variety of agents who are used to acting as principals in Canada and other countries. This framework is helpful in forcing us to focus on the role of various revenue sharing arrangements as a means of spreading risky outcomes, rather than known returns, among the participants.

In Section III, we shall briefly outline the history and nature of the Syncrude project and describe our modelling of alternative tax, royalty, and equity participation schemes. We shall concentrate on three basic alternative schemes plus a fourth combination involving various options

open to Alberta under the Syncrude arrangement. The three basic schemes
are represented by, first, a simple application of the Syncrude arrangements
developed in January 1975; second, a system comparable to that used for
the first oil sands mine and plant (GCOS), based on a single private
enterprise corporation subject to the corporation income tax and a non-
deductible gross royalty to Alberta, and, third, a more hypothetical system
involving private enterprise plus a net royalty coming into effect only when
the private participants have an accumulated surplus of revenues over costs.
The fourth combination extends the basic analysis of the Syncrude
arrangement by taking account of Alberta's options to take over a larger
equity interest, or to opt for a gross instead of a net royalty.

Section IV contains the main empirical results of our research, presented
in such a way as to focus on the effects of alternative values of the five
major factors influencing the size and distribution of the financial costs and
benefits of Syncrude or any future synthetic oil project—the relative price
of crude oil, operating costs, capital costs, interest rates (those paid to raise
capital and those used to find the present value of future revenues), and the
general rate of inflation. Changes in the first four factors affect the total
amount and the distribution of net revenues from the project, while
different rates of general inflation, accompanied by equivalent changes in
the project's costs and revenues, affect only the distribution of revenues
among the participants.

We focus on the effects of five different types of uncertainty, in the
context of three different systems of revenue sharing, to emphasize that the
consequences of uncertainty depend not only on the type of risk-sharing
arrangement but also on what one is uncertain about.

In Section V we discuss the changes in the June 1975 federal budget,
outline the limitations of our analysis, and reveal our tentative conclusions,
especially with regard to future oil sands developments and the allocation of
resource revenues and taxing powers between levels of government.

II. PRINCIPALS AND AGENTS IN RESOURCE DEVELOPMENT

The relationship between principal and agent has recently been used (e.g.,
by Ross [1973, 1974]) to illustrate some of the problems involved in the
design of payment schemes that will lead the agent to act in the principal's
interest even though he has different objectives and may have quite
different attitudes towards risk. In applying the same concept to the
relationship between the patient and his medical advisors, Feldstein (1974)
has characterized an agency relationship as an "incomplete" one if the
available payment schemes are not able, whether in principle or in
application, to fully align the agent's interests with those of his principal. In

a paper prepared for the conference on mineral leasing, Helliwell (1974) described the problems inherent in finding any payment scheme that obtains full resource value for the principal while retaining adequate incentives for efficient management by the agent. The problems are especially acute when the potential agents have more expertise than the principal, and where distribution of possible outcomes is known by neither principal nor agent, yet is to some extent under the control of the agent. Under these circumstances, it seems clear that the relationships between resource owning governments and producing firms will be incomplete agency relationships.

Under certain rather restrictive conditions, it is possible to characterize a fee schedule that will cause an agent to make resource allocation decisions just as the principal would have done. In general, this requires giving both parties a stake in the outcome. The problem for the principal is to find a fee schedule that gets the greatest net benefit for the principal consistent with the need to motivate the agent, taking into account the risk preferences of both parties. Even if the principal and agent had the same knowledge about the resources and risks provided by nature, the agent's desire for payment will in general mean that the fee schedule preferred by the principal will involve some trade-off between the agent's preferences and his fee. In short, if potential resource revenues must be paid to make the actions of private developers line up with the interests of the resource owners, then it will usually be in the resource owners' interest to seek some compromise between maximum expected net revenue and maximum alignment of the agent's actions with the preferences of the principal.

In the context of Canadian resource revenues, the issues are further complicated by the existence of two principals, each with a different stake in resource revenues and each with some power to alter the fees paid to the developing firms. The two levels of government represent different populations, so that there is no reason to expect their interests to coincide exactly even aside from the relevant mass of political, psychological, and bureaucratic factors. If it is not possible to decide which of the two levels of government is *the* principal with the ultimate responsibility for setting the fee schedule, then there could be no single solution to the principal's problem of choosing the most appropriate form of agency relationship.

In his 1974 paper, Helliwell argued, largely on constitutional grounds, that this indeterminacy should be resolved by treating the provincial governments as the principals, with the tax claims of the federal government being neutral as between industries, thus interfering as little as possible with the design by the provinces of appropriate tax and royalty arrangements. This solution was to be made consistent with national redistribution goals by means of a revamped equalization payments system based more directly on all provincial revenues and needs. These issues are more thoroughly covered this year by several other papers, and we shall say no more about them.

In the present paper, we are less concerned with the design of appropriate revenue sharing arrangements than with an assessment of how some key alternative schemes work in practice to allocate gains and losses among the participants.

III. SYNCRUDE

By concentrating our attention on Syncrude, we ignore the problems involved in exploring for and delineating a mineral deposit. However, the high degree of uncertainty surrounding the costs and revenues involved in applying known techniques to the extraction and processing of firmly established oil sands deposits illustrates that in some cases it may be almost as dangerous to ignore uncertainty at the production stage as at the exploration stage. In this section, we shall briefly outline the history of the Syncrude project, and describe the three revenue sharing arrangements whose effects we shall report in section IV.

The first commercial scale plant to obtain oil from the Athabaska oil sands was Great Canadian Oil Sands, completed in 1967 for a capital cost of about $260 million, or about $5,800 per barrel-day for its initial design capacity of 45,000 barrels per day (Govier, 1973, p. 64). By 1972, output was up to 50,000 barrels per day, and costs were reported as $3.36 per barrel.[1] Syncrude, the second plant in the Athabaska oil sands, is planned to commence production in 1978, and to reach its design capacity of 129,000 barrels per day in 1985 (Foster 1975, p. 1). In 1973, the capital costs of the Syncrude project were estimated to accumulate to $960 million by 1978, with total production costs amounting to $5 per barrel in terms of 1972 dollars.[2]

However, in December 1974, Atlantic Richfield abandoned its 30 per cent interest in the project, and news reports were circulated to the effect that the estimated total of capital expenditures had risen to over $2 billion, or $16,000 per barrel-day. The remaining participants stated that the entire project would be dropped unless an additional $1 billion were obtained from government or other sources by the end of January 1975. Government requests managed to extend the deadline for a few days, but the terms of the new arrangement were nevertheless worked out in great haste and agreed to at a meeting in Winnipeg on 3 February 1975. Under the new agreement, the remaining non-defaulting partners would retain their 70 per cent equity interest in the project by putting up $400 million of the additional $1 billion, obtaining $200 million of that amount by debenture loan from the province of Alberta. The 15 per cent, 10 per cent, and 5 per cent equity interests of the federal, Alberta, and Ontario governments involve corresponding percentage commitments to the total costs of the project.[3]

The available information does not permit us to disentangle the various causes of the doubling of the estimated Syncrude costs between 1973 and 1974. In evaluating the future role of the oil sands, it is important to know whether there has been a doubling forever in the real costs of mining and processing synthetic oil from the Athabaska sands rather than bad luck or bad management specific to the Syncrude project. Even allowing for a possible doubling of construction costs between the mid-1960's and the mid-1970's the $16,000 per barrel-day capital cost of Syncrude is almost twice the 1970's equivalent of the corresponding cost for the GCOS plant. Our way of reacting to uncertainty about the nature of the Syncrude cost increase is to treat the real costs of constructing and operating the plant as uncertain variables.

The other variables we treat as uncertain are the world price of oil, the rate of social time preference (and the opportunity cost of funds), and the general rate of inflation. We have performed some mixed experiments to test for interactions among the effects of the different risks, but our general procedure has been to assess the effects of each risk separately.

The most important elements in our model of the Syncrude project are the "rent equations" which allocate the costs and benefits of the project among the main participants. We have prepared separate sets of rent equations for three main "simple" tax, royalty, and equity participation systems and have also assessed the more complicated mixed options open to the Alberta government under the Syncrude arrangements.

Even the three main sets of rent equations are not as simple as one might wish. The first set relates to the simplest version of the Syncrude deal, in which the private participants maintain their 70 per cent equity interest and the federal, Alberta, and Ontario governments maintain their 15 per cent, 10 per cent, and 5 per cent interests. In addition, the Alberta government collects a 50 per cent "profit share" of total revenues net of operating costs, depreciation and 6 per cent of the book value of total capital employed. The federal government collects a 25 per cent corporation tax and Alberta an 11 per cent corporation tax, in both cases levied only on the private participants' share of profits. Taxable income is defined net of the profit sharing royalty payments to the Alberta government, an arrangement reached prior to the 1974 federal budgets and reaffirmed by the federal Minister of Finance in December 1974.

The second set of rent equations reflects the tax and royalty arrangements applicable to Great Canadian Oil Sands, the first operating oil sands mine and plant. The equations involve a two-part gross royalty with a marginal rate of 20 per cent, no equity participation by governments, and non-deductibility of royalty payments when determining the federal corporation income tax base. In addition, the enterprise is designated "non-consortium" because it is assumed to be taxed as a separate corporation rather than as a consortium or joint venture. Under the Syncrude consortium arrangements, capital cost allowances and pre-production expenses may be written off against other taxable income of the participating corporations. Thus the consortium or joint venture arrangement reduces the present value of tax payments by making tax deductions available sooner, to the extent that members of the consortium are themselves in taxable positions.

The third set of tax and royalty arrangements is based on a private enterprise consortium and the federal and provincial rates of corporation income tax applicable in early 1975. It includes an Alberta royalty that comes into play only after the accumulated net revenues to the private participants become positive, but is thereafter levied at a high rate (80 per cent) and is deductible from the federal and provincial bases for the corporation income tax. The resulting set of rent equations differs from the first two sets in that it represents an alternative to existing methods of sharing resource revenues. By being based on revenues net of all costs, it represents an attempt to find an "agents' fee schedule" that removes the gross royalty's discrimination against marginal projects. By making full and equal allowance for capital and operating costs, it should spread the various types of risk among the principals and agents in a more evenhanded way than do the two sets of existing tax and royalty arrangements.

Our final experiments indicate the consequences for revenue sharing of the three main future options to the Alberta government under the Syncrude arrangement:

a. The $200 million debenture loan from Alberta to Cities Service and Gulf Canada is convertible into a 10 per cent equity interest.
b. The provincially owned Alberta Energy Company has an option to acquire 20 per cent of the total equity of the joint venture, exercisable at cost when the plant comes into production.
c. In the fifth year of production, the Alberta government has the option of switching, once-and-for-all, from the 50 per cent profit-sharing royalty to a 7½ per cent gross royalty.

These options obviously increase the expected value and decrease the riskiness of Alberta's share of net revenues. In general, if costs are low or revenues high, Alberta will be likely to take up options a and b, while if costs are very high in relation to revenues option c will be chosen. Over some intermediate range of profitability, Alberta may choose not to exercise any of the options. We have modelled Alberta's decision process on the assumption that the major cost and revenue uncertainties will be settled by the time the equity and royalty options must be exercised or abandoned and that Alberta will choose at that time the option with the highest expected net present value. To the extent that all uncertainties will not be settled by those dates (when production commences, for the equity interest, and five years thereafter, for the gross royalty option), this method of analysis may overstate the value of Alberta's options.

For all of the four sets of economic rent equations assessed, we use dynamic simulations of the whole model to accumulate the year-by-year flows of costs and revenues accruing to each of the participants over the lifetime of the project. At the end of the project's 25-year operating life, the accumulated future values of net costs or benefits are discounted back to obtain present values, as at the beginning of 1975, measured in terms of end-1974 prices. The main output from each simulation is thus a set of present values, one for each participant under each of the revenue sharing systems modelled. Some of the results are shown in Figures 1 to 4, and are described in the next section. The underlying equations and data are reported fully in Helliwell and May (1975).

IV. DISTRIBUTION OF SYNCRUDE COSTS, REVENUES, AND RISKS

The five figures and two tables in this section show how the distribution of costs and benefits depends on some key variables whose values cannot be easily forecast. Figures 1 and 2 both have four segments, each showing the distribution under one of the four revenue sharing régimes analyzed. We shall discuss the figures separately and then make a combined assessment at the end of the section. We shall consider first the effects of crude oil price, then proceeding to deal with capital and operating costs, the general rate of inflation, and the interest rates used to charge an opportunity cost for capital and to discount future net flows to obtain present values.

When we calculate the net present values using various assumptions about the price of crude oil, or some other factor, we assume so-called "base case" values for all of the other co-efficients and variables in the model. The base case values are generally drawn from the Foster (1975) economic study prepared for the Alberta government, or are based on some historical averages, as with the real pre- and post-tax returns on capital.

IV.1 Syncrude under Alternative Oil Prices

The results in Figure 1 show the net present value of the Syncrude project, in total and to each of the participants, under four royalty régimes. In Figure 1A, for example, the horizontal axis shows various plant-gate prices for synthetic oil, in terms of end-1974 dollars, and the vertical axis shows the net present value of the project, at the end of 1974, in millions of end-1974 dollars. We represent an entire vector of future oil prices as a single number by assuming that the relative price of oil will be set at some value by the time Syncrude comes into operation in 1978, and will thereafter rise at the general rate of inflation. The prices are per 35-gallon barrel of synthetic oil at the plant gate. A Toronto price can be obtained by adding about .25 1974$ for transportation to Edmonton and another .60 1974$ for transportation to Toronto.

In Figure 1 we represent the various oil prices in terms of end-1974 dollars, which are then converted into future nominal oil prices, within the simulation runs, by escalation at the general rate of inflation, which is assumed in our base case to be 4 per cent per annum.

There are five curves plotted in Figure 1A. Curves 1 through 4 show the present value of net rents accruing to the federal government, the Alberta government, the private producers, and the Ontario government, respectively. Curve 5 shows the total economic rents accruing to the project as a whole. It is thus the sum of the amounts measured by curves 1 through 4. The net benefits of the project as a whole take account of the direct operating costs and the before-tax opportunity cost of the capital employed and are therefore independent of the tax and royalty structure. Thus it is not necessary to draw the curve for total net benefits in each part of Figure 1, because, for any oil price, the net costs or benefits from the project as a whole are unaffected by the changes in the patterns of ownership, taxation, or royalties.

Curve 5 in Figure 1A shows, quite naturally, that total rents are large and negative at low oil prices, pass through the break-even point at a plant-gate price just over $12 per barrel, and become increasingly positive at higher prices. Landed in Montreal by pipeline, synthetic oil would thus cost more than $13 per barrel in terms of end-1974 dollars. This is substantially more than the mid-1975 spot price for imported oil, and slightly more than the mid-1975 subsidized cost of Middle East oil landed at Montreal on long-term shipping contracts. 1975 world prices have been regarded by many analysts as being likely to fall in real terms in the future. For example, the three oil prices used in the U.S. Federal Energy Administration's analysis of Project Independence are $4, $7, and $11 in terms of constant 1973 U.S. dollars. The Foster estimates of plant-gate prices used in our base case start at $13.70 in 1979, or 10.85 in 1974$. If 1975 spot foreign crude oil prices were indexed to rise, in terms of Canadian dollars, with the general rate of inflation, Syncrude oil would cost about $1 per barrel more than foreign crude, assuming no Alberta royalty. The O.P.E.C. price increases hinted in mid-1975 for application in late 1975 or in 1976 have been specifically related to prior changes in the prices of O.P.E.C. imports, which over the longer term are likely to increase at the general rate of inflation. As will be shown later in the section, this conclusion depends heavily on the cost assumptions, including the "required" rate of return on capital. Our base case estimates utilize the Foster (1975) cost data and assume a real rate of return on capital (after royalties and corporation income tax) of 7.44 per cent and a corporation tax return of 3 per cent on capital. Both of these are based on historic economy-wide averages.

Curves 1 through 4 in Figure 1A show that the basic Syncrude arrangements provide positive net benefits to Alberta at any 1974$ oil price above $9.00, while the private producers have a "break-even" price of about $12 at the plant gate, and the federal and Ontario governments have a negative net return at any of the oil prices assessed. Using the Foster estimates for oil prices, and the rest of our base case assumptions, gives negative net benefits of about 450 million 1974 dollars for the project as a whole. Within this total, the Alberta government receives positive benefits of $350 million, with offsetting negative present values of $705 million, $60 million, and $35 million for the federal government, the private producers, and the Ontario government, respectively.

Referring to part B of Figure 1, we can see that the GCOS tax and royalty arrangements are in general much less favourable to the producers than are the Syncrude arrangements. Table 1 contains results from five simulations designed to show the relative importance of the four main differences between the GCOS and Syncrude arrangements. The left-hand column shows the Syncrude base case rents, the right-hand column shows the GCOS results, and the move from left to right across the intervening columns shows the effects of sequentially removing the main Syncrude advantages. The second column shows the effect of applying the GCOS royalty schedule instead of the Syncrude profit-sharing royalty, with all other provisions unchanged. Using the base case prices, total rents to each party are almost unchanged. However, it will be shown later that the gross royalty, relative to the profit-sharing royalty, shifts more of the revenue uncertainty, and much more of the cost uncertainty, from the Alberta government to the private producers. In the middle column of Table 1 the government equity positions are removed, causing a slight improvement in Alberta's position at the expense of the federal government and the private producers.

The fourth column of Table 1 shows the very large consequences of altering the tax treatment from a consortium to a non-consortium basis. This leads to a substantial delay of tax writeoffs, thus subtracting more than $600 million from the present value of rents accruing to the private producers; over two-thirds of the $600 million accrues to the federal government. The right-hand column shows the effects of moving from a

TABLE 1

SYNCRUDE VERSUS GCOS ARRANGEMENTS RENTS UNDER ALTERNATIVE
REVENUE SHARING SCHEMES (1974 $MILLION)

	Syncrude Base-Case	Syncrude GCOS Royalty Deductible	Private Enterprise Consortium GCOS Royalty Deductible	Private Enterprise Separate Corporation GCOS Royalty Deductible	Private Enterprise Separate Corporation GCOS Royalty Deductible
Federal	-706.4	-711.5	-727.5	-264.8	-193.4
Alberta	+346.8	+359.6	+367.1	+570.8	+570.8
Ontario	-36.7	-37.5	–	–	–
Private	-60.7	-67.6	-96.6	-763.0	-834.4
Totals			457.0		

deductible royalty to one that is deductible only from the provincial income tax base. This causes a shift of about $70 million, in terms of present values, from the producers to the federal government. We have now completed the transition from the Syncrude system to the GCOS system, so that the figures in the right-hand column correspond to those pictured in part B of Figure 1, for the base case oil price of $10.85 in terms of end-1974 dollars. The average tax and royalty rate is much higher in the GCOS system, giving rise to a "break-even" oil price, from the point of view of the producers, of about $15 per barrel, based on the Foster (1975) cost estimates for Syncrude.

By comparing parts B, C, and D of Figure 1 we can see the effects of the different tax and royalty systems. The most important features to note are the relative slopes of the lines in the four segments of Figure 1, as they indicate the manner in which oil price risks are shared among the participants. The relative heights of the curves in parts B and C may be less important than the slopes, as the illustrative 80 per cent "surplus sharing" royalty rate has no special basis in fact. Compared to the basic Syncrude arrangement, a private enterprise development with a gross royalty would shift more of the oil price risk to the firms, as illustrated by curve 3 being steeper than curve 2 in Figure 1B, while it is flatter in Figure 1A. The increasing steepness at the left-hand end of curve 3 in Figure 1B can be traced to the non-consortium feature of the second set of rent equations, as the deferral of tax write-offs becomes especially great when oil prices and hence revenues are low.

The "surplus sharing" royalty, by allowing a full return on capital before any royalty is charged, lowers the break-even price from the point of view of the private producers. However, there is no negative royalty if costs are not covered, so that curve 3 (showing the private producers' returns) in Figure 1C is very steep at oil prices below about $9. At low prices, the equity participation by governments in Figure 1A shares the losses, making curve 3 flatter relative to curves 1 and 2 in Figure 1A than in Figure 1C.

Finally, in Figure 1D we return to the actual Syncrude arrangements again, showing the effects of Alberta exercising its option to increase its equity interest from 20 per cent to 36 per cent (on top of the 50 per cent profit-sharing royalty) at high oil prices or to shift to a gross royalty at low oil prices. By comparing Figure 1D with Figure 1A, we see that the basic Syncrude arrangement is likely to be chosen by Alberta if oil prices are between about $9 and $14, with the 7½ per cent gross royalty chosen for lower prices and the increased equity for higher prices. The effect of the twin options is to increase Alberta's share of any large positive rents while decreasing its share of large losses. Given uncertainty about oil prices, these options increase the expected value of the Syncrude arrangements for Alberta, and lower them for the other parties. These net changes cannot be

164

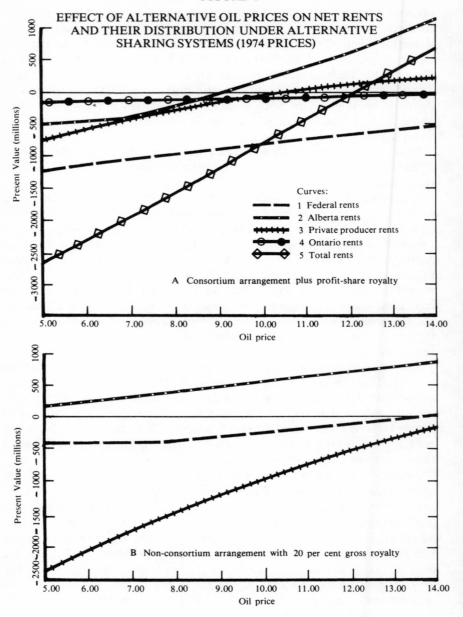

FIGURE 1

EFFECT OF ALTERNATIVE OIL PRICES ON NET RENTS
AND THEIR DISTRIBUTION UNDER ALTERNATIVE
SHARING SYSTEMS (1974 PRICES)

Curves:

1 Federal rents
2 Alberta rents
3 Private producer rents
4 Ontario rents
5 Total rents

A   Consortium arrangement plus profit-share royalty

B   Non-consortium arrangement with 20 per cent gross royalty

FIGURE 1

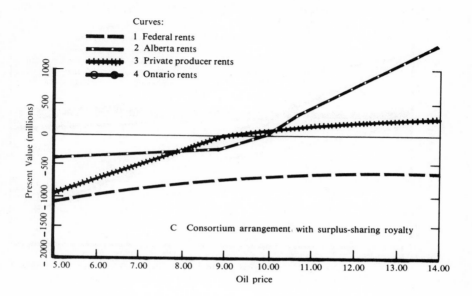

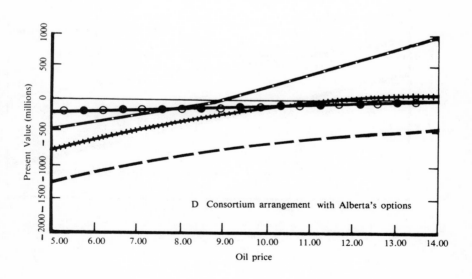

FIGURE 2

EFFECTS OF ALTERNATE CAPITAL COSTS
ON TOTAL NET RENTS AND THEIR
DISTRIBUTION UNDER ALTERNATE SHARING SYSTEMS (1974 PRICES)

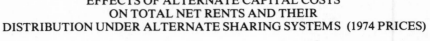

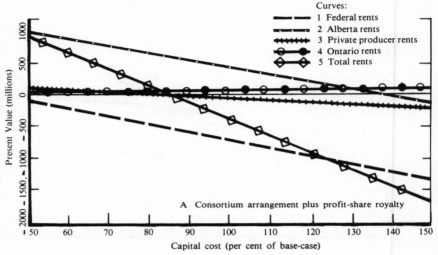

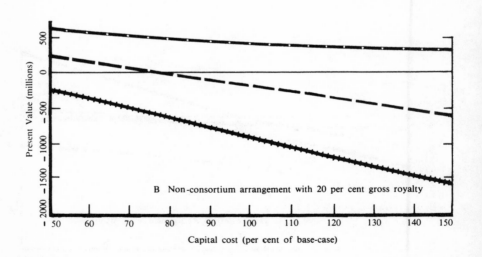

FIGURE 2

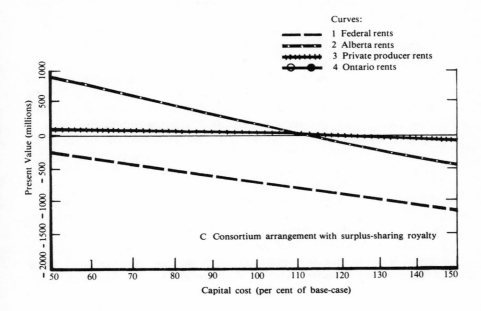

C Consortium arrangement with surplus-sharing royalty

Capital cost (per cent of base-case)

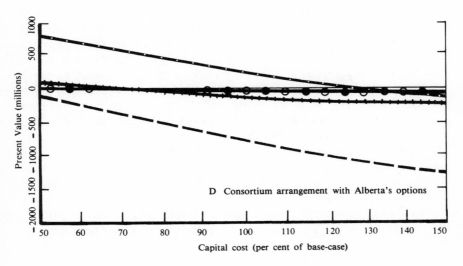

D Consortium arrangement with Alberta's options

Capital cost (per cent of base-case)

quantified without reference to a specific probability distribution of future oil prices. In the absence of that, we pass on to consider the impact of varying costs of development.

IV.2 The Effects of Uncertain Costs

In the context of a project whose anticipated real costs nearly doubled over the course of a year, it is scarcely necessary to state that there is a substantial amount of cost uncertainty to be shared among the participants. The four parts of Figure 2 show the effects of altering capital costs, in real terms, over a range between 50 per cent and 150 per cent of the costs estimated for Syncrude at the end of 1974. The various parts of Figure 2 reveal once again the key differences among the four revenue sharing arrangements, but there are some differences brought about by the fact that capital costs are only partially allowed for in the computation of the bases for the corporation income tax and the Syncrude profit sharing royalty, while no costs at all are allowed against the gross royalty. Thus the gross royalty system, which involved the least risk for Alberta under oil price variation, involves Alberta in even less risk if the risk relates to costs rather than revenues. At the other extreme, the "surplus sharing" royalty, which allows all costs to be set against the royalty base, shows a pattern of returns in Figure 2C similar to that in 1C.

The fourth part of Figure 2 shows that Alberta would not alter the basic Syncrude arrangements over most of the tested range of capital costs, only obtaining a higher present value from the expanded equity option at capital costs down about half of those presently estimated. Simulations run with variations in both capital and operating costs indicated a switch to higher equity at costs about 15 per cent below the current estimates, or a switch to the gross royalty at costs about 30 per cent abouve those currently forecast.

Another potentially useful way of assessing the impact on Syncrude of variable\$ costs is to chart the total per barrel costs, in terms of 1974\$, after allowing for a pre-tax real cost of capital of just over 10 per cent and a real social time preference rate of 7.44 per cent, but no royalties of any kind. These costs, which also measure the "break-even" oil price for the project as a whole, are shown in Figure 3. Curve 1 shows the effects of varying capital and operating costs, while curve 2 shows the impact of altering the capital costs alone. The capital and operating costs in both cases are measured as proportions of the base case costs.

IV.3 The Effects of General Inflation

The way we have modelled general inflation, it is very general indeed. In sections IV.1 and IV.2 we considered the effects of once-and-for-all changes

FIGURE 3

EFFECT OF VARYING COST ON
SYNCRUDE BREAK-EVEN PRICE (1974 PRICES)

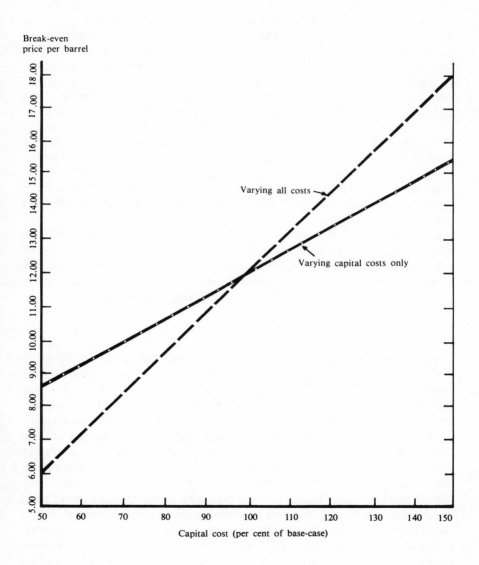

Break-even
price per barrel

Varying all costs

Varying capital costs only

Capital cost (per cent of base-case)

in oil prices or project costs, in each case relative to a general price level growing at 4 per cent per year. In this section, we hold relative prices unchanged and vary the trend rate of growth of all prices, making a corresponding adjustment to all nominal interest rates. In the equations underlying our estimation of economic costs, we have measured all our capital stocks, depreciation, and so on, so that they are unaffected by anticipated changes in the general price level. Thus when we graph the net benefits under various inflation rates, the total benefit line (curve 5) in Figure 4A is a horizontal line unaffected by the general rate of inflation. However, the distribution of net benefits does change because the various tax and royalty arrangements have not been designed to eliminate the effects of inflation. In particular, the Alberta profit sharing royalty and the corporation income tax are both higher in real terms at higher rates of inflation. Conventionally calculated depreciation allowances provide a smaller total real recovery of capital when inflation is greater, although higher nominal revenues mean that the recovery is faster. In addition, the Alberta profit sharing royalty's allowance for interest expense (8 per cent on 75 per cent of total capital employed) is a fixed percentage that does not increase with inflation.

Figure 4B shows the effects of different inflation rates under a gross royalty system and full private ownership. In this case the impact of inflation is much less, involving a shift of net advantage from the private producers to, principally, the federal government as the total real capital cost allowances become smaller at higher rates of inflation.

IV. The Cost of Capital and Social Time Preference

In our base case, we use a 10.44 per cent total cost of capital, of which 7.44 per cent is after-tax and 3 per cent is corporation income tax. As mentioned earlier, these are based on historical averages for the whole economy. To find present values in the base case we use a 7.44 per cent real rate of social time preference, a figure chosen to make the social time preference rate equal to the after-tax opportunity cost of capital to business. This facilitates comparison of our results with internal rate of return calculations. The uncertainty about these rates is different in nature from that assessed earlier—there is less likelihood that the two numbers will change markedly over time, but there are many different views about what the current cost of capital is and perennial problems in the estimation of a social time preference rate for discounting. In the face of diverging views, sensitivity analysis can be helpful, and we report some in Figure 5. For the experiments in Figure 5A we set the after-tax cost of capital equal to the rate

FIGURE 4

EFFECT OF VARIOUS INFLATION RATES
ON TOTAL NET RENTS AND THEIR DISTRIBUTION (1974 PRICES)

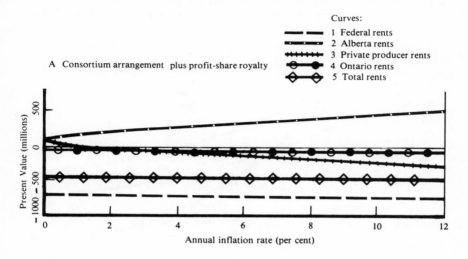

A Consortium arrangement plus profit-share royalty

Curves:

1 Federal rents
2 Alberta rents
3 Private producer rents
4 Ontario rents
5 Total rents

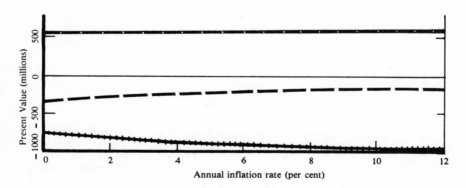

B Non-consortium arrangement with 20 per cent royalty

172

FIGURE 5

EFFECT OF ALTERNATE COSTS OF CAPITAL
AND SOCIAL TIME-PREFERENCE RATES
ON TOTAL NET RENTS AND THEIR DISTRIBUTION
IN CONSORTIUM ARRANGEMENT WITH PROFIT-SHARE ROYALTY

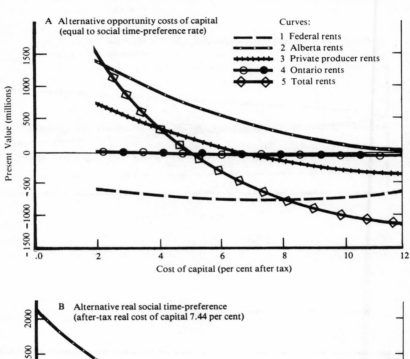

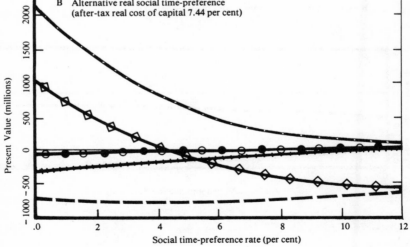

of time preference (an equilibrium condition for savers if net personal taxes on corporation income are negligible) and vary both over the range from 2 per cent to 12 per cent in real terms. The corresponding nominal interest rates are all 4 per cent higher, as we used the 4 per cent inflation rate along with the other assumptions from the base case.

Curve 5 in Figure 5A shows how sharply dependent are the total benefits on the assumed opportunity cost of capital. In our preliminary runs of the Syncrude model, we used a high cost of capital, and therefore found lower present values for the project as a whole. Figure 5 permits the reader to calculate the consequences of his own estimate of the opportunity cost of capital.

To test the separate effects of the cost of capital and the social discount rate, we report in Figure 5B the effects of varying the rate of real social time preference from 0 per cent to 12 per cent, with the after-tax real cost of capital set at its base case value of 7.44 per cent. A comparison of the two parts of Figure 5 shows that the project as a whole is much less affected if only the social time preference rate is varied, but the Alberta returns are still altered dramatically. This is because the Alberta 50 per cent profit sharing royalty produces its major cash flows for Alberta towards the end of the project's life, while the other participants get their returns on a more regular basis.

IV.5 Summary of Simulation Results

To help draw our many results together, we have prepared Table 2 showing, in the first row, the Syncrude base case rents accruing to each participant and, lower down, the changes due to variations in each of the uncertain variables assessed earlier in this section. In the left-hand column the cost changes are measured as percentages of total costs per barrel in the base case. In all of the other columns, the rents and changes in rents are measured in terms of 1974 cents per barrel. By comparing the changes in "total" column with those in the columns for each of the Syncrude participants, we can calculate the percentage distribution, or "marginal tax rates" applicable to the various cost and revenue changes. For example, if oil prices throughout the simulation are raised by 10 per cent of their base case values, then total rents rise by 108.5 cents per barrel, which is 10 per cent of the $10.85 base case oil price. Of this increase, 67.3 cents, or 62 per cent, accrues to Alberta, 15 per cent to the federal government, 2 per cent to Ontario, and 21 per cent to the private producers. Roughly the same percentage distribution would apply to a change in operating costs, but any change in capital costs falls more directly on the federal government. For example, a 10 per cent increase in the capital cost of Syncrude would lower

TABLE 2

RELATIVE EFFECTS OF CHANGING BASE-CASE VALUES FOR SENSITIVE VARIABLES ON TOTAL NET RENTS AND THEIR DISTRIBUTION IN CONSORTIUM ARRANGEMENT WITH PROFIT-SHARE ROYALTY (1974 PRICES)

	Percentage change in costs per barrel	Rents in cents per barrel				
		Total	Federal	Alberta	Ontario	Private Producers
Base-case: (price = 10.85 cost = 12.12)	—	-127.2	-196.7	+96.6	-10.2	-16.9
Changes relative to base-case:						
10% increase in 1974 $ oil price	—	+108.5	+16.3	+67.2	2.5	+22.5
10% increase in capital costs	5.63	-68.2	-31.8	-25.1	-2.1	-9.2
10% increase in capital and operating costs	9.94	-120.4	-39.4	-58.1	-3.3	-19.6
1 percentage point increase in inflation rate	—	0	-0.4	+9.1	-0.5	-8.2
1 percentage point increase in private cost of capital and discount rate for net rents	8.87	-83.2	-30.0	-18.5	-3.7	-31.0
1 percentage point increase in discount rate for net rents	2.87	-34.7	-22.7	-13.6	-1.3	+2.9

total rents by 68.3 cents per barrel, of which 46 per cent would come out of federal rents, 36 per cent out of Alberta rents, and 13 per cent out of private producers' rents.

Increasing the generally anticipated rate of inflation has only moderate redistributive effects, chiefly favouring the federal government at the expense of the private producers. By contrast, increases in the cost of capital, and in the discount rate used to find present values of net rents have substantial effects on the size and distribution of economic rents. If both rates increase by one percentage point, total rents decrease by 83.2 cents per barrel, of which 36 per cent comes out of federal rents, 22 per cent out of Alberta rents, and 37 per cent out of private producers' rents. The highest share comes out of producers' rents because we have raised the after-tax private opportunity cost of funds but not the tax opportunity cost. The high share is not because the private producers have to wait longer for their returns; on the contrary, the numbers in the last row of Table 2 show that a rise in the discount rate, with opportunity costs held constant, actually increases the present value of private producers' rents in the Syncrude base case. This is because the immediate tax write-offs permit an immediate reduction of corporation income taxes paid by private consortium members, while taxes are relatively high late in the project's life when there are fewer expenses left to deduct. This concludes the analysis of our main simulation experiments to date, leaving only the opportunity to make sage concluding comments.

V. CONCLUSIONS

We have four tasks in this concluding section. First we shall report briefly on our analysis of the effects of the new resource taxation measures introduced in the federal budget of 23 June 1975. Then we shall proceed to outline the limitations of the analysis, to assess the implications of the results for future oil sands developments, and to suggest some possible general implications for the sharing of resource revenues.

V.1 Effects of the June 1975 Federal Budget

The main proposal relevant to Syncrude was the raising of the federal corporation income tax rate applicable to oil sands plants from 25 per cent to 36 per cent, coupled with an extra deduction from taxable income equal to 25 per cent of production income from petroleum resources. For a firm whose production income and taxable incomes were equal to each other and unchanging over time, the net effect of these two measures would be very slight, depending on the provincial tax rate and the response of the provincial governments. In a province which continued to accept the federal definition of taxable income, and which applied an 11 per cent provincial tax rate, the combined marginal tax rate would rise from 36 per cent to 47 per cent, on a tax base reduced by one-quarter. In terms of the old base, federal taxes would be increased by two percentage points, while provincial taxes would be reduced by 2.75 percentage points, leaving the firms with slightly lower net taxes. In general, production income is larger than taxable income, so that tax reductions are the rule rather than the exception. This is especially so in the case of a consortium like Syncrude, with large immediate deductions from taxable income, all of which are now worth much more at a 36 per cent federal tax rate than they were at a 25 per cent rate. In modelling the new budget, we assumed that Alberta would continue to use the federal definition of taxable income, that royalties would not be deducted in determining production income, and that (in the absence of more precise information) 50 per cent of the Syncrude equipment expenditures would be classified as development expenditures. On this basis, the effect of the new proposals is very substantial, raising the net rents accruing to the private participants from $-67 million to $ + 86 million, measured as present values in terms of 1974 dollars. This $147 million increase is provided roughly 85 per cent by the federal government and 15 per cent by the Alberta government. To give some idea of the possible impact of our more problematic assumptions, the $147 million increase would be reduced by about $20 million if none of the Syncrude capital expenditures were treated as development expenditures in the calculation of production income, or by $50 million if the Alberta profit sharing royalty were subtracted in the calculation of production income. Results based on the June budget are analyzed more fully in Helliwell and May (1975); the main point we wish to make here is that the June budget apparently had important effects on the taxes paid by the private producers in the Syncrude consortium, involving a transfer to them with a present value of almost 150 million 1974 dollars. In terms of year-by-year flows, the reductions in federal income tax payments by the Syncrude members are estimated to be almost half as large, between 1976 and 1980, as the $40 million total annual cost estimated for those years by the Minister of Finance.

V.2 Limitations of the Analysis

Although we have come to grips with the economic and financial detail of the Syncrude project, and of the complicated dynamics of the sharing over time, and among the participants, of the economic costs and benefits, our analysis has some important gaps. We have assessed the Syncrude project without regard for foregone future uses of the oil sand leases devoted to the project. This means we are treating user cost as zero, a procedure that might be justified in this case, if at all, only on the basis of the fairly vast extent of the sands, the supposed requirement that extraction and processing techniques be developed in such large-scale experiments, and the likely slow pace of future developments.

Another limitation of our present analysis is that we have been able to assess the consequences of uncertainty only in a partial way. As we have been unable to find any normative principles for the allocation of project risks among principals and agents, and to find any joint subjective probability distributions (held by any of the participants, or by an outside observer) of the various risks to which the project is subject, we have been limited to a separate assessment of the consequences of different cost and revenue assumptions under alternative revenue sharing systems. Even in this case, we have simplified matters, probably to an unrealistic extent, by assuming only a single dimension to the uncertainty about each variable. If we had a better stock of information, we could model the future movements of uncertain variables as time dependent stochastic processes, and use multiple simulations to obtain frequency distributions of present values. At present, we think our inability to choose representative parameters for such processes limits the usefulness of the additional information obtainable from stochastic simulations. Finally, our current analysis ignores the positive and negative spillovers created by Syncrude and similar large projects. Environmental factors loom large here, as the Syncrude processing uses vast amounts of water and produces vast amounts of poisonous tailings liquids which do not settle out satisfactorily. The construction phase can put stress on the local economy, or provide a welcome stimulus, depending on the circumstances and one's point of reference. The latter factors can be roughly costed, while the inclusion of environmental costs is more likely to take place through regulations that limit the environmental impact and thus increase direct processing costs.

V.3 Implications for Further Oil Sands Projects

For all their limitations, our results do seem to indicate that under present estimates of the costs of current mining and processing techniques, there is no resource value in the oil sands at current world oil prices. When this result is combined with the substantial Alberta royalty and the related federal tax concessions in the November 1974 budget, the effect is to make further plants on the same basis unattractive from the point of view of either the private producers or the federal government. This conclusion becomes stronger when account is taken of the various options left open to the Alberta government, but is reversed for the private producers by the provisions of the June 1975 federal budget. If the current cost estimates are valid for future projects, and if the June budget measures are sustained, there is likely to be some enthusiasm from private producers and Alberta for further oil sands plants, even though the overall economic result is negative at current world oil prices. Under presently estimated costs, the net effect of the Syncrude arrangements is to achieve a very substantial payment from the taxpayers of Canada to those of Alberta, with a lesser transfer from the federal government to the private producers.

V.4 General Conclusions

What have we learned of more general applicability? For one thing, we have shown that most existing tax and royalty systems have substantial differences in their effects on risk-sharing, and that different types of risk have rather different effects. That conclusions such as these might seem novel, and that these effects have not been quantified previously, shows how far we are from a full understanding of the nature and consequences of various revenue sharing arrangements.

Second, we have seen that the tax and royalty arrangements for oil sands plants have been adapted, by tax changes and direct equity participation, to an extent that suggests that almost any pattern of revenue division could be developed consistent with the prevailing constitutional interpretations of the powers of the two levels of government. The Syncrude arrangements are thus an example in support of Professor Lederman's view that the ultimate solutions to resource revenue sharing conflicts reflect political accommodations that have not been, and need not be, constrained by narrow constitutional interpretations of the respective powers and duties of the two levels of government.

We have also seen from our simulation results that Syncrude represents a vast transfer from the federal government to Alberta, with the position of the private producers shifting from budget to budget. On behalf of all Canadians, the federal government has heavily subsidized what appears from available data to be a large elephant of pale hue, offering little promise of increasing the speed of development of more appropriate technologies. Can we make any conclusions from this about the responsibility for resource management and the rights to resource revenues? Only by conjecture, we suspect. It might be argued, in a conjectural way, that the great haste and relative ignorance accompanying the federal government's decision to invest were jointly responsible for the results and that resource developments might better be left in the more knowledgeable hands of the provinces, given the relative success of Alberta at the bargaining table. It might also be argued that the magnitude of the transfer created by secret bargaining requiring no prior public or parliamentary investigation or approval creates a dangerous precedent, one that is likely to be followed in the future if government participation in private ventures and special exemptions from taxation are to become standard methods for the federal government to acquire a larger role in resource management. While we find these issues intriguing, they take us beyond the results of our current research, about which we have by now said our piece.

Notes

1. Great Canadian Oil Sands, presentation to the Organization for Economic Cooperation and Development.

2. The 1973 capital cost estimates are from the February 1975 report prepared by Loram International for the Alberta government, as excerpted in the *Proceedings* of the House of Commons Standing Committee on National Resources and Public Works, 4 March 1975, p. 6:73. The per barrel costs are from p. 90 of vol. I of *An Energy Policy for Canada, Phase I*, published by the federal Department of Energy, Mines and Resources in 1973.

3. These and other features of the Winnipeg agreement were reported by Premier Lougheed to the Alberta legislature on 4 February 1975 (Alberta Hansard, IV, 9, pp. 318-21) and in *Oilweek* (10 February 1975, p. 9). According to *Oilweek*'s calculations, the equity interests of Imperial, Cities Service, and Gulf are to shift from 30 per cent, 30 per cent, and 10 per cent to 31.25 per cent, 22 per cent, and 16.75 per cent by dint of differing contributions towards the additional $400 million estimated to be required from the private participants. Another feature of the agreement is that Alberta will provide 100 per cent of the investment in the utility plant and the pipeline to Edmonton, as opposed to 50 per cent and 80 per cent in the original 1973 agreement. We ignore this element of Alberta's investment in our analysis as the services of the utility and the pipeline are to be priced to produce a normal utility rate of return.

References

Feldstein, Martin S., "Econometric Studies of Health Economics," in Intriligator and Kendrick, eds., *Frontiers of Quantitative Economics* II (Amsterdam: North Holland, 1974): 377-434.

Foster Research Limited, "Economic Evaluation of the Syncrude Project." Calgary, January 1975 (Report prepared for the Alberta government and tabled in the Alberta legislature on 4 February 1975).

Govier, G.W., "Alberta's Oil Sands in the Energy Supply Picture," in K.J. Laidler, ed., *Energy Resources* (Ottawa, 1973). (Proceedings of a Royal Society of Canada Conference, 15-17 October 1973).

Goyer, J.P., "Energy: A Look at Alberta's Oil Sands" (Vancouver, 1974). (Notes for a speech by the Minister of Supply and Services at the University of B.C., 7 February 1974).

Helliwell, John, "Overlapping Federal and Provincial Claims on Mineral Revenues," forthcoming in Michael Crommelin and Andrew R. Thompson, eds. *Mineral Leasing as an Instrument of Public Policy* (University of B.C. Press, 1977). (Proceedings of a conference sponsored by the B.C. Institute for Economic Policy Analysis, 18-20 September 1974).

Helliwell, John and Gerry May, "A Model for Assessing the Economic Costs and Benefits of Athabaska Oil Sands Projects." U.B.C. Department of Economics Discussion Paper, October 1975.

Ross, Stephen A., "The Economic Theory of Agency: The Principal's Problem," *American Economic Review* LXIII (May 1973): 134-39.

Ross, Stephen A., "On the Economic Theory of Agency and the Principle of Similarity," in Balch, McFadden, and Wu, eds., *Essays on Economic Behaviour under Uncertainty* (Amsterdam: North Holland, 1974): 215-37.

Note to Figures

In all of the following figures (except Figure 3) we show the consequences for shares of rent of varying the value of only one variable, holding all other variables constant at their base-case levels. For example, in all four panels of Figure 1 the 1974 oil price (set at $10.85 in the base-case) is varied between $5 and $14. Similarly, in Figure 2 capital costs are altered from 50 per cent to 150 per cent of their base-case levels.

The whole set of base values is given in the text, Section IV.

"Rent" is a measure of the net present value of the shares accruing annually to each partner and discounted at 7.44 per cent after allowing for inflation.

Figure 3, unlike the other figures, shows the effect on break-even prices, of changing current and capital costs.

A Comment on Natural Resource Revenue Sharing: The Links between Revenue Sharing and Energy Policy

JUDITH MAXWELL

Taxation and pricing policies are the primary instruments available to governments to manage the development, production, and consumption of a depletable resource. It is through taxes and prices that government can influence the incentives that will in turn determine the decisions made by explorers, developers, producers, and consumers.

Both the federal and the provincial levels of government have major responsibilities for the management of resources. The provinces own the resources located in their territories and have a major responsibility for ensuring efficient development and production. The federal government must formulate national energy policy decisions that synthesize the interests of both the producing and the consuming regions of the country. Thus, both levels of government require some influence over taxation and pricing.

The actual sharing of this power was not so important in the first thirty years of the development of the Canadian oil industry because there was a national consensus at the time that policies should emphasize rapid development. In that environment, governments were agreed that the industry needed help in the form of tax concessions, a protected national market, subsidies for transportation systems, and, finally, support for exports that not only boosted production but speeded up the depletion of reserves. We then endured a brief period in 1973 and 1974 when the sole goal of government policy was revenue maximization with each level of government competing for control of the revenues. This period had the opposite result of actively discouraging development. In the past two years, the policy pendulum has been swinging slowly back toward what I would optimistically characterize as a moderate middle ground where development goals will share priority with policies that actively encourage demand conservation and also modify the security risks facing this country.

Although I believe that the conflict over revenue sharing has in some respects stabilized, it is still intriguing to explore the question "Who should get the revenues?'' Professor Thompson has stated his position quite categorically as a "firm defender of the provincial position." He has quite appropriately tied the provincial position less to the revenues themselves than to control, and he defines control as

> who can develop what natural resources where, who can determine price, and who can determine what revenue share will belong to the resource developer and what share will accrue to the province?

I would agree that control is the issue, but I would argue that many of the powers he has mentioned must somehow be shared with the federal government because the peculiarities of the Canadian market make it impossible for the provinces to formulate many of the policy decisions he mentions on their own. There are at least three areas where there is a need for federal management of the crude oil resources.

The first is in the area of determining prices. Theoretically, the producing provinces could set prices by behaving as pure monopolists. They would sell their reserves at the international price, unless consumers were able to reduce their demand to the point where the provinces did not wish to accept further cuts in production. Presumably, they would be able to maximize revenues at a production level that was lower than that prevailing today and at a price that was higher. But in fact, the provinces have not behaved as pure monopolists. They have willingly agreed for reasons of the "national interest" to sell crude oil to other Canadians at prices well below the international level in order to cushion the shock of the jump in world prices, and they have agreed to forego the earnings from export sales at the international price in order to finance this consumer subsidy.

As long as we have a two-price system for oil, some national agency must take the responsibility for setting the export tax, paying the import subsidy, and administering changes in the domestic price. Even after the domestic price finally rises to the international level (as is now accepted by all levels of government, though there are disputes on the speed of the increase), there will be a need for a national agreement on the appropriate price of the expensive new supplies arriving on the market from the Alberta oil sands, the Arctic frontier, and so on. This means that the domestic price is likely to be an administered one for some time and a federal influence on pricing will be required as long as it is an administered price.

A second area where national decisions are required is in the development of new supplies. Alberta, Saskatchewan, and British Columbia are now mature producing regions with relatively limited potential. This means that future Canadian supplies will have to come primarily from other regions, particularly the Arctic and the continental shelf.

One of the primary objectives of national policy will have to be to ensure the development of these new supplies and it would be quite natural to use the economic rent generated by current oil production to promote this development. However, the primary economic objective of the three producing provinces is to ensure the diversification of their economies into an industrial structure that will prosper after oil production begins to decline. They are therefore anxious to divert their share of the economic rent into investments in other kinds of economic activity (although Alberta has been willing to invest a substantial amount of its economic rent in the oil sands as a means of diversifying its energy base). There is therefore a conflict in the objectives of the two levels of government and thus both need a share of the rent.

A third area where national decisions are required is security of supply or, in Professor Thompson's words, which markets will be served. The national oil policy of the 1960's provided a protected market for western crude in Ontario on the grounds that the industry needed protection from international competition. At the time, Canadians east of the Ottawa Valley retained the advantage of cheap imported oil but also bore the risk of possible supply interruptions.

Since 1973, the risk of such interruptions has increased significantly and the national response has been to try to reduce this insecurity by extending the Interprovincial Pipeline from Sarnia to Montreal. Moreover, this decision to extend the line has been pushed by the federal government despite two substantial drawbacks. First, this line could not be justified on pure economic grounds because the western provinces do not have sufficient reserves to keep the line running for its normal economic life. (Such pipelines are usually amortized over a period of twenty to twenty-five years.) Second, production to fill the extension even temporarily will have to be diverted from existing exports to the United States—which are sold at the international price.

If the western provinces had been setting this policy, and had been operating as pure monopolists, they would not be concerned about the security of supply issue in Canada because they would simply sell to the highest bidders, regardless of their geographic location.

Similar issues will arise in the next few years as Canada reassesses its commitment to self-sufficiency in energy. For example, some political judgement will have to be made about whether Canada should pursue high-cost energy sources in the oil sands (where Professor Helliwell has estimated a break-even price of over $11 a barrel in 1974 dollars) and in the frontier in order to reduce the security risk on imports.

None of these three examples of the need for a national presence in the control of resources provides a guideline for determining how the control should be shared. It is possible that the federal government could actually carry out its responsibilities using the powers it possessed prior to September 1973, that is, control over the resources in the Arctic and on the continental shelf, the power to tax corporate income, allowing full abatement for royalties, and control over export permits.

However, I suspect that it may also need some of the new powers over pricing and income taxation that it has absorbed in the past two years in order to manage the tasks ahead: that is, the tasks of maintaining the single domestic price for oil, of improving security of supply, and of resolving the conflict between the provincial desire for industrial diversification and the national need for energy supply diversification.

Finally, there are indications that some of the projects on the frontier are now so large as to be beyond the investment capabilities of the Canadian industry. This may mean that governments will also have to share the risks on the frontier by using their own revenue share to help finance these large projects. That would provide yet another argument for a combination of federal and provincial control and management of the resource base.

Note

* I will confine my remarks to crude oil since I am not as familiar as I should be with the other minerals.

Rent vs. Revenue Maximization as an Objective of Environmental Management

HARRY F. CAMPBELL*

I. INTRODUCTION

The other papers in this volume have been concerned with the taxation of rent from exhaustible resources. In these papers it was assumed that private management of the resource will generate rent and that maximization of this rent is in the interest of both society and the private firm. The tax which secures a portion of the rent for the public purse may, in many instances, be neutral in that its imposition does not substantially change the private firm's policy as to the rate or level of exploitation of the resource. In these circumstances it was possible to regard the resource rent as an already existing flow of revenue which the government can appropriate by means of a tax. "Which government?" is the question to which the other papers have largely been addressed.

There is another category of resource, however, the rent from which is unlikely to be maximized under private management. The full rent which, for example, the environment is capable of yielding is unlikely to be realized in the absence of public regulation of its use. In circumstances such as these, a tax is primarily a means of ensuring rent maximization, and its revenue-earning capacity is a secondary consideration. Indeed, much of the literature on the use of a pollution charge or fee fails to consider the generation of revenue as a likely consequence. In this respect, the literature resembles that on the use of the tariff in international trade which frequently concentrates on the "efficiency" effects of the tariff to the exclusion of its revenue-raising potential. In this paper, however, two interpretations of the word "rent" are developed: rent is considered as a maximand in the management of the environment; and it is considered as a potential flow of income from a publicly owned environmental stock. It is argued that these two conceptions of rent are inseparable in the economic analysis of environmental problems.

The subject of rent maximization through public management of a resource is probably most extensively treated in the fisheries economics literature. Consequently, this paper will exploit the familiarity of the analysis of the fisheries rent problem by developing the concept of environmental resource rent maximization through an analogy with rent maximization in a fishery. It then examines the potential revenue flow resulting from efficient environmental management and demonstrates that the maximization of this flow and its distribution among governments or members of the public are considerations which are inextricably linked in the process of efficient environmental management. Finally, an attempt is made to draw some conclusions about the appropriate jurisdiction over environmental policy from the characteristics of an efficient management scheme.

II. RENT MAXIMIZATION

It is convenient to develop the concept of an "environmental rent" and a model of environmental rent dissipation by analogy with the concept of rent and the model[1] of rent dissipation in a common property fishery. Consider an economy in which there are two industries—fishing and agriculture; land is privately owned, but the fish stock is a common property resource. It is assumed that there are diminishing returns to the units of "effort" (services of labour and capital) which combine with the stocks of fish and land to produce units of output. The prices of the outputs (fish and corn) are assumed to be constant—independent of the levels of output and of the distribution of income. There is a fixed supply of effort, and the wage of effort adjusts so as to clear the factor market. The landowner hires units of effort up the point where the value of the marginal product of effort in agriculture (VMP_E^A) equals the market wage; in this way he maximizes his property income. As H. Scott Gordon (1954), Scott (1955), and others have argued, the owners of effort will enter the fishery as long as their income from fishing is greater than or equal to the market wage: this implies that the value of the average product of effort in fishing (VAP_E^F) equals the market wage. In Figure 1, OA units of effort are allocated to the common property fishery, and OB units to agriculture. The owner of the land receives a rent of W_0EGH, while the common property fishery earns no rent.

If the fishery were transferred from a common property status to sole ownership, the sole owner would behave in a manner similar to the landowner: he would maximize his income from the fishery by hiring effort up to the point at which the value of the marginal product of effort (VMP_E^F) equals the market wage. Under the present assumptions this means that some effort is transferred from working the fish stock to working the land: in Figure 1, the new allocation of effort is OD units to fishing and OC units to agriculture ($OA + OB = OD + OC =$ the fixed supply of effort). The owner of the fish stock now receives a rent of

FIGURE 1
OPTIMAL ALLOCATION OF EFFORT TO A FISHERY

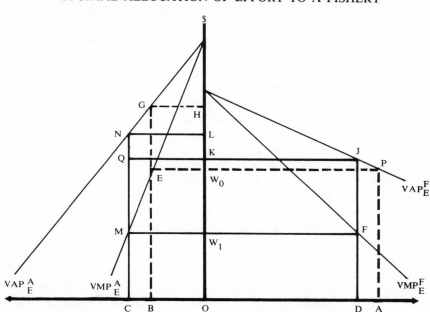

W_1FJK, and the landowner receives a rent of $W_1 MNL$. The value of output of the fishery falls from $OAPW_0$ to $ODJK$, while the value of agricultural output rises from $OBGH$ to $OCNL$; the total value of output is now at a maximum, as indicated by the equality of VMP_E^A and VMP_E^F.

While the total value of output of this two-industry economy increases as a result of sole ownership of the fish stock, not all factor incomes rise in consequence. The increase in rents of $W_1 FJK + (W_1 MNL - W_0 EGH)$ is larger than the increase in the total value of output, implying that there is a significant redistribution[2] of income from owners of effort, whose wage falls from W_0 to W_1, to owners of the land and fish stocks. In other words, efficient management of the fishery in this model results in a potential, but not an actual, Pareto improvement. Discussion of the significance of income distributional effects for efficient management of common property resources will be postponed to the next section of the paper.

Reverting for a moment to the initial situation of "bionomic equilibrium"[3] in the common property fishery, it is instructive to ask why the potential Pareto improvement, represented by the increased total value of output, is not achieved in the absence of property rights to the fish stock. Why do some units of effort not bribe others to shift from fishing to agriculture? It would be possible, in an accounting sense, for OD units of effort working the fishery to co-operate with the landowner in paying W_1MQK to bribe $OB + BC$ units of effort engaged in agriculture not to become fishermen; such a procedure would result in a Pareto improvement in that the landowner and the OD units of effort remaining in the fishery would be better off without the $OB + BC$ units of effort in agriculture being worse off. The reason for such a procedure not being followed (and for the common property fishery remaining in bionomic equilibrium) appears to be the size of the transaction costs[4] involved in organizing the purchase of a public good. In bionomic equilibrium, the exit of a unit of effort from the fishery is a public good as far as the remaining units are concerned because each unit is imposing external costs on its fellow units through its influence on the fish stock. If a unit of effort departs from the fishery the remaining units benefit in that the expected value of the catch per unit of effort increases. This probabilistic benefit has the public good characteristics of "non-rivalness" and "non-excludability": the good is non-rival in the sense that the benefit each unit of fishing effort receives, in the form of a higher expected value of catch, does not detract from the similar benefit accruing to other units; and the good is non-excludable in the sense that it is not possible, in a common property situation, to increase the expected value of one unit of effort's catch without at the same time increasing that of others. It has been argued that the transactions costs of working out a formula whereby DA units of effort would agree to quit the fishery, and the remaining OD units would combine to share, along with the landowner, the costs, W_1MQK, of bribing OC units of effort to remain in agriculture may be so high that they outweigh the potential gains. If this is the case, some form of public intervention will be necessary to achieve a maximum value of output in the economy.

The following characteristics of the model economy containing a common property fishery have been isolated: a. the total value of output is not at a maximum; b. the reason for (a) is a relative *overallocation* of effort to the fishery; c. a possible reason for (b) is the fact that departure of effort from the fishery creates a public good, so that the transactions costs of organizing the beneficiaries to purchase this departure are prohibitively high.

It can be argued that the above characteristics of equilibrium in an economy containing a common property fishery have close analogues in the equilibrium achieved by an economy with a common property environment: a. the total value of output (including an imputed value of pollution abatement) in the economy is not maximized; b. the reason for (a) is a relative *underallocation* of effort to pollution abatement; c. the reason for (b) is transactions costs and the public good nature of pollution abatement. A simple diagram [5] will serve to illustrate these points. Assume that society has a fixed quantity of effort to allocate between two activities—the production of goods, which has pollution as a by-product, and pollution abatement. Figure 2 shows the marginal utility from using effort in each of the two activities; these marginal utility functions MU_E^A and MU_E^C are analogous to the VMP_E^F and VMP_E^A schedules in Figure 1 For a maximization of social utility, the marginal utility of effort must be equalized in its two uses: this ocurs when OD units of effort are employed in abatement, and *OC* units in goods production.

Pollution abatement—the use of effort to reduce the flow of effluent— tends to have the public good characteristics of non-rivalness and non- excludability. It can therefore be assumed that less than the optimal amount of abatement will be undertaken in an economy with a common property

FIGURE 2

OPTIMAL ALLOCATION OF LABOUR TO POLLUTION ABATEMENT

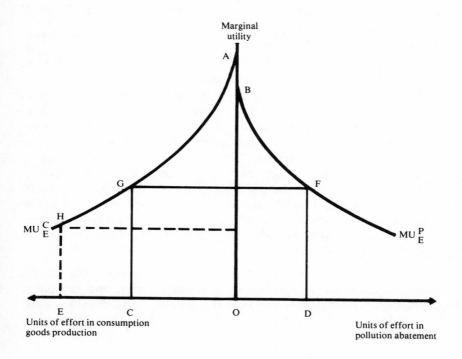

Marginal
utility

MU_E^C

MU_E^P

E

C

O

D

Units of effort in consumption
goods production

Units of effort in
pollution abatement

environment; indeed, for the purposes of the present discussion, it can be assumed that no abatement will be undertaken in the absence of public intervention. If public intervention succeeds in increasing the allocation of effort to pollution abatement from its initial level of zero to the optimal level of *OD* in Figure 2, total utility increases by the area (*BFDO - GHEC*). Some forms of public intervention are discussed in Part III of the paper.

III. REVENUE MAXIMIZATION

The importance of the income distributional effects of public regulation of the exploitation of a common property resource was stressed in the discussion of the fishery. The income distributional effects of environmental management will also be of concern to policy-makers.[6] In this section of the paper these effects are discussed first in a partial, and then in a general equilibrium framework of economic analysis.

A. *The Partial Equilibrium Framework*

(1) The Partial Equilibrium Model. The partial equilibrium approach to the analysis of environmental policy is summarized by a diagram (Figure 3) of the relationship between a polluter and the victims of pollution:[7]

   MAC: is the long-run marginal cost to the polluting firm of abatement at each level of effluent discharge; this may represent the marginal cost of adjusting inputs so as to produce less effluent and/or the marginal cost of treating effluent once it is produced;

   MAB: when effluent is discharged from the polluting firm, it is diffused in the environment where it may have harmful effects on individuals or on the production processes of firms. Assuming for the moment that an aggregate dollar measure of damage is available, the long-run marginal benefit of abatement (*MAB* in Figure 3) can be defined as the negative of the measure of the long-run marginal damage resulting from the emission of the polluting firm. In Figure 3, the flow of effluent discharged by the polluting firm in the absence of public intervention is assumed to be *OZ*. In view of the damage resulting from the discharge of effluent, the socially optimal flow of emissions is *OE*, with *EZ* being abated.

Two limitations of the analysis in Figure 3 are worth noting at this point. First, the analysis deals with only one polluter, and any policy implication derived from it applies to that polluter only. If, for example, it were decided to implement an effluent charge scheme on the basis of this analysis, the charges to be levied on each type of effluent emitted by

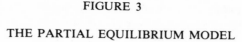

FIGURE 3

THE PARTIAL EQUILIBRIUM MODEL

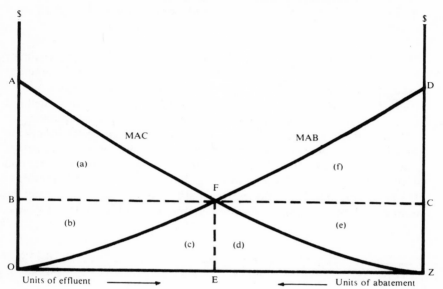

each firm would, in general, have to be computed individually. This point is discussed further in Part IV. Secondly, since pollution abatement is a public good to the group of victims, it will be difficult to ascertain the aggregate benefits of abatement and the amount by which each member of the group benefits. This problem is discussed briefly in the next section of the paper.

(2) Two approaches to environmental management. There are many possible approaches to the problem of environmental management, some depending on economic mechanisms and others on regulation or direct government action. The economic mechanisms are themselves numerous. Here we will outline two, the market failure and resource rent approaches. We show that they have quite different distribution effects, and that the frequently proposed effluent charge system is a modified version of the resource rent approach.

For both alternatives it is assumed that prior to the creation of the management mechanism, the polluting firms act as if they have full rights to dispose of their wastes in the environment. Under the market failure approach, these are full *de jure* rights, of which they cannot be deprived;

but under the resource rent approach, the firm's rights are only *de facto*, and are subsequently appropriated by the government. It is assumed that in this pre-management common property situation no resources are allocated to pollution abatement; in other words, there are *OZ* units of effluent (Figure 3).

The market failure approach. Under this approach, the government respects the rights of the polluting firms, and confines its environmental management role to that of compensating for a market failure.

The *MAC* and *MAB* curves can be regarded as supply and demand curves, respectively, for pollution abatement. The optimal quantity of abatement is *ZE*, but that quantity is not produced in any market because pollution abatement is a public good. The role of environmental management is to organize the victims of pollution to purchase *ZE* units of abatement at EF dollars from the polluting firm. The distributional effects of this purchase, under the market failure approach, may be summarized, on the basis of the areas enumerated in Figure 3, as follows:

	GAIN	LOSS	NET GAIN
Polluter	(4) + (5)	(4)	+ (5)
Victims	(4) + (5) + (6)	(4) + (5)	+ (6)
Government	(4) + (5)	(4) + (5)	-
Total net gain			(5) + (6)

The net result, when the government collects the area *FCZE* from the group of victims and uses this revenue to purchase *ZE* units of abatement at a price of *FE* per unit, is that the victims receive a consumer surplus of *DFC* (6) and the polluter receives a producer surplus of *FCZ* (5).

The resource rent approach. While the ownership of the environmental resource appears to lie *de facto* with the polluter in the pre-management situation, it is assumed under this approach (as in the case of other natural resources[8]) that ownership lies *de jure* with the public. If the public decides to assert its right to the value, or resource rent, generated by its resource under optimal management, then it can sell waste disposal facilities to polluters and environmental quality to victims. The *MAB* curve should be regarded as the polluter's demand curve for waste disposal services, and the *MAC* once again as the public's demand curve for pollution abatement. The supply linkage between these two markets is determined by the relative locations of the polluter and the victims and by the assimilative capacity of the environmental resource, which are already implicit in Figure 3. The price of $OB = ZC$ clears both markets: the price OB is an effluent charge and the price ZC is, as in the market failure case, the price of abatement. The distributional effects of the resource rent approach, as compared with the pre-management situation, can be summarized, on the basis of the areas enumerated in Figure 3, as follows:

	GAIN	LOSS	NET GAIN
Polluter	-	(2) + (3) + (4)	-[(2) + (3) + (4)]
Victim	(4) + (5) + (6)	(4) + (5)	+ (6)
Government	(2) + (3) + (4) + (5)	-	(2) + (3) + (4) + (5)
Total net gain			(5) + (6)

Under optimal management, the environmental resource yields a total rent equal to $AFEO + DFEZ$. Of this rent, ABF and DFC accrue to the polluter and the victims respectively in the form of consumer surpluses, and $BCZO$ accrues to the government. As compared with the pre-management situation, the polluter is considerably worse off, in consequence of losing the *de facto* right to pollute.

The market failure and resource rent approaches to environmental management have the same efficiency implications in this partial equilibrium context; both approaches result in the maximum net social gain of DFZ in Figure 3. It should be obvious, however, that policies which maximize net social gain do not necessarily maximize government revenue. The first approach produced none; and the amount produced by the second is not necessarily the largest sum that could be extracted from the two parties. For example, effluent charge revenues could be maximized by choosing an effluent charge corresponding to the point of unitary elasticity of the MAC curve; there is no reason to suppose[9] that this point will correspond to point F in Figure 3. In the following discussion it will be assumed that the government restricts itself to the class of efficient environmental management solutions.

Both the market failure and resource rent approaches, as defined here, call for the government to collect all, or part, of its revenues from the beneficiaries of pollution abatement. This is the amount $FCZE$ (areas d + e in Figure 3). But it is probable that this amount cannot be collected. As has been noted above, it is not easy to identify these beneficiaries, nor the magnitude of their benefits. In the fishery example of Part II, public management of the fishery secured the optimal number of units of effort for the fishery, or, what is the same thing, secured the optimal level of negative externalities among units. This optimum, as compared with the pre-management situation, was associated with a set of observable factor income changes which enabled the management agency to identify both the beneficiaries and the magnitude of the benefits of fishery management. Pollution abatement does not in general yield cash flows which can easily be identified as abatement benefits. Some attempts have, indeed, been made to place dollar values on the benefit firms [10] and individual consumers [11] have received from pollution abatement, but there is little prospect at present of defining a tax base in this way. For the purposes of the discussion of the market failure and resource rent approaches it will be assumed that the benefits of pollution abatement are so widespread that the general tax system is used to collect the resource rent *FCZE* in Figure 3, but this assumption is not crucial to the analysis.

Assuming that the general tax system is used to appropriate the benefits of pollution abatement, the role of an environmental management agency is reduced to paying a subsidy of *FCZE* to polluters under the market failure approach, *or* to collecting an effluent charge of *BFEO* from polluters under the resource rent approach. If Canadian governments had adopted the market failure approach, we should expect to observe abatement subsidies and no effluent charges; if they had adopted the resource rent approach we should expect to observe effluent charges but no abatement subsidies. In fact, as detailed in the following paragraphs, the issue is more complicated than this, since different levels of government may be using different approaches.

It appears that the only abatement subsidies which Canadian governments are currently offering private firms [12] are those in the form of special tax provisions for abatement equipment. For example, the federal Income Tax Act provides for accelerated depreciation of pollution control equipment, and the federal Excise Tax Act provides for refunds of the sales tax payable on certain classes of goods used for pollution abatement. Another example is a provision in the B.C. Taxation Act which exempts improvements or land used exclusively for pollution control purposes from taxation. The percentage subsidy afforded to the firm by such provisions should presumably be defined as the percentage by which the tax system lowers the cost of abatement equipment less the percentage by which the tax system lowers the cost of other forms of capital equipment.

While federal and provincial governments approach the problem of pollution control through various forms of subsidies to pollution abaters, some municipal governments have adopted the effluent charge approach. The only examples [13] of effluent charge schemes currently operating in Canada are those of sewerage charges levied by some municipalities on the "excess strength" of industrial effluent over "normal strength" household and commercial effluent. According to Demakeas (1974), ten municipalities, with approximately twenty per cent of Canada's population, collected $1.14 million in effluent charges in 1973.

(3) Potential government revenues from environmental quality management. The scanty evidence presented in the previous section of the paper might suggest that federal and provincial governments in Canada lean towards the market failure approach to environmental management, while some of the municipal governments lean towards the resource rent approach. Since the latter approach is similar to the approach adopted by governments to the exploitation of other natural resources, it will be pursued a little further. An attempt will be made to estimate the effluent tax revenues which the Province of British Columbia would receive as a result of applying the resource rent approach to pollution control in B.C.'s pulp and paper industry.

The B.C. provincial government has issued[14] two sets of environmental standards for the pulp and paper industry—effluent standards and ambient standards. There does not exist an invariant relationship between the quality and quantity of effluent discharged by a mill and the quality of the air and water affected; this is because of the varying assimilative capacities of different bodies of air and water, and because of varying levels of geographical concentration of industry. Nevertheless the Pollution Control Branch has issued a set of effluent standards which they regard as representative of those necessary to achieve the chosen set of ambient standards. There are three levels of effluent standards:[15] level *A* is the set of effluent standards recommended for new discharges; level *C* is the set of standards which most existing discharges are currently satisfying; and level *B* is an interim set of standards to which existing discharges are to be upgraded.

Suppose that the B.C. government decided to enforce level *C* or level *A* effluent standards for biochemical oxygen demand (*BOD*) and suspended solids (*SS*) through an effluent tax scheme; how much revenue would this resource rent approach to environmental management yield? A very rough estimate of the revenues resulting from effluent charges on these pollutants can be obtained from a model of an "average" pulp mill constructed by Stephenson and Nemetz (1974). These authors report a set of estimated responses of a Kraft mill producing 500 tons of bleached tissue paper per day[16] to effluent charges on *BOD* and *SS*. From the figures reported by Stephenson and Nemetz, the set of effluent charge revenues and abatement costs presented in Table 1 was calculated.

TABLE 1

REVENUES AND COSTS OF EFFLUENT CHARGE SCHEMES

	1 Effluent Standard	2 Effluent charge	3 Government revenues	3 Abatement costs	3 Total Firm costs
	Level A				
BOD =	15	$300	$834,937	$1,458,000	$2,292,937
SS =	15	$5			
	Level C				
BOD =	80	$50	$735,475	$286,000	$1,021,475
SS =	60	$0.5			

Notes: 1 Measured in lbs. per air dry ton of output.
2 Per 1000 lbs of effluent.
3 Annual figures.

The effluent charge revenue corresponds to *BFEO*, and the abatement costs correspond to *FEZ* in Figure 3. From Table 1 it can be seen that, assuming the firm decides to maintain its operation in B.C.,[17] the provincial government would collect $835 thousand per year from an effluent charge scheme designed to promote observance [18] of the level *A* standards. Of course, this figure does not represent a net revenue to the government since there will be enforcement and administrative costs associated with the operation of an effluent charge scheme.

The estimates reported in Table 1 are for a model pulp mill which may not correspond precisely to any mill currently operating in B.C. Nevertheless, these estimates can be used to derive a very rough estimate of the total effluent charge revenues which would be obtained from B.C.'s Kraft pulp industry under level *A* and *C* standards. Since B.C.'s output of Kraft (bleached and unbleached) is around 28 times that of the model mill, the figure in Table 1 can be multiplied by a factor of 28 to give estimates for the Kraft pulp industry:with level *A* standards, annual effluent charge revenue is $23.4 million and annual abatement costs are $40.8 million; with level *C* standards, annual effluent charge revenue is $20.6 million, and annual abatement costs are $8.0 million.

These estimates of potential revenues from effluent charge schemes applied to B.C.'s Kraft pulp industry can be considered as no more than very rough guesses. Furthermore, they are gross of the enforcement and administrative costs of the schemes. Nevertheless the estimate of $23.4 million as the potential gross revenue from an effluent charge scheme applied *to the Kraft pulp industry alone* is 15.2 per cent of the figure of $154.4 million reported by Scott (1975) for B.C.'s comprehensive natural resource revenues, gross of collection costs, in 1971. Thus it would appear than an effluent tax scheme applied to all industrial discharges in the province would account for a significant proportion of natural resource revenues.

B. The General Equilibrium Framework

The partial equilibrium analysis of the previous section proceeded as if it were possible to define an efficient solution to an externality problem independently of any income distributional effects which the policy mechanism used to implement that solution might have. For example, it was suggested that the appropriate public policy towards *BOD* and *SS* discharges might consist of effluent charges of $300 and $5, respectively, per 1000 lbs., and that such a policy would yield $23.4 million in effluent charge revenue from the Kraft pulp industry alone. An effluent charge scheme of this type would affect the distribution of income in various ways, the most obvious of which is the collection and disposition of effluent charge revenues. A set of effluent charges which is deemed efficient on the basis of the pre-management income distribution may turn out to be inefficient when assessed on the basis of the post-management distribution.

The significance of income distribution effects can be illustrated by a simple general equilibrium model of an economy containing two firms, one of which inflicts a negative externality on the other. [19] The model is presented in general functional form in the appendix to this paper; the specific functional forms and the set of parameter values chosen to simulate the adjustment of the economy to various effluent tax schemes are reported in Campbell (1975).

The simulation results reported in Appendix Table 1 illustrate the proposition that there is no correct level of effluent charge independent of the distribution of the effluent charge revenues. The level of effluent charge which maximizes social welfare will change with changes in the institutional framework for distributing effluent charge revenues. It can be seen from Figure 4, which summarizes the simulation results, that an effluent charge of 207 maximizes social welfare under Distribution 2, while an effluent charge of 214 maximizes social welfare under Distribution 1. This result should not be surprising: we expect a change in income distribution to result in shifts of market demand curves, and, assuming non-constant costs, changes in market prices; while the price for the discharge of effluent is not determined in a market (for reasons discussed in Part II), it is nonetheless a shadow price—an estimate of the price which would be established in a perfectly functioning market in rights to discharge effluent —and, consequently, it too is influenced by changes in the distribution of income.

The significance of the income distributional effects of environmental

FIGURE 4

VALUES OF THE SOCIAL WELFARE FUNCTION

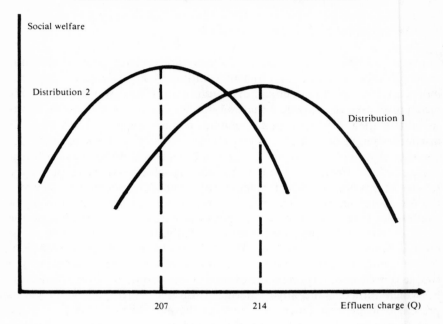

management in a Canadian context may be illustrated by the following simple example, which follows fairly closely the argument of the general equilibrium model in the appendix. Suppose there are two firms in British Columbia, one of which produces paper and the other of which produces some form of water-based recreation; the paper mill's discharge of effluent into a watercourse is assumed to cause an increase in the costs of supplying recreation. In addition, suppose that Ontario residents are the consumers of the paper mill's products, while B.C. residents are the consumers of the recreation firm's product. Furthermore, assume that if the B.C. government has jurisdiction over environmental management, revenues resulting from a charge on the paper mill's effluent will be distributed to B.C. residents, but that federal jurisdiction over environmental problems would result in any such revenues being distributed to Ontario residents. It can now be argued, within the framework of this simple example, that the optimal effluent charge will be higher if the B.C. government has jurisdiction than if the federal government has jurisdiction. The reasoning underlying this argument is that the marginal abatement benefit curve of Figure 3, which can be regarded as the demand curve for pollution abatement, will shift to the right as the incomes of consumers of recreation rise; since B.C. jurisdiction involves higher incomes for B.C. recreationists than does federal jurisdiction, the intersection of *MAB* with *MAC* in Figure 3 will be at a higher level of the effluent charge.

The foregoing example, which is a very simple representation of a very complex problem, suggested that the choice of jurisdiction over environmental management will influence the appropriate level of effluent charge to be imposed upon a polluter. In the following part of the paper it is recognized that environmental management may require the use of an effluent charge scheme in which the appropriate level of the effluent charge varies from locality to locality, and the implication of this feature of the scheme for the choice of the appropriate jurisdiction is discussed.

IV. JURISDICTION OVER ENVIRONMENTAL MANAGEMENT

In the discussion of the partial equilibrium model in Part IIIA, it was suggested that the optimal charge to be applied to the effluent of an individual polluter was determined by three sets of considerations: first, the nature of the abatement cost curve; secondly, the relative locations of the polluter and the victims and the manner in which the effluent is assimilated or diffused in the environment (which is implicit in Figure 3); and, thirdly, given the diffusion of the effluent, the nature of the victims' damage functions. An implication of the existence of these three sets of determinants of the optimal effluent charge is that even if the pulp and paper industry, for example, consisted of twenty-eight identical mills as was assumed earlier, each mill might be subject to a different optimal level of the effluent charge depending upon its location relative to that of the potential victims of the effluent.

If each polluting firm is to be assessed its own effluent charge on the basis of local air and water flows, the amount and spatial distribution of local economic activity, and the preferences and incomes of local residents, it can be argued that the charge should be decided upon at a local level. The case for local environmental decision-making has been persuasively made by Scott (1973) and need not be elaborated upon further. The implication of this argument for federal and provincial environmental management agencies is that they should be designed for decentralized decision-making, possibly in co-operation with existing local governments.

V. CONCLUSION

The paper has argued that an efficient, or rent maximizing, policy towards environmental management need not result in maximum government revenue: the market failure and resource rent approaches are "efficient" in the context of the partial equilibrium model, but they have very different implications for revenue. Even if authorities opt for the resource rent approach as a source of revenue, the set of charges which maximizes the environmental rent is not necessarily the set which maximizes government revenue. Nevertheless, the perfunctory calculations reported in Part III of the paper indicate that an efficient environmental management policy may be a relatively significant potential source of natural resource revenue.

The discussions of income distributional and geographic considerations in Parts IIIB and IV suggest that the task to be entrusted to the environmental management agency is not an easy one. In consultation with local representatives, the agency must define, for each discharger, an efficient effluent charge, taking into account abatement costs, pollution damages, and the income distributional effects of collecting and disbursing the effluent charge revenues. In view of the substantial amount of local information which is necessary for efficient environmental management, it would appear that this function should be assigned to a local jurisdiction; spill-overs among jurisdictions would probably have to be regulated by a formalized process of interjurisdictional negotiation.

Notes

* I am especially grateful to Anthony Scott for many provocative discussions of this topic, and for comments on an earlier draft of this paper. I also wish to thank Chris Archibald, John Butlin, Tony Dorcey, and David Dorenfeld for helpful comments, Frank Flynn for assistance with computer programming, and Gerry May for research assistance. The financial support of the Canada Council and the U.B.C. research grants committee is gratefully acknowledged. None of the above named individuals or institutions should be held responsible for the views expressed in this paper.

1. Static models will be used for the exposition of the concepts discussed in this paper. For a discussion of the dynamics of rent maximization in a fishery, see Clark and Munro (1974).

2. This point is made by Scott (1958), Samuelson (1974), and Weitzman (1974). If the assumptions of the model were changed so that the agriculture industry could absorb the

extra BC units of effort without there being a fall in *VMPAE* (and hence in the market wage), then the increase in the total value of output in the economy would correspond to the newly created rent in the fishery.

3. For a discussion of this term, see H. Scott Gordon (1954), Part II.

4. This point has been emphasized by Cheung (1971).

5. For a discussion of the dynamics of environmental rent maximization, see Neher (1973).

6. For example, Fox (1974) has listed income distributional effects as one of four categories of information needed to evaluate an environmental policy mechanism.

7. For an elaboration, see almost any text on the economics of environmental management, e.g., Kneese and Bower (1968), chapter 6.

8. For a discussion of the ownership of natural resources in Canada, see Gibson (1970), pp. 8-12.

9. In fact the demand curve for effluent rights derived for an "average" pulp mill by Stephenson and Nemetz (1974) corresponds fairly closely to a rectangular hyperbola over much of its range; this means that effluent tax revenues are more or less constant over this range.

10. For example, Crocker (1971) has attempted to identify increases in the value of agricultural land resulting from air pollution abatement in Florida.

11. Dornbusch and Barrager (1973) have attempted to measure increases in property values resulting from water pollution control in various parts of the United States.

12. Excluded from consideration are CMHC and provincial subsidies to municipalities for the construction of sewage treatment plants.

13. See Demakeas (1974).

14. See Water Resources Services (1972) for a description of these standards. Although the present discussion is concerned only with the *BOD* and *SS* standards, it should be noted that governments are concerned with additional effluent quality parameters.

15. The federal government has also issued a set of pulp and paper effluent regulations under the Fisheries Act which differ somewhat from the B.C. guidelines. For example, the federal standard lies between B.C.'s *A* level and *C* level standards; see Fisheries Act (1971).

16. The model mill constructed by Stephenson and Nemetz produces 500 tons of bleached tissue paper per day, has a Kraft pulping process, uses softwood as the primary input, and has a mechanical wood preparation process.

17. In 1972 the U.S. Council on Environmental Quality estimated that 329 out of 752 U.S. pulp and paper mills had profit margins significantly lower than the industry average. Of these marginal mills, which were responsible for 15 per cent of U.S. production, 30-35 were expected to close in the period 1972-76 because of low profit margins, and an additional 60-65 mills, representing 16,000 jobs, were expected to close on account of pollution abatement regulations.

18. Stephenson and Nemetz report that all B.C.'s Kraft mills meet Level *C BOD* standards, and only 3 fail to meet level *C SS* standards; 5 mills fail to meet level *A BOD* standards and 6 fail to meet level *A SS* standards.

19. See Maler (1974), chapter 6, for a model in which a firm inflicts a negative externality on a consumer.

References

Archibald, G.C. and C. Wright, 1974, "Alternative Solutions for the Control of a Production Externality in a General Equilibrium Model," *Claremont Economic Papers*, 88, p. 29.

Council on Environmental Quality, *Third Annual Report* (Washington: U.S. Government Printing Office, 1972).

Cheung, S.S., "Contractual Arrangements and Resource Allocation in Marine Fisheries," in *Economics of Fisheries Management: A Symposium*, A.D. Scott, ed., (Vancouver: Institute of Animal Resource Ecology, U.B.C., 1971): 97-108.

Clark, C.W. and G.R. Munro, "The Economics of Fishing and Modern Capital Theory: A Simplified Approach," U.B.C. Department of Economics Discussion Paper 74-20 (1974), p. 39.

Campbell, H.F., "The Significance of the Income Distributional Effects of Environmental Management," U.B.C. Department of Economics Discussion Paper 75-27. (1975), p. 11.

Crocker, T.D., "Externalities, Property Rights, and Transactions Costs: An Empirical Study," *Journal of Law and Economics* 14 (1971): 451-64.

Demakeas, J., "Effluent Charge Schemes in Canada," presented at the Comparative Review of the Management Options, OECD, p. 10.

Dornbusch, D.M. and S.M. Barrager, *Benefit of Water Pollution Control on Property Values* (U.S. Environmental Protection Agency, 1973), p. 148.

Fisheries Act, "Pulp and Paper Effluent Regulations," in *Canada Gazette*, Part II, Vol CV, No. 22 (1971).

Fox, I.K., "Air and Water Pollution Control: Some Concepts for Use in Policy Development" in conference on the Use of Economic Incentives for Air and Water Pollution Control, Victoria, B.C. (1974).

Gibson, D., *Constitutional Jurisdiction over Environmental Management in Canada* (Ottawa: Queen's Printer 1970).

Gordon, H.S., "The Economic Theory of a Common Property Resource: The Fishery," *Journal of Political Economy* 62 (1954): 124-42.

Kneese, A.V. and B.T. Bower, *Managing Water Quality: Economics, Technology, Institutions* (Baltimore: Johns Hopkins University Press, 1968), p. 328.

Maler, K.-G., *Environmental Economics: A Theoretical Enquiry* (Baltimore: Johns Hopkins University Press, 1974), p. 267.

Neher, P.A., "Democratic Exploitation of a Replenishable Environment," U.B.C. Department of Economics Discussion Paper 73-23 (1973), p. 11.

Samuelson, P.A., "Is the Rent-Collector Worthy of His Full Hire?" *Eastern Economic Journal* 1 (1974): 7-13.

Scott, A.D., "The Fishery: The Objectives of Sole Ownership," *Journal of Political Economy*, 63 (1955): 116-24.

Scott, A.D., "Optimal Utilization and the Control of Fisheries," in *The Economics of Fisheries*, R. Turvey and J. Wiseman, eds. (Rome: F.A.O., 1957).

Scott, A.D., "The Defense of Federalism, or, the Attack on Unitary Government," *The American Economist* 17 (1973): 162-69.

Stephenson, J. and P. Nemetz, "Pulp and Paper in British Columbia" in conference on the Use of Economic Incentives for Air and Water Pollution Control, Victoria, B.C. (1974).

Water Resources Service, Department of Lands, Forests, and Water Resources, *Report on Pollution Control Objectives for the Forest Products Industry of British Columbia* (Victoria, B.C.: Queen's Printer, 1972), p. 25.

Weitzman, M.L., "Free Access vs. Private Ownership as Alternative Systems for Managing Common Property," *Journal of Economic Theory* 8 (1974): 225-34.

Appendix

Suppose the economy has two firms producing goods X and Y according to the following production functions:

$$X = F(X_1, X_2), F_i > 0; F_{ii} < 0, i=1,2; F_{12} = F_{21} > 0; \tag{1}$$

$$Y = H(X_3, Z), H_1 > 0; H_{11} < 0; H_2 < 0; H_{22} > 0; H_{12} = H_{21} < 0, \tag{2}$$

where X_1 and X_2 are quantities of labour used in X production, X_3 is the quantity of labour used in Y production, and Z is a pollutant discharged by the X producers:

$$Z = G(X_1, X_2), G_1 > 0; G_2 < 0; G_{11} < 0; G_{22} > 0; G_{12} = G_{21} < 0. \tag{3}$$

The more labour the X firm uses in the X_1 function, the higher is the discharge of Z; and the more labour it uses in the X_2 function, the lower is the discharge of Z. Thus the X firm has the capacity to abate, whereas the Y firm has no abatement technology; the technology of the model corresponds to the $(1, 0)$ technology described by Archibald and Wright (1974). The economy has a resource constraint:

$$X_1 + X_2 + X_3 = \bar{K}. \tag{4}$$

The two firms are assumed to be price-takers in both product and factor markets, and to maximize the following profit functions:

$$\Pi_x = P_x X - W(X_1 - X_2) - QZ; \tag{5}$$

$$\Pi_y = P_y Y - wX_3, \tag{6}$$

Where P_x, P_y and w are the product and factor prices, and Q is an effluent charge imposed by the environmental management agency. First order conditions for profit maximization are:

$$P_x F_1 - w - QG_1 = 0; \tag{7}$$

$$P_x F_2 - w - QG_2 = 0; \tag{8}$$

$$P_y H_1 - w = 0. \tag{9}$$

The economy contains two consumers whose utility functions are:

$$U_A = U_A(X_A, Y_A), U_{A_i} > 0; U_{A_{ii}} < 0, i=1,2; U_{A_{12}} = U_{A_{21}} > 0; \qquad (10)$$

$$U_B = U_B(X_B, Y_B), U_{B_i} > 0; U_{B_{ii}} < 0, i=1,2; U_{B_{12}} = U_{B_{21}} > 0. \qquad (11)$$

Assuming that each individual maximizes utility subject to a budget constraint, the utility functions yield the following demand functions:

$$X_i = D_{X_i}(I_i, P_x), i=A,B; \qquad (12)$$

$$Y_i = D_{Y_i}(I_i, P_y), i=A,B; \qquad (13)$$

where

$$X_A + X_B = X; \qquad (14)$$

$$Y_A + Y_B = Y. \qquad (15)$$

The individuals in the economy have three sources of income: labour income, shares in the profits of the two firms, and share in the effluent tax revenues collected by the environmental management agency:

$$I_i = v_i w \bar{K} + u_i \Pi_x + r_i \Pi_y + s_i Q \cdot Z, i = A,B, \qquad (16)$$

where v_i, u_i, r_i, and s_i are shares in labour income, the profits of firms X and Y, and effluent charge revenues. For the purposes of the simulation, it will be assumed that the two individuals share equally in labour income and profits. Two possible distributions of effluent tax revenues are considered: Distribution 1 which preserves the equality of income distribution by setting $s_A = s_B$ and Distribution 2 which gives all the revenues to individual A.

Equations (1)-(9), and (12)-(16) constitute a system with 17 equations and 17 unknowns: X, Y, Z, X_1, X_2, X_3, P_X, P_Y, w, I_A, I_B, X_A, X_B, Y_A, Y_B, Π_X, Π_Y. Since the system determines only relative prices, the wage is chosen as the numeraire: $w = 1$. One equation is superfluous because of the accounting identity between incomes and the value of output; equation (6) may conveniently be dropped from the system. A simple social welfare function

$$SWF = U_A + U_B \qquad (17)$$

was used to evaluate the impact of alternative levels of the effluent charge, Q, and alternative distributions of the effluent charge revenues, QZ.

The values of the social welfare function for a range of effluent charges are obtained by solving the 16 equation system, by means of a computer algorithm, for different values of Q, S_A, and S_B, and using the solution values of X_A, X_B, Y_A, and Y_B to compute U_A and U_B. The solution values, which are reported in Appendix Table 1, are those reported in columns 3 and 4, respectively, of Table 1 in Campbell (1975). For Distribution 1 the optimal effluent charge is 214, whereas for Distribu-

TABLE 1

VALUES OF THE SOCIAL WELFARE FUNCTION

Effluent Charge	SWF	
	Distribution 1 $(S_A = S_B = 0.5)$	Distribution 2 $(S_A = 1.0, S_B = 0.0)$
0.0	88.59281905	88.59281905
150.0	88.85584552	88.90446947
200.0	88.87647020	88.92606273
205.0	88.87706351	88.92637457
207.0	88.87723004	88.92640981*
210.0	88.87740468	88.92636760
214.0	88.87749841*	88.92613515
220.0	88.87734441	88.92541305
250.0	88.87145737	88.91529585

* denotes a maximum.

tion 2 it is 207. The relationships between the effluent charge and the value of the social welfare function for different distributions of effluent charge revenues is diagrammed in Figure 4. These relationships illustrate the importance of taking income distributional effects into account in formulating an effluent charge scheme.

The Ontario Mining Profits Tax:
An Evaluation

J. CLARK LEITH

The Ontario Mining Tax Act of 1972 is the primary economic policy instrument currently employed by the provincial government in its treatment of the mining sector. The Act, together with the accompanying administrative regulations, bears significantly on the level and distribution of mining activity in the province. The purpose of this paper is to examine the main features of the tax and to evaluate its effectiveness in achieving its primary policy objective.

I. OBJECTIVE

The 1972 Ontario Mining Tax Act has a number of possible objectives. By far the most important objective, however, is to capture for the province at large a payment for the raw natural resource. [1]

Since 1908 the province has not retained mineral rights for itself. In giving up the mineral rights to private interests, Ontario did not abandon all claim to profit from the minerals. [2] In 1907 the province instituted a mining profits tax whose base was regarded as the return to the raw mineral deposit. A few years later (1914) the tax was formally embodied in the first Mining Tax Act. At that time the fundamental reason for a tax on mining profits was articulated:

> It was considered right to claim for the public interest some share in the bounty of nature, especially when lands sold for $2.00, $2.50, or $3.50 per acre were found to contain great riches, sometimes a veritable Golconda. [3]

In brief, the argument is that there exists some bounty of nature over and above the economic costs of obtaining the minerals which the province regards as a legitimate base for a tax. [4] Note that the province lays claim to a *share* of the bounty of nature—not the entire return to the raw mineral deposit.

The bounty of nature is, of course, the economic rent attributable to the differential quality of deposits. This means that for a continuum of workable deposits whose outputs are sold at a common price, there is a range of deposits from the most profitable through to the marginally profitable. At the margin, if all factors of production are paid their opportunity cost, there is no rent accruing to the owner of the mineral rights. On infra-marginal deposits, however, the difference between the value of the mineral and the opportunity cost of the productive factors used in extracting the mineral is rent attributable to the fixed supply of the total mineral. Because of the continuum of deposit quality, the rent component per unit of output will differ between deposits.

The primary purpose of the Ontario Mining Profits Tax is to capture a share of the rent attributable to the differential quality of the deposits. If this ideal were achieved, the marginal deposit would thus pay no tax, and infra-marginal deposits would pay taxes as a function of their rents.

II. OUTLINE OF TAX

The Ontario Mining Tax is levied on profits from the *mining* stage.[5] Whether or not this succeeds in capturing some of the rent without falling on other productive factors or on users depends crucially on the types of revenue and expenses included in the calculation of the tax base.

The tax base is the profit for a year, defined as the difference between the value of mineral substances at the pithead and the expenses incurred in producing the mineral to that same stage. Consider first the issue of determining the value of the mineral at the pithead.[6] If the ore is sold or has a readily ascertainable market value as ore, the question is easily resolved. However, when there is no clear market test for the value of the ore, the mine assessor has to appraise the value. This is done by determining the amount of revenue arising from eventual sale of the processed mineral at a later stage, and deducting normal processing costs up to the point of sale, plus an allowance for profit on the processing stages. It is here that the administration of the tax makes one of the most notable departures from the primary objective. If the allowance for normal profit in each of the processing stages did not discriminate between stages of production or locations of processing, it would not have any broad policy implications. It does, in fact, discriminate in both these ways. As a result, total revenue for tax purposes, and hence total taxable profit, is not independent of the degree and location of further processing activities. In other words, considerations other than the bounty of nature enter into the determination of the tax base.

I have shown elsewhere that the effective mining tax rate for a typical mine can be reduced dramatically by carrying processing through the refining stage, and by locating the refining stage in northern Ontario.[7] It should be noted, however, that the potential total processing incentive is strictly limited because it takes the form of a reduction of profits taxes payable. Further, the processing allowance does not affect the cost of independent downstream producers, who remain free to purchase their inputs on world markets.

Turn now to the expense side. It is noteworthy that the following expenses *are* allowable: (1) all working expenses; (2) depreciation on plant and equipment; (3) exploration and development expenses (except for acquisition of mineral rights). There are a few important items which are *not* allowable as expenses under the Act: (1) return on capital invested; (2) depletion; (3) royalties or purchases of mineral rights. The precise definitions of these expenses are spelled out in the Act and accompanying regulations. Without taking up a number of minor matters, this summary provides us with enough information to distinguish between true economic costs which are, and those which are not, allowed in the Ontario system.

The rate of tax in Ontario was for some time a progressive function of total mining profits (see Table 1). In 1969 the tax free base was increased to $50,000 and the rate on all profits over that amount was unified, as recommended by the Smith Committee,[8] at 15 per cent. The 1974 Act returned to a progressive schedule, set out in Table 2, apparently to permit adequate leverage for the processing incentives to bear on the companies large enough to establish processing plants in northern Ontario.

III. EVALUATION OF THE TAX

To what extent does the Ontario tax capture a share of the bounty of

TABLE 1
THE MINING PROFITS TAX IN ONTARIO:
OLD MARGINAL TAX RATES

Profits	Marginal Tax Rate on Profits			
	1914	1930	1947	1958
0 to $10,000	0%	0%	0%	0%
Next $990,000	3%	3%	6%	6%
Next $4,000,000	5%	5%	8%	11%
Next $5,000,000	6%	6% max. marginal rate	9% max. marginal rate	12% max. margina rate
Next $5,000,000	7%			
Subsequent $5 million increments	add 1% increments			

Source: *Report of the Ontario Committee on Taxation* (Ontario: Queen's Printer, 1967) and *Ontario Budget*, various years.

TABLE 2

NEW MINING PROFITS MARGINAL TAX RATES 1974

Profits	Marginal Tax Rate on Profits
0 to $100,000	0%
Next $900,000	15%
Next $9,000,000	20%
Next $10,000,000	25%
Next $10,000,000	30%
Next $10,000,000	35%
Over $40,000,000	40%

Source: *Ontario Budget*, 1974.

nature for the province without introducing other effects? There are two dimensions to the issue: at one point in time, and over time. First, in a given year, we want to know the extent to which the tax base corresponds to the true economic rent. The answer, as we noted earlier, depends on the way revenues and expenses are considered in computing profits. The Ontario tax has one major departure from the concept of true economic rent attributable to the differential quality of deposits. The law does not permit a return on capital to be charged as an expense. Hence, the tax base includes both the rent and the return on capital. In the extreme case of a marginally profitable deposit where no rent is earned, the tax falls entirely on capital. In all other (infra-marginal) cases the tax falls on both capital and rent.

For the sake of completeness, we should also note that the Act is perfectly correct in not allowing depletion as an expense while exploration and development expenses are allowed. To allow both would be to permit the mine operators to charge twice for what is fundamentally the same thing. Also, the Act is correct in not allowing payments for mineral rights as an expense, for such expenditures are in fact payments for the rent which the Act is attempting to tax.

A second dimension of the Ontario tax is the 1974 increase in rates designed to capture a greater share of the windfall gains arising from the recent sharp increases in mineral prices. As the provincial treasurer put it in his budget speech:

> Increased demand by major industrialized countries has resulted in sharply higher metals prices and substantial windfall gains for the mining industry in Ontario. . . it is (therefore) only fair that we secure for the people a higher return from our natural resources. [9]

The tax rates were adjusted to yield an expected doubling of the total tax take.

In analyzing this aspect, note that an increase in metals prices has two effects. It increases the rent collected by all existing producers, thus increasing the tax payable to the province, and it extends the margin of profitable deposits. An increase in the tax *rate* in response to the higher metals prices also acts on both: it increases the *share* of the rent collected by the province, and it contracts the extensive margin from its new point. The tax rate increase thus captures more of the windfall gains accruing to infra-marginal producers. But the increased rate also has the side effect on the allocation of resources. [10]

IV. A PURE RENT TAX

To achieve the primary objective of the Ontario tax policy toward the mining sector—to capture for the province a share of the rent due to the bounty of nature—what adjustments to the present system might be introduced? An attempt to convert the current Ontario mining profits tax to a tax on economic rent would require one major change. The return on capital would have to be removed from the tax base. This could be accomplished, as suggested in the report of the Smith Committee, by permitting an "investment allowance" which would be chargeable as an expense in computing taxable profits. The allowance would be the allowable rate of return on the gross investment of the mine operator in all assets employed (including unamortized exploration and development expenditures) with one exception. Investment in mining rights would not be included.

The key issue in such a provision would be the determination of the allowable rate of return on capital invested. Clearly the allowance should reflect the normal return on capital invested in similar circumstances, including risk. Any concrete measure is bound to have an element of arbitrariness involved in setting it. Granting this, the calculation of the rate of allowance proposed by the Smith Committee seems to have been particularly haphazard. Their approach was to examine price earnings ratios on the Toronto Stock Exchange during the two and one-half year period of 1 April 1964 to 31 October 1966. This examination yielded an after-tax rate of return of 7.84 per cent which, when grossed up for federal and Ontario income taxes, amounted to a 12 per cent allowance. Such a computation, however, uses an extremely short period in a relatively thin market, and fails to take into account the myriad of special concessions that interpose between the gross and net rates of return. A simple alternative measure is the rate of "base profits" on total assets as computed by Statistics Canada. Base profit is a term they employ to provide a consistent measure of profits unaffected by tax concessions. It includes in profits depreciation, depletion and amortization, provision for current and deferred income tax, non-cash allowances, and provisions charged against profit. Consider the rates contained in Table 3. The mean all industries base

TABLE 3

MEAN AND STANDARD DEVIATION OF BASE PROFIT RATES ON
TOTAL ASSETS, CANADA, SELECTED INDUSTRIES 1962-73 (PER CENT)

Year	All industries	Total mining	Metal mining	Mineral fuels	Other mining	Manufacturing	Trans-portation
Mean	12.0	14.1	14.1	13.7	14.3	13.0	10.3
St. dev.	1.03	1.70	2.49	1.73	3.42	1.41	1.18

Source: D.B.S., *Industrial Corporation Financial Statistics.*

profit rate in the twelve years considered is the 12 per cent proposed by the Smith Committee. The mean rate in metal mining, however, is 14.1 per cent. The latter rate seems more appropriate. Exclusion of a normal return on capital from the base of the tax would leave the base as an approximate measure of the rent due to the bounty of nature.

The economic effects of such a change would be of two types: allocational and distributional. First, regarding the allocational effects, in contrast with the existing tax, a pure rent tax imposes no distortion at the margin. As a result, there would be some gain, probably small, in allocative efficiency to be had by moving to a pure rent tax. This arises because mine owners currently work to the point that their *after* mining tax marginal productivity of capital is the same as elsewhere in the economy. As a result, there is currently underinvestment in the mining sector. By switching to a pure rent tax, the before mining tax marginal productivity of capital in mining would be equal to that elsewhere in the economy. Potential mines that are currently just beyond the margin would become profitable. Higher cost (lower grade) ores would be extracted, and the rate of extraction would be increased. In the absence of offsetting distortions, all of these effects move the static intertemporal allocation of provincial mining activity closer to the optimal state.

Second, there would be a redistribution of mining income. Infra-marginal mines would be less profitable because of the tax on pure rent. Owners of these mines would suffer a reduction in their expected flow of income from the mine, and thus take a capital loss to the benefit of the government. Owners of marginal mines would reap a capital gain at the expense of the government. Whether or not the total take from mining as a whole would rise or fall depends on the extent to which the rate is adjusted to compensate for the shrunken base. In any case the share of the taxes paid by owners of marginal mines (with a high ratio of return on capital to total mining profits as presently calculated) would fall, while the share paid by owners of the richer mines (with a lower ratio of return on capital to total mining profits) would rise. However, when it is recognized that most mining companies own both marginal and richer mines, it is clear that the redistribution of tax shares between companies would probably be relatively small.

Once a mining rent tax is in place, the level of activity in the mining sector is unaffected by the rate of tax (within reason). This follows from the fact that the ex ante rate of return at the margin is independent of the amount of pure rent. Put another way, a change in the rate of the pure rent tax (but only a pure rent tax) changes the distribution of income from mining between the government and the mine owners. It does *not* change the level of mining activity.

Such a state of affairs raises the distinct possibility that the government would be tempted to increase the tax rate substantially, and thus increase its total take from the mining sector. Beyond the question of whether or not such a move would be equitable to the mining shareholders, this raises the potentially important problem that the mining companies might dissipate their rents in excessive costs as the rate of tax on pure rent rises. Undoubtedly some of this sort of effect exists at present due to both the mining and the corporate profits taxes. As a problem peculiar to the rent tax, then, it would arise only when the rate of rent tax exceeds the rate of corporate income tax.

On balance, the economic effects of a change in the Ontario mining tax to a tax on pure rent would not be substantial in any direction. The major advantage has little to do with the economic effects. The major advantage would arise from clarifying the jurisdictional question of which level of government should tax which revenues from the mineral sector.

The unique feature of the mineral sector is that part of profits from mining may be attributable to the bounty of nature. The provincial right to tax that bounty of nature is well established: the provinces have an indisputable claim to *sole* jurisdiction in taxing rent due to the bounty of nature (differential quality of deposits). Hence, a move to convert the province of Ontario's mining tax to a pure rent tax would stake out the province's claim to sole jurisdiction in taxing mineral rents. No other mineral tax or royalty has this feature.

The area of sole provincial jurisdiction is strictly limited, however. It does *not* include windfall profits in the mineral sector which arise from unexpected changes in prices or costs. These are not unique to the mineral sector. As noted earlier, inclusion of these in the tax base for the mineral sector will introduce an allocative distortion. Instead, a windfall profit accruing in the mineral sector is simply a capital gain and should be treated in the same way as a capital gain elsewhere in the economy.

The distinction between pure rent and windfall profit thus provides a useful guide to resolution of the jurisdictional issue. The province should have sole jurisdiction in the taxation of pure rent, but only of pure rent. Further, a pure rent tax should be deductible in computing income for corporate income tax purposes. Beyond the tax on pure rent, there is nothing to distinguish the minerals sector from other sectors, and the general jurisdictional principles apply.

Notes

1. It is worth noting that one objective *not* attributable to the Ontario Mining Tax is regulation of the rate of exploitation.

2. The province did, however, effectively preclude subsequent resort to several alternative systems such as a royalty on minerals extracted or leasing of mineral rights. The reason for the exclusion of the latter option is obvious. The reason for the former lies in the fact that a royalty paid to the province would not be a payment to the owner of the mineral rights. Rather it would be an indirect tax which is *ultra vires* of provincial jurisdiction.

3. T.W. Gibson, equivalent to Deputy Minister of Mines for Ontario at the time. Quoted in the *Report of the Ontario Committee on Taxation, III, The Provincial Revenue System* (Ontario: Queen's Printer, 1967), p. 304.

4. This justification has been repeated recently in the report cited above, p. 314.

5. This discussion refers exclusively to the Mining Tax Act, 1972, as amended by the Mining Tax Amendment Act, 1974 (passed 14 February 1975) and the accompanying Ontario Regulation 126/75, *Ontario Gazette*, 8 March 1975.

6. This is generally taken to mean after the ore has passed through the primary crusher.

7. J. Clark Leith, "Exploitation of Ontario Mineral Resources: An Economic Policy Analysis," draft of a study prepared for the Ontario Economic Council, May 1975.

8. *Report of the Ontario Committee on Taxation*, 1967, referred to as the Smith Committee after its chairman.

9. The Honourable John White, Treasurer of Ontario, *Ontario 1974 Budget*, p. 14.

10. For a more detailed analysis of this proposition see H.G. Grubel and S.S. Smith, *Canadian Public Policy* I, 1 (1975).

Governments and Mineral Resource Earnings: Taxation with Over Simplification?

PAUL G. BRADLEY

I.

In his leadoff paper in this volume Professor Scott addresses the question of which level of government should receive natural resource revenues. The revenues to which he refers are residual earnings which remain after "necessary earnings" have been allocated to compensate the suppliers of capital, labour, and other inputs required for the production of the resources. That such residual earnings should be assigned to government, at one level or another, is a premise based upon a concept of equity. This premise is reinforced by identifying them as economic rents: the significance of rents is that their bestowal does not affect the level or mode of the production by which they were created.

The neutrality aspect of the disposition of rental income is illustrated by considering the implications of assigning non-rental income to governments. Thus: "governments cannot in the long run successfully tax any part of resource sales revenues except the rent; attempts to do so would result in the contracting of industry to those shows and sites where the tax could be shifted from necessary factor earnings to rent."[1] The issues posed when one delves into the division among levels of government of taxes derived from resource income are complex, as the reader of Professor Scott's careful exegesis will realize. There is therefore ample reason for undertaking this analysis with the stricture *ceteris paribus*—"other things," in this instance, being the outputs of the resource industries which are being taxed.

It is nevertheless noteworthy that in the debates which have taken place in various provinces it has been shown that taxation of mineral industries often does change "other things." The type of taxation chosen—for example, gross royalties as against levies on profits—can, of course, change output. It is necessary to go farther and to inquire whether, even when the "right" *type* of tax is chosen, there may not be circumstances where output will be affected, incidentally or by design. Are there reasons why provinces may prefer taxation which changes the level of activity? Or, may there be resource industries where it is impossible to identify the rent component of earnings? Neither of these eventualities would undermine the premise that resource industry earnings should be subject to special taxation. However, to reject or circumscribe the applicability of the concept of economic rents would dictate a much broader range of concerns for government. Taxation policy would no longer be restricted to questions of distribution or even allocation, as the latter is identified in the Scott paper. Different levels of taxation would be associated with different levels of activity in the resource industries, so that tax policy would of necessity involve governments in the management of resource development. This responsibility, which would be multifaceted, would bear on the question which is the theme of this volume: what is the appropriate division among governments of tax receipts from natural resource industries?

My objective in this paper is to examine whether government tax policy *should* or *could* be neutral with regard to the use of mineral resources, as posited by Professor Scott for resource development in general. After considering in the next two sections the nature of the residual earnings, or surpluses, associated with the extractive industries, I conclude that such neutrality is unrealistic. In the first of these production from known deposits is examined under the assumption that one factor required to produce the mineral is available only at increasing cost. In the second the implications of depletion and replenishment are analyzed; these are two features of mineral resources which distinguish them from agricultural land, the prototype in most discussions of resource rent. In the following section I consider the type of analysis which is feasible for governments which levy taxes upon the receipts of a mineral industry. I conclude with an unresolved query: if taxation of resource earnings may, or indeed must, involve responsibility for the rate of resource use, is this realization helpful in deciding at what level of government that taxing power should reside?

II.

Erich Zimmerman, an economic geographer, contributed to the development of resource economics by his insistence that substances be defined as resources not with reference to particular physical characteristics but rather to their usefulness as inputs to economic activity. His thoughts are epitomized in a remark that is frequently quoted: "Resources are not; they become."[2] This remark, as might be expected, has found great favour with those who emphasize the ingenuity of miners and prospectors and the willingness to accept risk of their backers. We can agree with its substance while extending its content if we add a phrase so that it reads: "Resources are not; they become, but some become better than others." Different physical characteristics determine how well various minerals "become."

For petroleum, size and depth of reservoir and productivity of wells are important in determining the unit cost of production. For metallic minerals, concentration of ore is crucial, along with size and location of the deposit.

In order to examine how quality differences among resource occurrences can give rise to surplus earnings, or rents, it will be useful to consider a very simple model. Assume that a particular mineral is obtained from ore bodies which differ only in their respective grades of ore. Production requires a single input, which is initially assumed to be available in any required quantity at constant cost.[3] It is further assumed that the deposits are long-lived, postponing until later consideration of depletion and discovery. Figure 1 portrays the derived demand *DD* for the various known ore bodies, assuming the price of the mineral to be unaffected by the level of total output. Owing to the high quality of ore found in deposit 1, its production generates a substantial surplus, shown by the shaded area. Lesser surpluses are generated by producing deposits 2 through 8, while under the assumed conditions there is no demand at all for ore body 9—it could only be produced at a loss. These surpluses, where they exist, yield the rents attributable to the natural resource. In this simple model they are eminently eligible for appropriation by the taxing authority because their distribution will not affect the economic incentives which dictate that the first eight ore bodies be produced, but not the ninth and tenth.

Although rents are defined with reference to factor demand, as shown for the ore bodies in Figure 1, it is more common in discussions of mining to consider the demand for, and supply of, the mineral product. One can easily transform the variables of the simple model. Thus Figure 2 shows the costs and outputs of mineral from the different ore bodies. It is assumed that any output can be sold at the going price. The areas bounded above and below by price and unit mining cost, respectively, are the same surpluses as before. So far our assumptions about mining have not diverged from Ricardo's assumptions about agriculture, so that Figure 2 is the conventional depiction of differential rents. As far as resource allocation is concerned, in this simple model economists need only make certain that the form of taxation is appropriate for capturing the rents attributable to the different ore bodies. No ambiguity arises over returns to other factors of production, nor is there any question about the preferred level of output of the industry.

In this simplified description of the mining industry, the assumptions coincide with those made by Professor Scott when defining potentially taxable resource income, the so-called tax base. He assumes that "the services of labour and capital used in Canadian resource industries are highly mobile and versatile—in fact, elastic in supply."[4] This phraseology appears to imply perfect, or nearly perfect, elasticity of supply for factors

FIGURE 1
VALUES OF TEN ORE BODIES OF DIFFERING QUALITY
(ALL INPUT COSTS CONSTANT)

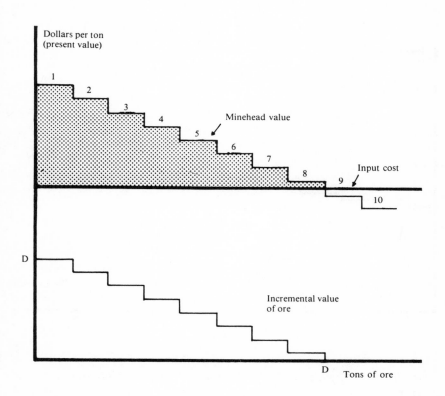

other than the natural resource itself. As we have seen, in these circumstances all surpluses associated with resource production are contained within the tax base, which is evaluated by summing for each resource occurrence the income from the sale of the product net of factor costs.

Because the validity of assuming perfectly elastic supplies of all inputs is not self evident, it is worth considering the implications of relaxing this assumption. Suppose additional increments of one factor, capital, are at any given time available only at successively higher cost, the situation depicted in Figure 3. Circumstances in Figure 3 are otherwise similar to

FIGURE 2

MINERAL SUPPLY FROM TEN OREBODIES
(COMPUTED AS STOCKS)

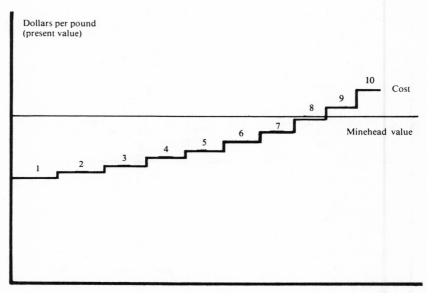

those of Figure 1, with the demand for known mineral deposits portrayed under a particular set of price and cost expectations. Now deposits 1 through 6 are utilized. The total economic surplus resulting from production is the area bounded on top by the stepped values of ore output and on the bottom by the marginal cost of capital.

We wish to identify the total surplus *attributable to the resource*, restricting consideration to points corresponding to full utilization of successive ore bodies. If the return to capital is limited to *uc*, so that only deposit 1 is developed, this surplus is the area *abcd*. If the return to capital is allowed to rise to *vk*, which permits the development of deposit 2, it is the combined rectangles *abef* and *ghke*. In the neutral case, with the return on capital rising to *lw*, deposits 1 through 6 are developed. The total surplus

FIGURE 3

VALUES OF TEN OREBODIES OF DIFFERING QUALITY
(ONE INCREASING-COST INPUT)

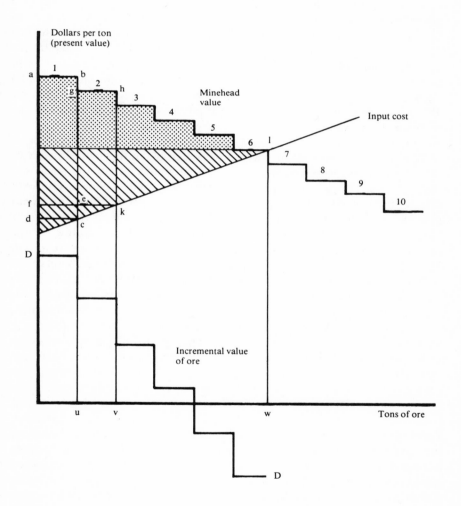

attributable to the resource is shown by the shaded area, while the surplus accruing to the special factor, capital, is shown by the diagonally-marked area. In Figure 3 increments to the aggregate resource surplus associated with the development of successive mines are shown by the lower line *DD*. Although some individual mines after number 4 can earn positive rents, their net effect on the tax base is to reduce it, since the higher return needed to attract additional capital lowers the rents earned on earlier ore bodies. [5]

In the circumstances just described, a taxation policy predicated upon neutrality with respect to the output of the mining industry, and hence to the rate of utilization of mineral resources, would not necessarily be the one which generated the most tax revenue. If increasing amounts of capital for mine development are only available at increasing cost, then rents must also be attributed to the inframarginal units of capital; these rents are often called producers' surplus. Varying the allowable return to capital affects the division of total surplus income between governments, as claimants to the resource share, and investors, while at the same time altering the level of output of the industry.

Whether higher tax revenues would be preferable to the neutral policy of maximum output would depend upon the circumstances of the particular industry. For example, in a closed economy, the surplus income accruing to investors would contribute to the national income, whereas to the extent that foreign ownership was substantial, this surplus would go abroad. In the latter case the government might regard the surplus accruing to the resource, not the total surplus, as the appropriate quantity to be maximized. This preference would be reinforced if there was sentiment to conserve the resource (to be considered in the next section), but it would be weakened if a lower level of activity, and hence fewer employment opportunities, was regarded as undesirable. Foreign ownership, conservation, and employment are issues relevant to the Canadian mining industry. As a consequence, governments may see taxation policy as extending beyond the appropriation of neutral resource rents to embrace a variety of resource management concerns.

III.

We now must expand our analysis to include discovery and depletion, two distinguishing features of the mineral industries. Economists classify resources in a variety of ways, using such terms as replenishable or non-replenishable, renewable or non-renewable, stock or flow. It may be confusing to find minerals designated as non-replenishable, non-renewable, or exhaustible, inasmuch as mining and petroleum companies advertise their continuous investment in building up stocks. This they accomplish both by exploration and by cost-reducing technical innovation which makes available low grade deposits. The confusion in terminology probably springs from failure to indicate the time span or scope for action which is contemplated. In the traditional short-run mineral availability is confined to those amounts which can be produced with installed capacity, but this time frame is of little relevance to taxation policy or resource management. The longer-run which has been considered so far embraced all activity required to produce known deposits; these comprise a stock which is not replenished by natural forces as it is used. However, if more scope for action is allowed, so that search and research can proceed, producible mineral stocks can be replenished.

Engineers and economists working in the petroleum and mining industries apply the term "reserves" to known deposits which are economic to produce at current price-cost relationships. The term "resources," though used less precisely, describes the physical stock from which reserves are drawn. Mineral resources may be known but uneconomic to produce or they may exist in the earth's crust as yet undiscovered. In analyzing production from known deposits I have included as part of the cost of minerals the investment to establish producing and concentrating capacity. Over the longer term the supply price of minerals must also reflect the investment required to create reserves out of resources. One is tempted to picture a cost component, exploration cost, which would be tacked on to the costs depicted in Figures 1-3, reducing the areas which were identified as surplus earnings in those figures. Specifying the magnitude of this exploration cost, however, appears to lie beyond the capabilities of present-day analysis. If this is the case, then the definition, not just the desirability, of a tax base consisting of resource rents is at issue.

To examine this problem we must consider the surpluses associated with resource production in a long-run which embraces exploration activity. In this time frame I deal not with known deposits but with prospects. Figure 4 portrays the derived demand for prospects, and hence the level of exploration, as being determined by the expected value of prospects and the cost of exploring them. Prospects are arrayed in order of declining expected value, with the line *ab* approximating the stepped function. The expected value of a prospect is the sum of the values of all possible outcomes—big finds, little finds, nothing—multiplied by their respective probabilities of occurrence. The value of each outcome is the capitalized value of the revenue it will yield net of development and operating costs; this is what was identified in Figure 1 as surplus. To simplify Figure 4 it is assumed that the same capital expenditure is required to explore each prospect. The supply price of exploration funds is assumed to be constant, as indicated by the line *xy*.

FIGURE 4

VALUE AND COST OF EXPLORATION
OF MINERAL PROSPECTS

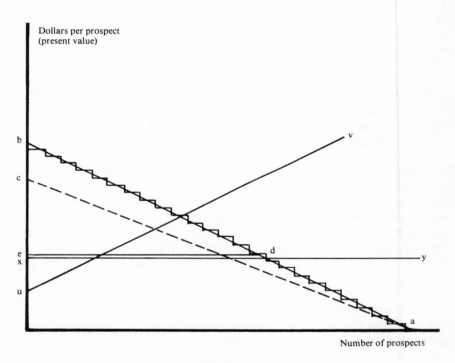

ab-Value of prospects
xy-Input cost (constant)
uv-Input cost (increasing)

Surpluses might be identified in Figure 4 in a manner analogous to Figure 1. They exist for each prospect where expected value exceeds exploration cost. Assuming no subsequent taxes at time of production and accepting the absence of risk aversion (as implied by the use of expected values), these surpluses could be appropriated without changing the level of exploration activity, that is to say, they could be regarded as economic rents. To tax resource revenues—or, more accurately, potential resource revenues—at the exploration stage would be a radical departure from current practice. I avoid examining the problems it would raise, however, and instead consider whether taxation *at the time of production* could be designed so as to appropriate the long-run surpluses defined in Figure 4 rather than those of Figure 1.

Taxes levied on receipts from production can be assumed to enter the calculations of companies searching for new ore bodies. The value of each prospect will in general be affected by a reduction in the after-tax returns to mines of any quality, since the prospector does not know what type of deposit he will find. Suppose, for example, that all the surplus identified in Figure 1 for the best ore body, labelled 1, were certain to be taxed away while the others were to be free of tax. This would lower the expected value of all the prospects shown in Figure 4, perhaps in the manner indicated by the dashed line *ac*. This would not be neutral in its effect on exploration, since fewer prospects would have a positive expected value net of exploration cost.

To capture the surplus depicted in Figure 4, it would be necessary to design a tax policy for the producing mines of Figure 1 such that the value of prospects would be reduced to the level *ade*; ideally this new curve would intersect the cost-of-exploration curve *xy* at the same point as before, so that the level of exploration activity would remain unchanged. To design such a neutral production tax is not feasible. Appropriation of *all* the surpluses attributable to mineral reserves (that is, those to be earned by developing known deposits) would extinguish the value of prospects. Enough must be left to cover the cost of exploration, as depicted in Figure 4. In addition, the expected returns from "successes" must contribute to the cost of exploration where the only reward is knowledge, since many prospects will fail to yield new reserves. In order to know the correct amount to claim from each mine in taxes in Figure 1, governments would need to have a model completely specifying the exploration process. Indeed, this description understates the difficulty of the problem because it is based upon the simplest of possible assumptions regarding the behaviour of prospectors. Analysis of decision-making under uncertainty ought to account for attitudes toward risk: perhaps capital is attracted by the prospect that the rare success will be a bonanza.

In the preceding section I dealt with the possibility that capital may only be available to the mining industry at increasing cost. Empirical evidence is needed on this point, but rising marginal cost for exploration capital would seem to be even more likely than rising marginal cost for development capital. If so, the capital supply schedule in Figure 4 should appear as the line *uv*, and the design of a neutral tax policy on production revenues becomes yet more complicated. Certainly it would be much more difficult to measure the cost of capital. Furthermore, as discussed in connection with development investment, governments might not find neutrality an appealing goal, when compared, for example, with the maximization of tax receipts.

Though kept offstage so far, there are other issues which undermine the plausibility of a neutral tax policy. Several writers—Gaffney, for example[6]— have argued that there is a tendency in a competitive mining industry to dissipate potential surpluses through premature exploration. So long as exploration is motivated by the right to lay claim to discoveries, it will take place sooner than it would where ownership had already been established. The force of this argument is again to weaken the appeal of neutral taxation, even if it could be achieved. Taxation more severe than the neutral rate would be preferred because it would serve to capture resource surpluses which would otherwise be dissipated.

In the long-run view the discovery process is an integral part of mineral production, and, as we have just seen, its incorporation into an analysis of the industry greatly complicates the task of defining resource rents, those earnings whose disposition does not affect mining activity. Discovery is necessitated by depletion, but we might inquire whether the fact that a particular orebody is used up over time poses in itself problems with regard to the definition of surplus resource earnings. The answer is in the negative. Although I stipulated that the mines depicted in Figures 1-3 be long-lived, imposing the condition that their reserves be limited would only have the effect of altering production plans: the volume constraint would necessitate that their managers consider user costs. Under the optimal production plan, a surplus could still be identified as before—the difference between receipts and total input costs.

Once again, however, the longer view should be considered. Whereas governments and private interests may not diverge in the matter of producing known deposits,[7] governments, by virtue of their responsibility for resource management, may feel compelled to take account of natural limitations in the supply of prospects. Thus depletion, in the sense of using up prospects, may imply a user cost which will enter government calculations but not those of individual companies. This would cause the desired rate of exploration, as perceived by the government, to differ from that which would appear to the mining industry to be the neutral rate. This possibility will be one of my concerns in the next section.

IV.

I have argued that governments may neither desire, nor be able, to view resource taxation as simply a matter of designing taxes that will funnel off economic rents. In this section we will try to develop a more realistic picture of their role, one in which fiscal responsibilities are commingled with those of resource management. As a means of describing surplus earnings attributable to a resource, a supply curve for a highly simplified, hypothetical mining industry was portrayed in Figure 2. Supply analysis of this sort is analytically possible, as has been demonstrated in studies made of the British Columbia copper industry.[8] However, in light of the preceding discussion, the deficiencies of such analysis with regard to the determination of taxation policy are all too evident.

A government seeking to define a tax base comprising surplus earnings might proceed by specifying allowable costs. This situation is illustrated in Figure 5, which isolates a single mine from the group which together account for industry supply as in Figure 2.[9] For simplicity I assume the ore grade is assumed to be homogeneous. The lower shaded area to height a in the sketch depicts unit operating costs. The margin between these and minehead price represents quasi-rent. Obviously this cannot all be appropriated by governments if continuing investment is to be forthcoming to develop mines.

If the government could confidently estimate a single value for the opportunity cost of capital, it could impute to output a development cost, like that labelled b in Figure 5, which would cover the capital expenditure required to install producing capacity. Here it encounters the problem considered in Section II: it may be unreasonable to suppose that the supply of capital will be highly elastic at a single value. The opportunity cost of capital as perceived by a mining company will depend upon the returns it can earn elsewhere; these in turn will depend upon the quality of foreign deposits and upon the extent to which foreign governments generously forego their power to capture resource earnings. A government may wish to attract more development capital by permitting a high rate of return. Or, as already suggested, it may wish to discourage investment and to retard the rate of use of resources by allowing only a low rate of return. Therefore, a single value for development cost cannot be specified in Figure 5, not at least until a choice has been made as to the desired level of total investment.

If an extractive industry is to maintain its level of output or expand, exploration must continue. Hence a further portion of the quasi-rent shown in Figure 5, perhaps the amount c, must be attributed to exploration cost. However, as we saw in Section III, it is not possible, given our present understanding of the discovery process, to know what this allowance must be in order that exploration activity remain unaltered. It is not even clear that such neutrality is desirable, since with the existing organization of the industry and prevailing institutions for rewarding exploration, the so-called neutral rate may in fact be inconsistent with maximization of the social

FIGURE 5

COSTS AND REVENUE:
SINGLE HYPOTHETICAL DEPOSIT

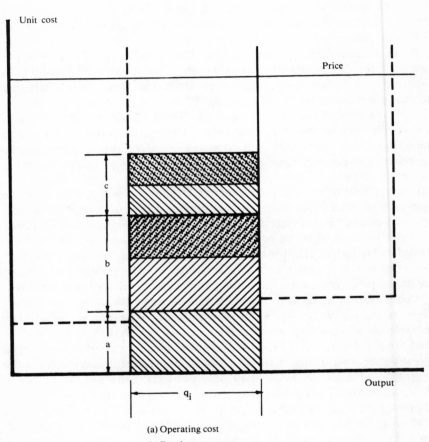

(a) Operating cost

(b) Development cost

(c) Exploration cost

value of mineral resources. Furthermore, as with development investment, the allowable return on capital may be a decision variable. In sum, governments cannot expect to isolate a definite component of the earnings of a mine which can be said to be economic rent and therefore a neutral tax base.

It appears that for the present governments must accept that changing the level of taxation of mineral industry earnings, implying variation in the rates of return to investors, will affect the pace of development of the industry. Taxation policy, therefore, must involve a good deal more than the division of tax revenues among various levels of government. It is of necessity intertwined with resource management, with the taxing authority in a position to control the rate of investment in the extractive industries and hence the rate of use of mineral resources.

The fiscal alternatives confronting governments can be characterized, admittedly roughly, by the diagram of Figure 6. [10] It depicts three possible *types* of taxation: *A*, *B*, and *C*. For each of these it portrays different *levels* of taxation, ranging from those which encourage very rapid development of mineral resources to those that lead to slow rates or even stagnation. With reference to the curve marked *A*, a tax policy yielding the outcome indicated by point 1 would be one which appropriated a very large share of industry earnings net of costs, stifling the incentive to search for or develop new mineral deposits. The point 2 shows the results of negligible taxation: government near-term receipts are small, but so are long-term ones, since it is assumed that the generous tax policy will be adhered to. Point 3 envisages a compromise under which mining activity is maintained, but governments claim a significant share of resource revenues.

The type of taxation or leasing measures imposed will affect revenues because private investment is responsive not only to expected return but also to risk. Uncertainty enters the mining industry in a variety of ways; these are commonly classified under the headings engineering and geological, economic, and political. [11] New processes which make available new sources, world business cycles, nationalization and curtailment of production in a foreign country—all of these cause variation in mining revenues which cannot be anticipated in advance. These risks will be shared among the various claimants to mining industry revenues. The manner of the division depends upon the taxation and leasing arrangements which are in effect. For example, a government which was desirous of reducing the risk associated with its revenues from mining would favour cash bonus bidding or royalties over profits taxes or direct participation. It would choose a position on curve *C* rather than on curve *A*.

When taxation policy involves a government in resource management, it

FIGURE 6

REVENUE POSSIBILITIES OPEN TO GOVERNMENT

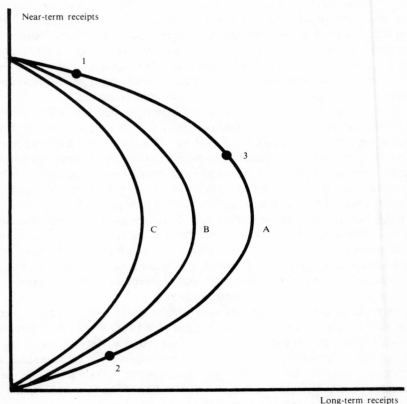

Near-term receipts

Long-term receipts

Level of risk to government:

A > B > C

should be cognizant of a fundamental proposition of resource economics, the idea that resources are a form of social capital, comparable to conventional capital goods. [12] This introduces a further dimension to the problem of maximization of natural resource revenues because it implies that governments should take the anticipated quantity and nature of mineral resources into consideration. For example, if it were expected that high quality deposits of a particular sort were limited relative to current and foreseeable rates of use, a government which subscribed to the principle of intergenerational equity and therefore discounted future revenue at a low rate might desire to slow down their development. This could be accomplished by regulation, but it could also be achieved through tax policy.

The ability to manage natural resource capital depends upon the ability to measure it. A great deal of effort by mineral economists has gone into classifying mineral stocks according to economic potential and degree of certainty. [13] However, only very limited progress has been made in Canada towards accumulating information about mineral stocks which can be related to government economic policy. In particular we appear to be a long way from viewing decisions about resource revenue as conditioned by our endowment of resource capital.

Finally, we should recall that in popular discussion as well as in most government reports, the central concerns differ from what has been discussed here. Creation of employment and economic activity, on the one hand, and environmental protection, on the other, are important issues and therefore must be taken into account in governmental decisions about mineral development. While particular incentives or regulations may be justified, it must not be overlooked that, if the argument of this paper is valid, employment in mining and trade-offs between environmental preservation and industrial development are concerns which cannot be divorced from tax policy.

v.

The various papers in this volume deal with legal, political, and economic issues raised by the taxation of natural resource revenues. In the economic sphere some resolution can be perceived between questions of income distribution and questions of resource allocation. Professor Scott's paper describes allocational issues seen from the standpoint of public finance. He considers relating taxation to the provision of benefits, so as to increase the likelihood that the appropriate level of public expenditure will be forthcoming both at the beginning of resource development, when provision must be made for public services, and at the end, when resettlement must be accomplished. In this paper I have considered allocational issues from the viewpoint of resource economics, arguing, with reference to the extractive industries, that the question of how large a share of resource revenues should be claimed by governments must stand prior to the question of how these tax receipts should be distributed among governments. Taxation policy is seen to be inseparable from resource management.

I am led to a final question: if taxation of resource earnings is bound up with how and at what rate mineral resources are used, does this awareness put us any further ahead in deciding what level of government should have the taxing power? I have touched on some of the complexities of managing resource use for the public benefit. What level of government should be vested with this responsibility? Which might be most sensitive to public preferences? No less important, can one level of government mobilize the required skills better than another? We long for a modern counterpart of Shakespeare's Henry V, assuming that the Archbishop of Canterbury was right when he declared: "Turn him to any cause of policy, the Gordian knot of it he will unloose."

Notes

1. A.D. Scott, "Who Should Get Natural Resource Revenues?" this volume, p. 3.

2. E.W. Zimmerman, *Introduction to World Resources* (New York: Harper and Row, 1964), p. 21.

3. Factors other than the single input have not been dealt with explicitly. However, in this fixed-proportions production model, product value could be interpreted as net of other factor costs. For example, where the specified input is capital, product value would be net of operating costs.

4. Scott, "Who Should Get Natural Resource Revenues?" p. 3.

5. It is assumed that the tax collecting government is unable to discriminate among mines with respect to capital cost. This would be true for most types of taxation: royalties, profits taxes, or income taxes. It would not be true if mining rights could be individually auctioned, so that for a particular deposit the company with lowest opportunity-cost capital would be favoured in the bidding.

6. M. Gaffney, ed., *Extractive Resources and Taxation* (Madison: University of Wisconsin, 1967), pp. 385-88, 391-92.

7. Some economists have argued that public and private discount rates might be markedly different, so that private investors would prefer a more rapid rate of use. I ignore this possibility.

8. Early work is reported in P.G. Bradley, "Some Issues in Mineral Leasing and Taxation Policy: Preface to a Simulation Study," in M. Crommelin and A.R. Thompson, eds., *Mineral Leasing as an Instrument of Public Policy* (Vancouver: University of B.C. Press, 1977).

9. In Figure 5 price and cost are related to the output of the mine (a flow). This is a slight departure from Figure 2, where they were related to reserves (a stock).

10. This diagram is a revised version of one appearing in Bradley, "Issues in Mineral Leasing and Taxation Policy."

11. Uncertainty and its implications for mining taxation were discussed more fully in Bradley, "Issues in Mineral Leasing and Taxation Policy."

12. For a complete discussion see Anthony Scott, *Natural Resources: The Economics of Conservation* (Toronto: McClelland and Stewart, 1973).

13. For a survey of this work see David B. Brooks, "Mineral Supply as a Stock," in Vogley, ed., *Economics of the Mineral Industries* (New York: Society of Mining Engineers of of A.I.M.E., forthcoming).

Note on Federations and Risk Aversion

In this brief note I wish to concentrate on the capacity of junior levels of government to bear risk in various types of federal systems. Canadians should be reminded that such issues are of interest well beyond North America. Two other federations should be noted.

In Australia, the first socialist government in twenty-four years brought down its first budget in August 1973. The budget was noteworthy, *inter alia*, for the measures taken to increase the federal government's share of the rent accruing to mining companies from mineral exploration and extraction.[1] The reaction by the state governments was strong and immediate. There were even suggestions that Western Australia, the state whose economy depends most heavily on the mining industry, would secede from the Commonwealth of Australia. (To Canadians this story should not be unfamiliar.)

More striking than the case of Australia, but in the same vein, is the relationship between the discovery of North Sea oil and the development of the devolution movement in Scotland. Since the Second World War there have been three fairly distinct periods when pressure for self-determination has mounted in Scotland. The first was immediately after the war, the second in the mid-to-late 1950s, and the third has spanned the last five years. The first two periods were brief and, essentially, abortive. In contrast, the third has resulted in the machinery for a Scots parliament being established, almost precipitously, by the British government. The most obvious explanation for the success of the most recent Scottish Nationalist lobby is the proximity of the North Sea oil field to the Scottish coast. Were Scotland to separate from the remainder of the United Kingdom, the cost to the other three countries in terms of lost revenue and of higher oil prices would be substantial. In summary, a tentative claim on an important natural resource gave the Scots in the 1970's the political power that they had lacked in earlier attempts to win a greater degree of independence.

This brief excursion into political analysis seems to indicate one main conclusion: in a world where resource constraints are becoming ever more strongly felt, the political, as well as economic, power afforded by the ownership of any scarce natural resource is likely to give rise to disputes concerning the right to ownership of the resource. It is to be expected that together with such disputes will go disputes concerning the portion of the Ricardian surplus that should accrue to the various parties disputing ownership. A brief comparison of Saudi Arabia in the 1920's with Saudi Arabia today should convince anyone that this phenomenon is not uniquely Canadian.

With this background, I wish to concentrate on the newly-opened question of risk-sharing by different levels of government (in both old and new federations) in the exploitation of natural resources. (The term "exploitation" is used throughout these comments as embracing both the exploration for, and the primary extraction of,these resources.) It is useful to consider the problem raised by the explicit introduction of risk into the discussion, and to review briefly the economic aspects of this problem.

The crux of the problem lies in the fact that, if both parties are not risk-neutral, decisions concerning the proportion of risk borne by a particular level of government will have allocational significance. There are two ways of looking at the problem. The first is that taken by Arrow and Lind.[2] They show that if the risk on a particular project is shared between a number of individuals, then, as the number of individuals (who are assumed to be risk-averse) becomes increasingly large, the risk apportioned to any individual becomes increasingly less significant. Hence, society should take a risk-neutral approach when evaluating alternative natural resource development projects. The key question to ask at this juncture is: "How large is large?" The answer presumably depends on the size of the project in question, and no general answer can be given. Nevertheless, this approach suggests that, for a particular project, and assuming general risk-aversion among individuals, the smaller the population the greater the proportion of the risk that is borne by any individual, and therefore the more risk-averse that group.

An alternative way of looking at the problem is to regard governments as entities in themselves, whose attitude towards risk is determined largely by the constraints that impinge upon them. The most important of these is the extent to which a particular level of government is able to pool the overall risk it assumes by spreading it over a number of projects. This has been dealt with in more detail elsewhere but the essentials of the argument are given below for convenience.

Governments typically have choice sets of projects from which they have to choose the subset, or portfolio, of projects which will (by some criterion) maximize the welfare of the population over which they have jurisdiction. Assume that both governments have the same degree of absolute risk-aversion. In the absence of an infinitely large, perfectly divisible, riskless investment the portfolio of projects that a government undertakes is likely to be diversified as much as possible to reduce the overall risk. To what extent can each level of government effect this type of self-insurance in an imperfect world? (that is, a world without a complete set of contingency markets that are all perfectly competitive). The senior level of government is likely to have a larger choice set, and thus is likely to be able to assume some projects that are too risky for the subordinate level of government to hold in its portfolio, which is likely to have been chosen from a smaller choice set. By spreading the risk of the more risky projects, the more senior level of government can maintain the return on the portfolio of projects at the desired rate of return, while not increasing the overall risk that it assumes.

Much of the above discussion points to there being more to be said about risk-sharing at different levels of government than the current literature suggests. Arguments have been advanced, from two points of view, that suggest that the more junior the level of government the more risk-averse the behaviour that will be displayed towards a particular risky project. For particularly large projects even national governments may not be risk-neutral. To approach questions of project evaluation, revenue-sharing, or budget-allocation using the assumption that all levels of government are risk-neutral seems likely to lead to incorrect allocative decisions.

Notes

1. Editor's note: See, for example, Michael Crommelin, "Australian Energy Policy and Management," paper presented at the 13th Pacific Science Congress, 18-30 August 1975, Vancouver.

2. K.J. Arrow and R.C. Lind, "Uncertainty and the Evaluation of Public Investment Decisions," *American Economic Review* 60 (1970): 364-78.

A Note on the Economics of Oil–Financed Recovery Projects

G.C. WATKINS

The purpose of this note is to illustrate how neither the amount of rent nor the rent forthcoming is independent of the level of royalty charged. That is to say, the revenue policy can affect the tax base itself. Taxes and charges are therefore not neutral instruments to be handed back and forth between governments.

At the present time, new supplies of crude oil in Canada are obtainable from three sources: oil sands (synthetic crude oil) and related heavy oil deposits; discovery of new conventional crude oil reservoirs; and recovery of a greater volume of oil from existing reservoirs. This note concerns the economic cost of the latter source of supply.

Under natural methods of production, an oil reservoir usually approaches the end of its primary life having recovered only a small fraction of its oil-in-place.[1] Enhanced recovery (ER) refers to the artificial augmentation of reservoir energy to increase recovery of oil-in-place.[2] Increases in recovery due to implementation of an ER scheme can range from just a small percentage to approximately one-half the oil-in-place, depending on reservoir characteristics and the type of scheme utilized.[3] The two most common ER techniques used in Alberta are water and solvent flooding.[4]

As at 31 December 1973, some 34 billion barrels of crude oil-in-place have been discovered in Alberta; about 11.2 billion barrels are estimated to be recoverable under prevailing technology (and prices). Of these 11.2 billion barrels, about 67 per cent, or some 7.5 billion barrels, would be produced by primary extraction; some 3.7 billion barrels or 11 per cent of oil-in-place would be recovered through enhanced recovery operations.[5] Thus, ER schemes account for a significant portion—about one-third—of Alberta's conventional crude oil reserves. Each percentage point in recovery attributable to the introduction of ER means an additional 340 million barrels of oil reserves in Alberta. As exploration prospects become depleted, the importance of enhanced recovery as a source of "new" oil is correspondingly increased.

The AERCB has approved 370 schemes in Alberta located in 230 reservoirs.[6] Large reservoirs account for the predominant portion of *ER* reserves; the five largest account for one-half of *ER* reserves.[7]

Clearly, then, economic aspects of the enhanced recovery schemes are important. More specifically, derivation of a unit cost of supply for *ER* oil would provide useful information for any formulation of a long-term Canadian oil supply curve.

As is now familiar in the attribution of costs where expenditure and related output streams vary,[8] we can define a supply price by the expression:

$$S_p = \sum_{t=1}^{T} \frac{I_t + Y_t}{(1 + r)^t} \bigg/ \sum_{t=1}^{T} \frac{F_t}{(1 + r)^t} \tag{1}$$

where S_p = supply price, \$ per barrel
r = discount rate
F_t = production of crude oil in year t, barrels
I_t = investment expenditure in year t, \$
Y_t = operating expenditure in year t, \$
t = time, years $t = 1, 2, \ldots T$
T = length of period considered.

Thus, the calculation of supply price for oil recovered by *ER* schemes requires data on production attributable to enhanced recovery over time (Ft), relevant development and operating expenditures (It and Yt) and the discount rate. Note this formulation of the supply price here excludes rental type expenditures—royalties, lease payments, and the like—since our concern is with real costs.

Comprehensive data on all *ER* schemes in Alberta were not readily available. Instead, examination was confined to thirteen *ER* schemes, based on information supplied from industry sources.[9] However, these schemes account for about 40 per cent of total *ER* reserves in Alberta and thus constitute a strong sample.

Generally, the production data supplied by scheme operators were in the form of a production schedule under primary extraction and a corresponding gross schedule under combined *ER* and primary operation. The difference between the two schedules defines production attributable to enhanced recovery. The normal pattern of such incremental production is to peak within ten years of the inception of a scheme, and then to fall rapidly over the remaining project life. No such easy generalization applies to operating expenditures—constant, increasing, and decreasing series were shown. Development capital tended to follow a pattern of substantial expenditures in the early years of the project life, followed by lower incremental amounts thereafter. In many instances, negative expenditures were relevant because the introduction of an *ER* scheme would alter the timing of and obviate the need for certain investments—for example, additional wells that would have been required to maintain production under primary depletion.

All cost data were adjusted to 1973 dollars. Accordingly the discount rate of 12 per cent adopted for the results listed below should be considered to be in real terms. As indicated beforehand by the exclusion of rental type payments, all supply prices were calculated on a pre-tax basis. [10]

Calculated supply prices at a discount rate of 12 per cent for the thirteen enhanced recovery schemes examined are shown in Table 1.

TABLE 1

SUPPLY PRICES FOR ENHANCED RECOVERY SCHEMES,
ALBERTA (1973$/BARREL)

Number	Scheme	Supply Price
1	Swan Hills, Beaverhill Lake A and B, Swan Hills Unit 1, Water Flood	0.248
2	Swan Hills, Beaverhill Lake A and B, Inverness Unit No. 1, Water Flood	0.781
3	Nipisi, Water Flood	0.791
4	Swan Hills South, Beaverhill Lake A and B Water Flood	1.141
5	Swan Hills South, Beaverhill Lake A and B Solvent Flood	2.349
6	Virginia Hills, Beaverhill Lake, Unit No. 2, Water Flood	0.486
7	Swan Hills, Beaverhill Lake C, House Mountain Units 1, 2, & 3, Water Flood	0.923
8	Kaybob South, Triassic A Extension Area, Water Flood	1.995
9	Mitsue, Gilwood Unit, Water Flood	0.279
10	Kaybob, Beaverhill Lake A, Water Flood	0.539
11	Rainbow IS Unit No. 1, (Rainbow A,D,E,G,H,O, EEE, B, and F; Rainbow South A,E, and G; Tehze A) Water and Solvent Flood	0.584
12	Countess, Upper Mannville H, Water Flood	0.560
13	Lathom, Upper Mannville A, Water Flood	0.400

The supply prices shown in Table 1 range from a low of $0.248 per barrel to a high of $2.349 per barrel, with a reserve-weighted average price of $0.831 per barrel. [11] The range in prices is due in part to the different nature of the reservoirs and the manner in which the schemes were developed and operated. Most of the *ER* schemes investigated use water as an injection fluid; an exception is the Swan Hills South solvent flood, which also has the highest cost.

1973 field prices of crude oil for the reservoirs listed in Table 1 range from $3.00 to $4.00 per barrel, depending on location. [12] A comparison of the market and supply prices shows, then, that the enhanced recovery production of conventional crude oil in Alberta enjoys significant economic rents. [13]

Estimated costs for finding and developing new discoveries in Alberta vary, but recent industry analysis suggests a figure for marginal finding and development costs of around $3.50/barrel in 1973 dollars. Whatever the precise figure may be, at this order of magnitude the conclusion is that at least in relation to the schemes examined, additional recoverable reserves acquired by enhanced recovery are significantly cheaper than those resulting from current discoveries.

While marginal costs of further enhanced recovery may rise steeply, the relatively attractive economics of such schemes to date encourage and justify emphasis on technological research directed towards recovering a higher fraction of the oil-in-place. [14] Moreover, it follows that insofar as mineral taxation policies seek to encourage new supplies (by shifting supply curves) or avoid truncating supply curves (restricting movements along supply curves), economic efficiency will be served by uniform treatment of all supply sources. Specifically, in the context of oil, royalties and related taxation measures to capture economic rent should not discriminate against additional reserves resulting from enhanced recovery operations.

It also follows that neither a single revision to the form of provincial royalty nor of the exemptions from federal tax can easily encourage enhanced recovery. In discussing who should get the revenues it is necessary to remember that the taxable base itself is very sensitive to the level and form of revenue chosen.

Notes

1. The term oil-in-place means the volume of oil existing in a reservoir, whether or not it is recoverable.

2. The Alberta Energy Resources Conservation Board (A.E.R.C.B.) has defined enhanced recovery as: "The fraction of the oil or gas in place that is considered to be recoverable due to the artificial improvement of the recovery process over a part or the whole of the pool." See A.E.R.C.B. Report 74-18 *Reserves of Crude Oil, Natural Gas Liquids and Sulphur, Province of Alberta*, Calgary, p. 1-9.

3. For example, in northwest Alberta the Rainbow Keg River B pool has a scheme with a recovery factor of 12 per cent of oil-in-place; the scheme in the Rainbow Keg River E pool enjoys a recovery factor of 40 per cent.

4. Of reserves attributable to enhanced recovery, water flood accounts for 90 per cent and solvent flood for 10 per cent (source A.E.R.C.B. *Conservation in Alberta,* Calgary, February 1974, Chart 16, p. 11).

5. All reserve data are taken from A.E.R.C.B. Report 74-18, *Reserves of Crude Oil, Natural Gas Liquids and Sulphur, Province of Alberta*, Table 2-2, pp. 2-78.

6. *Conservation in Alberta,* p. 11.

7. A histogram of reservoirs versus size of *ER* scheme suggests a log normal type distribution. This no doubt reflects the approximate log normality of the underlying distribution of primary reserves; see R.S. Uhler and P.G. Bradley, "A Stochastic Model for Determining the Economic Prospects of Petroleum Exploration over Large Regions," *Journal of the American Statistical Association* LXV (June 1970): 623-30.

8. For example, see P.G. Bradley, *The Economics of Crude Petroleum Production* (Amsterdam: North Holland Publishing Company, 1967).

9. Namely, *ER* scheme operators, including Home Oil Company Ltd., Amoco Canada Petroleum Company Ltd., Shell Canada Ltd., Hudson's Bay Oil and Gas Company Ltd., Chevron Standard Ltd., Acquitaine Company of Canada Ltd., and Pan Canadian Petroleum Ltd.

10. Taxation structures of individual firms differ considerably. Elimination of tax enables uniform analysis to be applied between reservoirs and is consistent with our primary concentration on real costs.

11. Recall that these calculations exclude taxes, royalties, and other rental type payments. The calculations were also repeated for different discount rates, but the results for several schemes were relatively insensitive to such variations.

12. Source: A.E.R.C.B.

13. In relation to current prices of around $6.50 per barrel, and after allowance for cost increases of 25 per cent or so, the economic rent has increased substantially. Note that not all the difference between the calculated supply price and the market price represents economic rent—a portion relates to relevant research and development expenditures and other overhead excluded from the analysis.

14. For example, see activities of the Petroleum Recovery Institute, University of Calgary, Calgary.

The Concept of a Nation and Entitlements to Economic Rents

A. MILTON MOORE

It is doubtless indicative of the present state of Canadian federalism that a large proportion of those who presented papers at the natural resource revenue conference wanted to talk about federalism or the equalization payments. This is appropriate. Surely the current controversy over claims to the economic rents generated by petroleum resources owned by the Crown in the right of a province cannot be—and should not be—resolved in isolation. The treatment of revenues from natural resources has posed severe difficulties from the start of the federal/provincial tax agreements, the equalization payments, and, indeed, ever since Confederation.

In a previous incarnation, I must have been a disciple of St. Thomas Aquinas or Plato. For as long as I can remember, my instinctive approach to a problem always has been to look for first principles and to deduce a conclusion from them. This inclination has been evident particularly in matters of taxation and concerning the Canadian federation. And, of course, the deductive method is the stock-in-trade of economists.

For the purpose at hand, I need two principles and an answer to one question.

The first principle has to do with entitlements to pure economic rents. How do nations or states regard them? Are entitlements to rents less securely in the private domain in a nominally free enterprise country than are other forms of income, or wealth drawn from other sources? The personal or individualistic view is familiar enough: witness the vast volume of tracts that assert a special status for capital gains. The individualistic view is that windfall gains are sacrosanct: you may tax my income but keep your grubby hands off my unrequited gains.

In the literature of economics, the contrary view holds sway. Since, by definition, economic rents and other windfall gains can be taxed away without affecting the behaviour of the rational person, it is received theory that rents are specially suitable for taxation. The pre-emption of rents by the community is invited. Also, the notion that accretions of wealth that are attributable to the growth of the community rightly belongs to the community surely antedates Henry George.

I shall take as my first principle that economic rents belong to the community.

For my second principle I must know which political unit of a country constitutes the community. Is it the smallest or largest unit; or something in between? Is the entire metropolitan area of a large urban centre a single community or is each component municipality a separate community? Is the community the small city or town with a huge industrial real property tax base, or the larger political entity of which it is part? These questions imply their answers. The trend to equalization of government services that has occurred in provincial/municipal relations in recent decades indicates that their community is at least as large as the provinces. Few persons now question the propriety of the equalization across school districts of the public schools portion of the real property tax. Every postwar inquiry dealing with provincial/municipal financial relations with which I am familiar has reflected a general public sentiment that the financing of all general services, and not only education, health, and welfare, should be at least the residual responsibility of the provincial government. The parochial view is on the wane in all provinces.

It follows that, for unitary government countries, the community is the nation. Hence the national government has the right and responsibility to pre-empt economic rents for the benefit of all members of the community.

One can arrive at the same conclusion by reasoning directly from first principles. One simply defines a community as the largest political entity within which all members are treated as equals, which we may interpret as meaning that the welfare of each counts equally, at least in conception. Hence the nation is the community and the national government has the right and responsibility to pre-empt rents for the benefit of all members.

To complete the deductive exercise, I must discover whether a particular country, Canada, that has a federal form of government, is a single community or only a loose confederation or coalition. It is clear that the E.E.C. is not a community in the sense defined. Perhaps Switzerland is not either. But I suspect that Australia is, and that the United States may be in the process of becoming one. And I like to think that, despite the misfortune (or political necessity) of 1867, Canada is a single nation, is a single community. Many anomalies are present, of course. But I would argue that the evolution of the welfare state, the general acceptance of the tax equalization payments, the assertion by the Government of Canada of its right to set oil and natural gas prices, and the disallowance of royalties payable to provincial governments as deductions for purposes of the income tax—these developments alone are sufficient evidence that Canada is a single community.

There is yet another way of reaching the conclusion that, de facto, no provincial government has the right to keep to itself the rents from the natural resources owned by the Crown. It would be unreasonable to expect the residents of any province to continue to share the costs of health, education, welfare, and general government services of other provinces if rents from the natural resources are not to be shared also. The logic of the welfare state, initiated by the national government with the acceptance of the provincial governments, and the logic of the tax equalization payments demand that the economic rents from natural resources be treated as a national asset. Political necessity takes priority over constitutional form.

We cannot be simultaneously ten countries and one country, ten communities and one community. For a time we can be, and are, two nations: Quebec and the rest. But that is not a stable situation; it is a transitory state. The marriage between Quebec and the other provinces has broken down. I expect that the breakdown will be formally recognized within a decade. There may be no divorce in this century but the fact that the partners to the marriage are no longer living together will be ratified in one way or another.

It may be argued, also, that Canada is a single community to a greater degree than is any province because the federal-provincial equalization payments and health and welfare programmes enable provincial governments to provide a national average level of services while imposing an average weight of taxation. But with the exception of education and the federal-provincial programmes, provincial and municipal services are not yet uniform within provinces nor are tax efforts. Equalization payments from provincial governments to municipalities are the exception, not the rule.

The present strained relations between the federal government and some of the provincial governments calls to mind the strained relations of the early 1950's. Then, out of the desire to retain their bounty, Ontario, British Columbia, and Alberta resisted the attempts of the federal government to take over the corporation and personal income taxes. Quebec did also for different reasons. To buttress their claims to the direct taxes, appeal was made by these provinces to the constitution. (The devil may quote scripture to his purpose.) It was even argued by some defenders of provincial rights that it was unconstitutional for the Government of Canada to raise revenues to finance expenditures in fields that were assigned to the provinces by the B.N.A. Act, notably health, education, and welfare. By parity of reasoning, it was claimed to be unconstitutional for the federal government to raise revenues to transfer to the provinces as fiscal equalization payments. Such appeals to the constitution did nothing to resolve the conflict between provincial rights and federal power in the 1950's and I cannot think that appeal to the constitution offers any solution to the conflicts of interests today.

In the 1950's I was opposed to the position taken by Ontario just as I am opposed to the stand taken by Alberta and British Columbia today. If these provinces are to be allowed to keep most of the revenues from oil and natural gas to themselves, I would expect Ontario to argue that the rules of fair sharing gradually developed during the last two decades had been rescinded. In consequence, Ontario might lay claim to the entire revenue from the income taxes and might well take the position that the federal revenues raised in a province should be no greater than the cost of the federal services received by the residents of that province. And, of course, the equalization payments should be terminated; in logic, there should be no interprovincial transfers whatever.

Reference has been made to the danger that Alberta might develop a sense of grievance and hence separatist sentiments if the Government of Canada pre-empts a substantial proportion of the revenues from oil and natural gas. Is there not a greater danger that Ontario might become militant and support the election of a Conservative government in Ottawa, after exacting from the party a pledge that all interprovincial transfers be terminated?

I have argued that we should not appeal to the constitution for a solution to the present impasse. I also would argue that the conflict will not be resolved by consultative or co-operative federalism or by bargaining. What a mess the United States would be in if the president had sought to resolve conflicts of interest between regions by consultation and compromise with the governments of the fifty states, rather than seeking their resolution in Congress. In my view, the premier of Ontario has since 1974 acted in the national interest as well as the self-interest of his province when he insisted that the Government of Canada accept full responsibility for determining the domestic prices of oil and natural gas. Bargaining would serve only to split the nation into two or more regions, each nursing a grievance. Before bargaining could begin, there would have to be agreement concerning the *status quo ante bellum* to which the confederation would revert if no compromise were reached. The federal government would argue that the *status quo* was the situation prevailing in 1972, while Ontario would insist upon 1939. Alberta probably would be unable to find a period that was ideal for its purposes. There would be no agreement concerning the *status quo*, hence bargaining could never begin. Surely the long, troubled, and comic history of the postwar federal-provincial tax agreements conferences decisively demonstrates the futility of expecting the premiers of the ten provinces to agree publicly to any sharing of public revenues that might leave them vulnerable to criticism in their provinces. One of the most divisive aspects of Canadian federalism is that it usually is assumed that a substantial proportion of the electorate of each province expects their premier to put the interests of his electorate ahead of the interests of other Canadians.

The only hope for the resolution of today's conflict between regional interests lies with the Government of Canada asserting its paramount power by imposing a solution that will be seen by most Canadians to be reasonable.

If the federal cabinet does not know and wants to determine what would constitute fair sharing, I suggest that it play a Rawlsian game by constructing the revenue allocations to which, say, ten Canadians representatives of various regions and backgrounds could agree if they were totally ignorant of the present and future financial and economic circumstances of the particular groups from which they were drawn.

In the currently popular mode of model building for the analysis of federal-provincial and other intergovernment relations, it is assumed that each participant pursues his self-interest unconstrained by multiple loyalties and develops strategies, forms coalitions, and makes side payments to maximize some self-centred objective. I am convinced that politics does not work that way. Like most individuals, most politicians have multiple loyalties and are under the constraint of justifying their actions in their own eyes and of convincing the public that their demands are justified. If you do not like the indeterminacy that such assumptions produce and if you insist upon using the postulate of the singleminded pursuit of self-interest, I suggest that you must impose the constraint that a necessary condition for success is that the leader of a provincial government appear to be acting in the national interest. I have already asserted that a premier must be seen by many of his constituents to be acting in the narrow self-interest of his province. Consequently, the premier is constrained to argue that the narrow self-interest of the province is either fair and just or is coincident with the national interest, or is both simultaneously. By doing so, a premier may consolidate his political position in his own province but he cannot win out in a confrontation with the federal government if he is isolated from the other provinces. The implication is that the share of the revenues from natural resources taken by a producing province must be accepted as reasonable by the other provinces, by the national government, and by the general public. Any outcome that lacks that attribute cannot be a stable one.

One last point: it has been said that the efficient management of the natural resources is facilitated if the revenue from the resources accrues to the political unit that does the managing. This proposition sounds attractive when stated at a high level of abstraction. But does it have any substance? It is received theory that a substantial proportion of the economic rents can be excised by a government without affecting the behaviour of the rational owner of a resource, whether the owner is a natural person or a corporation. It also is received theory that a tax on net profits does not affect the profit-maximizing behaviour of the firm. Does the behaviour of governments differ crucially? I could be persuaded that some provincial governments have been so inept in their endeavours to capture the economic rents of the natural resources they own that the public interest would have been better served if the governments had been content to take half the rents. I could be persuaded also that the combined incompetence of the federal and provincial governments and their agencies has made it unprofitable for private companies to undertake the exploration and development drilling of the petroleum resources under provincial jurisdiction on the scale that the public interest requires. But I am far from being persuaded that the root cause of the incompetence of the provincial governments is to be found in the federal government's pre-emption of what some provincial governments claim to be their birthright.

The Volatility of Rents

I.

One of the reasons why, among all the social sciences, economics has progressed so far can surely be traced to the ability displayed by economists in breaking down into manageable entities the mass of problems facing their discipline. One breakdown that can be found in each of the various specializations is that of allocation, distribution, and stabilization. Economists, of course, all know that most real world problems have all of the allocational, distributional, and stabilizational dimensions, but they have found it useful in thinking of these real world problems to focus on one dimension to the exclusion of others.

It must be emphasized, however, that even if one can use the breakdown mentioned above to analyze a policy problem, such a usage yields negative results when the object of the exercise is policy prescription. In such circumstances, all aspects of a problem have to be considered and weighed.

I suspect that much of the attractiveness in the concept of rents, that is in the concept of a sum which can be taxed or alienated without allocational effects, springs from the fact that if rents can be identified, the simple distinction between the allocational and distributional dimensions of real world problems could be carried directly from the world of theory to that of policy prescription. It is therefore important that we look carefully into the concept of rent in each specific area and ascertain whether it exists or not.

II.

It is for this reason that I wish to stress that to be able to accept Milton Moore's first principles as first principles it is necessary to accept the sometimes useful, but always dangerous and essentially incorrect view, that it is possible to formulate policies for which one can separate allocational and distributional aspects. How simple the world would be if one could formulate public policies that had only allocational or distributional effects depending on what one sought. May I suggest that this is one of the reasons why the idea of rent, that is the idea of a sum which can be captured and disposed of without allocational effect, is so attractive.

One of the things that Paul Bradley and Clark Leith made clear was the important idea that supply functions characterized by zero elasticities in the range of relevant prices do not really exist. Any tax or subsidy will therefore affect supply and hence will have allocational as well as distributional effects. The absence of zero supply elasticities has other implications, one of which is highly relevant to the subject of this book. Let us continue to follow Bradley (and Keyes) and implicitly assume that all the elasticity in the supply curves comes from the responses of capital to changes in supply conditions, responses which depend among other things (that is, *ceteris paribus*) on the number and quality of alternative opportunities open to capital, not only incidentally in other jurisdictions and in other countries in which resources can be exploited, but in other alternatives which, in the long run, include the alternative of consuming the capital.

If this is the case, the maximum revenue that can be raised at the national level by taxing a given industry will generally be larger than the sum of the revenues that provincial jurisdictions acting independently of each other can raise. The crucial words in the preceding sentence are "acting independently of each other," because clearly if they can get together, the provincial governments can raise exactly the same revenue as can the central government. If we are preoccupied with efficiency in the organization of the public sector, which, to simplify, I assume is composed of only two levels of government, then the time and money resources used up in co-ordinating the efforts of various provincial governments should surely be one of the factors which we should consider in deciding who should tax the proceeds from the sale of resource industries.

It would seem that the smaller the elasticity of supply co-efficient, the easier (i.e., the less costly) it will be for provincial governments to co-ordinate their activities and therefore the more one would expect taxes to be levied by junior governments.

I cannot pursue this line of analysis here, a line which reflects the work that Anthony Scott and I have been doing over the last four years, because I do not have the space for that. I would like instead to point to another response (in addition to the response of capital) that will result from changes in the price of output of resource industries and emphasize a very important point made at the conference by John Bossons, develop it further, and bring it together with an idea advanced by Meyer Bucovetsky.

To make my point, which I believe is crucial to the question of assigning responsibility over natural resources, let me develop it in the form of a story.

Imagine an hypothetical country divided into ten provinces, but in which there is also one central government. Suppose that in one or two of these provinces are located stocks of a given natural resource, such as crude oil. Assume further that from a position of virtual equilibrium, the price of oil is increased as a result of some exogenous event. Let us also postulate that the government of the hypothetical province or provinces in which the oil stocks are located decided to tax the income—gross or net is not really important for my argument—of the companies engaged in extracting that oil. We know from the Bradley-Leith-Keyes discussion that that tax will elicit a response on the part of capital which can be summarized by saying that the supply of oil will be less with the tax than it would be otherwise.

The tax, however, will also increase government revenues. The government of our hypothetical province can decide to dispose of these revenues in one or both of two ways: (1) reduce other sources of revenues, by cutting retail sales taxes, for example, or (2) increase expenditures. Both of these responses will have the consequence of attracting population to our hypothetical province from the other eight or nine hypothetical provinces. This may create "ghost towns" in the latter provinces, but will certainly require the host province or provinces to spend part of their new revenues on so-called infrastructures.

This mobility and the consequent arrangements and rearrangements will be costly to those who move, to those who remain behind, and possibly to those in the host province. Whether these costs should be incurred depends to some extent on both technological and economic considerations which help determine the expected value of the resource over its lifetime. Both technological and economic factors are important, as is obvious from a recognition of the fact that what we are dealing with is a resource which is exhaustible and non-renewable and from a recognition of the additional fact that the exogenous force which led to the higher price in the first place may not endure or that other forces may lead to a fall in the world price of the resource.

Specifically, whether the mobility, the consequent depopulation and production of ghost towns, and the new expenditures on infrastructures should be made depends in part on whether one expects the size of the asset to be large enough and the length of its life to extend far enough in the future to "compensate" as it were for all these adjustments. This size of asset is similar in effect to its "exhaustibility" referred to by Scott (pp. 3—45). If the asset is known to have a short life because one knows the exact size of stocks, then the efficient management of the resource would have to include the implementation of policies that would reduce or possibly eliminate the mobility of the population and the costs of adjustment consequent on this mobility. The problem, of course, is not made simpler if one is uncertain about the inventory of oil deposits. Indeed, as with many problems of that kind, one would expect that the presence of uncertainty would operate in the direction of forcing policies that would reduce still further the costs of mobility and of its attendant adjustments.

The question of whether one level of government is more able than another to make the "correct" decision about resource management when it cannot be assumed that supply curves have zero elasticities in the relevant range is a difficult one to answer. If we assume that all governments at all levels are Benthamite institutions seeking the maximization of the common good (somehow defined) *in their own jurisdiction*, then one would have to conclude that since the more senior government is better located to compute not only all the costs of adjustment in capital uses resulting from taxation, but also all the costs of adjustment in population location, it should be given the responsibility for managing the natural resource.

On the other hand, if governments are taken to be institutions that are essentially motivated by the pursuit of their own interests, then the assignment of responsibility for the management of natural resources will depend, as indicated above, essentially on the costs of co-ordinating the activities of the various governments of our hypothetical country.

A Comment on Decentralized
Resource Control

IRENE M. SPRY

The essential problem at issue in considering who should get natural resource revenues is not which level of government should get them, but which individuals should get them, as Milton Moore and Mason Gaffney have so justly reminded us. Governments are after all the agents of society (a community), not the society (or community) itself. The people of each province are also citizens of Canada; their well-being is affected by the taxes they pay and other contributions they make to the federal government and the benefits they receive in return, as well as by levies and returns at the provincial and municipal level. The problem is not so much the relationship of provincial governments to the federal government as of the relationship of the provinces to each other through the co-ordinating machinery provided by the federal government.[1]

The British North America Act and subsequent jurisprudence have established the right of the provinces to property in and control over natural resources within their boundaries, apart from a few specific exceptions.[2] Even the natural resources of the prairie provinces, which, at the inception of these provinces, had been reserved by statute to be "administered by the Government of Canada for the purposes of the Dominion," were in 1930 transferred to the control and ownership of these provinces.[3]

Revenues from the provinces' natural resources now enter, quite properly, "equalization" computations. Historically, revenues from Crown lands (and other natural resource revenues) have been an important element in defraying the costs of government.[4] Anthony Scott's ingenious computations give quantitative clarity to their early importance.[5] Any return reaped by a province from the use of its natural resources or by selling those resources or the right to use their services (whether by means of a price charged for those resources or a price charged for their use, or by means of a tax levied on the owners or users) therefore becomes an element in the balance of comparative "fiscal capacity." One result of the use of taxes where it is difficult to devise a way of charging a price has been that the necessary role of prices in the *allocation* of any resource among alternative possible uses and through time has been obscured by reason of a concentration of attention on intergovernmental assignment of taxing powers. Moreover, as Mason Gaffney in an unpublished contribution to the Victoria conference emphasized, and as the chapter by Moore also stresses, the importance of the the ultimate personal distribution is lost sight of in jurisdictional disputes.

Until the drastic change in the world price of crude oil, however, identifiable revenues from natural resources have in recent years played a minor and decreasing role in total government finances, which perhaps accounts for the fact that they have attracted relatively little attention in the overall calculation of fiscal capacity.[6] Then the abrupt change in price of crude oil precipitated a sharp dislocation of accustomed patterns of consumption of petroleum products and upset the precarious financial balance of Confederation.

The suddenness of the shift in the comparative prosperity of the various provinces in favour of the leading oil-rich province has created a crisis that calls for a renegotiation of the fundamental principles of co-operation within Confederation. Unilateral action by the federal government has only added to the complexities of the problem. The basic issues at stake in the current controversy are (a) a national price for oil; (b) the diversion of proceeds of oil and gas production from the Alberta treasury to a federal consumer subsidy; and (c) the problem of whether returns accruing from higher prices should be devoted, not to mitigating the effects of the sudden disruption of the customary distribution of costs and benefits among users of petroleum products, but to stimulating and financing the development of new sources of energy.

a. Federal response to the consequent social and political problems seems to have lost sight of the fact that oil and gas are not the only sources of energy used in Canada. In the past there is little doubt (despite the notorious difficulty of making valid comparisons of the cost of electrical energy)[7] that hydro-rich provinces have benefited from "cheap power." The Hydro-Electric Power Commission of Ontario, now Ontario Hydro, for example, had no doubt that "Hydro played a most important role in projecting the province into a position of leadership in the economic life of Canada."[8] No one, to my knowledge, has suggested that there should be a national price for hydro-electricity, to the disadvantage of the citizens of Ontario (and other hydro-rich provinces) and to the advantage of citizens of less hydro-rich provinces. Perhaps the fact that hydro-electric energy is mostly consumed within the province in which it is generated while a large proportion of oil and gas are exported from Alberta for use in other provinces and in the United States may be taken to be not only a constitutional basis for federal intervention, but also a possible social justification for the difference in treatment. This, however, seems to imply a drastic modification of the fundamental structure of a confederation that has long accepted the principle of provincial ownership and control of natural resources, despite great differences in the richness of the natural endowment of the various provinces. If the principle of a national price is to be accepted for one source of energy, perhaps it should be accepted for all equally. If it is to be accepted for one kind of natural resource, perhaps it should also be accepted for all natural resources: What about forest resources? And minerals?

b. Even if the principle of a national price is accepted, the question remains: How is its implementation to be financed? The citizens of Alberta seem to have some reasonable grounds for thinking that if the subsidy needed to reduce prices to consumers in eastern Ontario, Quebec, and the Atlantic provinces is to be paid, it should not come out of a special impost on their oil, but from the normal tax and equalization procedures.[9] It is very doubtful whether petroleum resources should, unilaterally, be given different treatment by the federal government from other natural resources, just because the drastic and sudden change in the international price has engendered a dramatically critical situation for consumers of oil products. Surely the situation called for consultation and agreement with the provinces involved. Moreover, concern arises that an artificially low price may check necessary curtailment of the use of oil and gas. [10]

c. There remains the further problem of whether keeping prices down creates a danger that incentives to seek out and develop new sources of supply may be stifled and the flow of funds to finance new exploration and innovation curtailed.

To the extent that price controls and subsidies distort the operation of the price-market mechanism in allocating nature-given resources and the capital and enterprise required to bring them into the "highest and best use," so rightly stressed as vital by Mason Gaffney, schemes to block or limit price changes and modify their impact deserve close and critical scrutiny. However, it is evident that in the energy field market forces do not operate with the untramelled efficiency assumed by economists in models that presuppose atomistic competition; full, free, and equal information to all involved in the bargaining process; a discount rate that accurately measures society's time preference; a perfect capital market; and the absence of any significant externalities that create social and economic inefficiencies by distorting the results of decisions made by owners, investors, producers, and consumers. In general, one must agree that the best results would ideally be attained by distributing windfall gains and rents to individuals,[11] applying returns from nature-given resources owned by the public as citizens of a province to reducing tax rates in the province concerned and, through the appropriate equalization mechanism, throughout the body politic within which the government has, in Milton Moore's phrase, "the right and responsibility to pre-empt economic rents for the benefit of all members of the community." What is most needed seems to be the elaboration of some sort of agreed machinery for co-ordinated planning for the development and use of nature-given resources to allow them to be exploited in the most efficient possible way and at the most efficient possible rate on the basis of a careful and comprehensive cost-benefit calculation. This would also make possible the full "socialization of rents" and the equitable distribution of those rents, as well as the inclusion of externalities and intangibles in the social calculation in addition to the more obvious and easily reckoned cash outlays and returns.

Such an exercise would necessitate drawing a clear distinction between (a) charging a *price* for the use or acquisition of a scarce natural resource, which is essential to secure the efficient allocation and rationing of such resources, and for the proper calculation of user costs; [12] and (b) *taxing* income and capital gains to secure revenues needed to finance general government expenses, the provision of public goods, and such transfers of income as the community considers essential to obviate intolerable discrepancies in well-being among its members. It is also essential to distinguish between (a) specifically beneficial taxation which is, in effect, a charge for inputs of public services (such as transportation amenities, water supply, etc.) into a mining or other natural resource-based enterprise, and (b) taxation levied to secure revenues needed to finance *general* government services to the public at large, as well as the type of transfer payments mentioned above. [13]

As the papers in this volume suggest, we are still a long way from accepting this principle on a national basis, though, as Milton Moore indicates, we have started to move in this direction.

We have not yet, however, recognized the need to include all elements of rent from natural resources in calculating fiscal capabilities, nor have we devised mechanisms that will make this possible even under normal conditions, let alone under conditions of extreme and unforeseen fluctuations in provincial fiscal capacity.

At present the longstanding Canadian tradition persists of allowing rent from increasingly scarce nature-given resources to be alienated to private owners (as in the case of western homestead lands), or to accrue to enterprises which make use of the resources in question or to final consumers without any payment being made, or at least no payment commensurate with the full scarcity value of the services of the resource in question. In such cases a hidden subsidy is bestowed on the resource users, either by inadvertence or as a deliberate policy designed to promote population increase and economic expansion in the hope of increasing the power and, supposedly, the prosperity of the jurisdiction concerned. An outstanding example is the use of increasingly scarce waterpower potential for which no payment (or, at most, only a trifling payment) is made. Does not the recent proposal of Ontario Hydro to raise its charges sharply to defray the cost of new capacity indicate that existing relatively cheap hydro-electric power sites yield a considerable rent? The Hydro-Electric Power Commission of Ontario was a splendidly effective institutional innovation designed to overcome the problems inherent in a natural monopoly and to prevent the rent of a public nature-given asset falling into the hands of a few enterprising capitalists, but the policy of supplying power "at cost" in Ontario (and in other provinces where a similar type of public enterprise in is operation) means that purchasers of electrical energy are getting the rent accruing from the low cost power potential of the falling waters of the provinces. Might not that rent go more efficiently to all the citizens of the province, since it is they who are the public owners of that resource? Why should it be power users who get the benefit of the rent of the superior efficiency of scarce power sites? Should this not be preempted "for the benefit of all members of the community" at the provincial level and taken into account in the national equalization computation?

The persistence of policies based on an erstwhile abundance of natural resources into a period of increasing pressure on a limited resource base not only distorts equalization calculations, it also distorts the allocation of resources. Power that is unduly cheap because it includes no charge for rent encourages inefficient extensions of the use of electricity.

Such policies are being increasingly called in question as the danger becomes increasingly evident of overuse of resources in the public domain and of free, open access resources or, in Mason Gaffney's terms, of the need to "protect the commons." The public is becoming ever more sensitive to the possibly destructive impact of economic growth on the quality of life, though it is surely overoptimistic to say with Mason Gaffney that "the anti-growth rage is now now in the ascendant." Be that as it may, insistence on the importance of imposing adequate user costs, charges for the use of open access resources (such as effluent fees), and full rents for scarce nature-given resources must command agreement, as does the suggestion that "inverted rate structures" are desirable to curb excessive consumption and to encourage mass transit and other mass systems in place of socially costly individual amenities.

The problems that emerge are the very difficult problems of (a) identifying and measuring all rents yielded by nature-given resources; (b) creating social mechanisms that will allow as much individual freedom as possible, along with flexibility and full play for local interests and knowledge; and (c) creating some means by which it may be possible to adjust entrenched constitutional structures and usages to meet the social and political needs of the entire community.

Notes

1. Mason Gaffney's statement that "provincial governments relate to national governments as their own local governments relate to them" seems to overlook the sovereign status of provinces within Confederation.

2. Elmer A. Driedger (1967); Gérard La Forest (1969).

3. Driedger (1967); Chester Martin (1938), pp. 220-43, 466-94.

4. La Forest (1969), pp. 17-21.

5. Scott, first paper in this volume.

6. Statistics Canada, pp. 68-202 (annual). This is not, of course, to say that specific points, such as mining taxation, did not become controversial issues, as, for example, Perry (1955) makes clear. The dwindling importance of receipts from the public domain among provincial revenues (Scott, first paper in this volume) is surely a normal result of the progress of the Canadian economy towards maturity.

7. Only by contrasting specific bills for electricity is a meaningful comparison possible. Even so, in this outstanding instance of unavoidably "administered prices," this gives an idea of comparative *charges* but not necessarily of comparative costs. However, for a comparison of domestic, commercial, and small power bills see Statistics Canada, pp. 57-203 (annual).

8. Hydro-Electric Power Commission of Ontario ([1956] p. 40).

9. Compare the letter from the Minister of Energy, Mines and Resources published in *The Ottawa Citizen*, 18 July 1975.

10. It may, of course, be argued that the high price is artificial. One view is that O.P.E.C.'s action was a long overdue recognition of impending scarcity; another view is that it was simply monopolistic profit-taking by a cartel newly aware of its bargaining power.

11. It is to be noted that windfall gains are quite different from rents in both character (except for being unearned) and function. Much confusion has resulted from neglect of this important difference. (Scott, first paper in this volume).

12. Scott (1967). User costs of the nature-given resource itself and of social capital, the cost of

which is so often external to the cost-benefit calculations of a firm exploiting exhaustible resources.

13. Compare Scott, section II, 4, in first paper in this volume.

References

Driedger, Elmer A., *A Consolidation of the British North America Acts 1867 to 1965* (Ottawa: Queen's Printer, 1967).

Hydro-Electric Power Commission of Ontario, *Hydro Progress in Ontario 1906-1956* (Toronto: O.H.E.P.C.[1956])

La Forest, Gerard V., *Natural Resources and Public Property under the Canadian Constitution* (Toronto: University of Toronto Press, 1969)

Martin, Chester, "Dominion Lands Policy," in A.S. Morton and Chester Martin, *History of Prairie Settlement and "Dominion Lands" Policy* (Toronto: Macmillan, 1938)

Minister of Energy, Mines and Resources, letter (undated) published in *Ottawa Citizen*, 18 July 1975

Perry, J. Harvey, *Taxes, Tariffs, & Subsidies* (Toronto: University of Toronto Press, 1955)

Statistics Canada (annual), *Consolidated Government Finance* Publication #68-202 (Ottawa: Information Canada)

Scott, Anthony, "The Theory of the Mine under Conditions of Certainty," Mason Gaffney, ed., *Extractive Resources and Taxation* (Madison, Milwaukee, and London: University of Wisconsin Press, 1967)

Biographical Notes

Paul G. Bradley is professor in the Department of Economics, University of British Columbia.

Albert Breton is professor in the Department of Political Economy, University of Toronto.

John Butlin is a lecturer in the Agricultural Economics Department, University of Manchester.

Harry F. Campbell is assistant professor in the Department of Economics, University of British Columbia.

Douglas H. Clark is with the Federal-Provincial Relations Division, Department of Finance, Ottawa.

Thomas J. Courchene is professor in the Department of Economics, University of Western Ontario.

W.D. Gainer is professor in the Department of Economics, University of Alberta.

John Helliwell is professor in the Department of Economics, University of British Columbia.

W.R. Lederman is professor in the Faculty of Law, Queen's University.

J. Clark Leith is professor in the Department of Economics, University of Western Ontario.

Judith Maxwell is director of economic policy analysis for the C.D. Howe Institute, Montreal.

A. Milton Moore is professor in the Department of Economics, University of British Columbia.

Gerry May is research associate in the Department of Economics, University of British Columbia.

T.L. Powrie is professor in the Department of Economics, University of Alberta.

Anthony Scott is professor in the Department of Economics, University of British Columbia.

Donald V. Smiley is professor in the Department of Political Economy, University of Toronto.

Irene M. Spry is professor in the Department of Economics, University of Ottawa.

Andrew R. Thompson is professor in the Faculty of Law, University of British Columbia and Chairman of the British Columbia Energy Commission.

G.C. Watkins is professor in the Department of Economics, University of Calgary and affiliated with Data Metrics Ltd., Calgary.

Index

Alberta: industrial strategy of, 67; unique position of, in Canadian federation, 66-67
Alberta Energy Company, 158
Alberta Energy Resources Conservation Board (AERCB), 236
Alberta-Ottawa conflict, 7, 67-68, 82-84, 86
Arrow, K.J., 233
Athabaska oil sands. *See* Syncrude Project

Bennett, R.B., 67
Berry, Glyn R., 69
Bionomic equilibrium, 187-88
Bossons, John, 247
Bradley, Paul G., 247-48
British Columbia Petroleum Corporation, 115, 120
British Columbia Pollution Control Branch, 195
Bucovetsky, Meyer W., 68-69, 247

Campbell, Harry F., 197
Carter Commission, 116
Carter Report, 68
"Centralized" resource revenue series, 33-35
Clark, Douglas, 92
"Comprehensive" resource revenue series, 18-31, 39-49
Continental economic integration, 63-65
Courchene, Thomas J., 36, 68, 108-9
Creighton, Donald, 62

"Decentralized" resource revenue series, 32-33
Demakeas, J., 195
Depopulation. *See* Mobility (population)

Economic growth, 61, 254
Effluent charge scheme, 190-91, 193-94: and revenue maximization, 193-200
Energy crisis, 74: and American policy changes, 64-65: government intervention in, 69, 86, 251; and self-sufficiency goals of Canada and U.S., 64, 183
Energy prices, rising, 75, 83-84, 86-87, 93, 118, 251

Enhanced recovery of oil, 235-38: sensitivity of taxable base of, 235, 238
Environmental management: income distributional effects of, 190-93, 197-200; jurisdiction over, 198-200; market failure approach to, 191-95, 200; resource rent approach to, 191-95, 200. *See also* Effluent charge scheme; Pollution abatement
Equalization formula, 6-7, 18, 33-35, 68, 74, 76-82, 95, 112, 240-43, 250, 252-54: and energy prices, 75, 83-84, 86; and Federal-Provincial Fiscal Arrangements Act (1967), 76, 90-91, 94, 109; Gainer-Powrie proposal for, 88-89, 93; and government intervention, 86; Helliwell proposal for, 89-90; and increasing dominance of resource revenues, 108-11; Musgrave proposal for, 87-88, 90, 93; Turner/Ottawa proposals for, 92-96. *See also* Redistribution; Revenue sharing
Exhaustibility of resources. *See* Mineral resource earnings, depletion; Resource rent assignment, and exhaustibility of resources
Export tax, 137-38: model for, for crude oil, 138-49; optimal, 137, 149-51

Federal-Provincial Fiscal Arrangements Act (1967). *See* Equalization formula, and Federal-Provincial Fiscal Arrangements Act (1967)
Feldstein, Martin S., 154
Foster Research Limited, economic study by (*Economic Evaluation of the Syncrude Project*), 159-61
Gaffney, Mason, 224, 250-52, 254
Gainer, W.D., 74-75, 88-89, 93
George, Henry, 9, 240
Gordon, H. Scott, 186
Government intervention in economy: affecting relations with U.S., 64-65; as reflecting declining confidence in market as allocative mechanism, 63; role of, during energy crisis, 69
Great Canadian Oil Sands (GCOS), 154, 156: tax and royalty arrangements of, 157-58, 161, 163
Grey Report on Foreign Direct Investment in Canada, 63

Harkness, Douglas, 67
Helliwell, John F., 75, 89-90, 155, 159, 176, 183
Hicks, Ursula, 8
Hydro-Electric Power Commission of Ontario. *See* Ontario Hydro

Interprovincial Pipeline, 182

Lambert, Marcel, 67
Land speculation tax, 62
Lederman, W.R., 5-6, 178
Leith, J. Clark, 247-48
Lind, R.C., 233

Macdonald, Donald, 66
Management of crude oil resources: and development of new supplies, 182-83; and export tax. *See* Export tax; federal responsibilities in, 181-84; and price determination, 182, 184; provincial responsibilities in, 181. *See also* Enhanced recovery of oil
Management of mineral resources, government involvement in, 215, 220, 224, 227, 229-30
Management of natural resources, 112-13, 116-17: co-ordinating costs of, 247, 249; need for federal-provincial cooperation in, 71-72, 250, 252-53. *See also* Environmental management
Marshall, Alfred, 8
May, Gerry, 159, 176
Mineral resource earnings: depletion and, 215, 220, 224; exploration and, 118, 129-30, 215, 220-25; neutral taxation of, 128, 215, 218, 220, 222-24; and non-homogeneity, 130; and quality differences of resources, 126, 216-20; and rate of resource use, 215, 220, 224-25, 227, 230; and revenue maximization, 220, 224, 228; risk and uncertainties in, 118, 129, 133, 223, 227; taxation of, 118, 130-31, 214-16, 220-25, 227, 229-30. *See also* Ontario Mining Tax Act (1972)
Mineral resource management. *See* Management of mineral resources, government involvement in
Mining industry, client relation of, to provinces, 68
Mobility (population), 8-9, 11-14, 29, 110-11: adjustment costs of, 248-49
Moore, A. Milton, 112, 246, 240-51, 253
Munro, Ross H., 64
Musgrave, R.A., 75, 87-88, 90, 93

National price: for crude oil, 251-52; for other resources, 252
Neher, Philip A., 16
Nemetz, P., 195
Nixon, Richard M., 64
North Sea oil field, 232

Ontario Committee on Taxation, 1967. *See* Smith Committee
Ontario Hydro, 251, 254
Ontario Mining Tax Act (1914), 206
Ontario Mining Tax Act (1972), 206: evaluation of, 208-10; objectives of, 206-7; proposed change to pure rent tax, 210-13; tax base for, 207, 209-10
O.P.E.C., 63-64, 116, 160-61
Ownership of resources, 11, 52, 116-17: and federal trade and commerce rights, 53-56, 114; and political power, 232-33; and provincial property and civil rights, 3-6, 53-55, 62, 114-15, 250, 252. *See also* Resource rent assignment
Pollution abatement, 188-94, 199: subsidies for, 194. *See also* Environmental management
Polyani, Karl, 62
Powrie, T.L., 74-75, 88-89, 93

Redistribution: areas of, 6-8; as equalization of fiscal capacity, 7. *See also* Equalization formula; Revenue sharing
Rent, definition of, 1, 114, 185. *See also* Resource rent
Rent maximization, 185-86, 200; fishery example, 186-90, 199-200
Resource development, government involvement in, 64-65, 215. *See also* Syncrude Project
Resource industry-government relations: declining importance of market mechanism in, 63, 70; decreasing sensitivity to private corporation interests in, 68-69; and energy crisis, 69; and joint private-public projects, 69, 70. *See also* Syncrude Project
Resource rent, 109-11, 118-19, 125-26, 131-33: alternate taxation schemes for, 120-21; collection of, 114-16; and fiscal capability, 34, 250-51, 253; as national asset, 242; from non-homogeneous resource, 126-28; non-taxability of, 56, 120; and risk, 133; taxation of, 3-5, 56-57, 119-20. *See also* Mineral resource earnings; Rent, definition of; Rent maximization; Taxation, federal and provincial powers of
Resource rent assignment: allocational criteria for, 8-17; benefit theory in, 8-10, 17;

definition of, 2; entitlement to, 240-45; and exhaustibility of resources, 10-14, 17, 248; institutional criteria for, 3-8; lack of efficient criteria for, 37. *See also* Ownership of resources

Revenue assignment. *See* Resource rent assignment

Revenue maximization, 186, 190, 200. *See also* Equalization formula; Redistribution

Ricardian rent, 72, 121, 124, 127-28, 216, 233

Risk (uncertainty), 17-19, 115, 127, 250: principal-agent approach to, 154-56; sharing of, by governments, 233-34. *See also* Mineral resource earnings, risk and uncertainties in; Resource rent, and risk; Syncrude Project, risk and uncertainties in

Ross, Stephen A., 154

Rowell-Sirois Commission, 10-13

Royalties, not deductible for corporation income tax, 82, 86, 91, 93, 116

"Saudi-Arabian" estimate of resource revenues, 35-36

Scarcity rent, 122-26, 128, 253-54

Scott, Anthony, 108, 112-13, 116-17, 186, 196, 214-16, 229, 247-48, 250

Senate Special Committee on Science Policy, 63

Sharp, Mitchell, 108

Smith Committee (Ontario Committee on Taxation, 1967), 208, 210-11

Stephenson, J., 195

Syncrude Project, 70, 153-54: default by Atlantic Richfield, 156; effects of alternative oil prices on, 159-68; effects of capital costs and time preferences on, 170, 173, 175; effects of general inflation on, 168, 170, 175; effects of uncertain costs on, 168, 173; and June 1975 Federal Budget, 154, 175-78; risks and uncertainties in, 153-55, 157-59, 161, 163, 168, 177; tax, royalty and equity arrangements for, 153-54, 156-61, 163, 170, 178

Taxation: federal and provincial powers of, 55-57; of net profits, 115. *See also* Resource rent

Thompson, Andrew R., 182-83

Tiebout, Charles, 8

Time preference, 14, 16-17, 113, 116-17, 252. *See also* Syncrude Project, effects of capital costs and time preferences on

Trudeau, Pierre-Elliott, 66

Turner, John, 76, 86, 90-93

Uncertainty. *See* Risk (uncertainty)

Western Economic Opportunities Conference (1973), 66

Western provinces: as economic colony of Canadian heartland, 65-66; revolts against position in Confederation by, 66

Windfall, 3, 8-9, 109, 133, 209-10, 212, 240: distribution of, 74, 116, 119, 121, 252-53

Zimmerman, Erich, 215